UFOs
Over New York

A True History of Extraterrestrial Encounters in the Empire State

By Preston Dennett

Schiffer
Publishing Ltd

4880 Lower Valley Road Atglen, Pennsylvania 19310

Schiffer Books are available at special discounts for bulk purchases for sales promotions or premiums. Special editions, including personalized covers, corporate imprints, and excerpts can be created in large quantities for special needs. For more information contact the publisher:

Published by Schiffer Publishing Ltd.
4880 Lower Valley Road
Atglen, PA 19310
Phone: (610) 593-1777; Fax: (610) 593-2002
E-mail: Info@schifferbooks.com

For the largest selection of fine reference books on this and related subjects, please visit our web site at **www.schifferbooks.com**
We are always looking for people to write books on new and related subjects. If you have an idea for a book please contact us at the above address.

This book may be purchased from the publisher.
Include $5.00 for shipping.
Please try your bookstore first.
You may write for a free catalog.

In Europe, Schiffer books are distributed by
Bushwood Books
6 Marksbury Ave.
Kew Gardens
Surrey TW9 4JF England
Phone: 44 (0) 20 8392-8585; Fax: 44 (0) 20 8392-9876
E-mail: info@bushwoodbooks.co.uk
Website: www.bushwoodbooks.co.uk
Free postage in the U.K., Europe; air mail at cost.

Other Schiffer Books by Preston Dennett
UFOs Over California: A True History of Extraterrestial Encounters in the Golden State, 0-7643-2149-9, $14.95
California Ghosts: True Accounts of Hauntings in the Golden State, 0-7643-1972-8, $14.95
Supernatural California, 0-7643-2401-2, $24.95

Other Schiffer Books on Related Subjects
Spooky Creepy Long Island, 978-0-7643-2814-5, $12.95
Ghost of New York City, 0-7643-1714-8, $12.95
Greetings from Buffalo, 978-0-7643-2888-6, $19.95

Type set in: Zurich BT

ISBN: 978-0-7643-2974-6
Printed in China

Contents

"There's UFOs over New York, and I ain't too surprised."

-- John Lennon

Introduction

New York State is undeniably one of the most famous and influential places on the planet. Although it is the thirtieth largest state in the Union, New York holds the second largest population of all the states (nearly twenty million people), almost half of which is located in New York City. The population is one of the most diverse in the world. New York City is a phenomenon in itself; it has been called the center of human civilization, containing virtually the entire range of human diversity and culture. It is an undisputed world leader in economics, politics, theater, publishing, fashion — you name it, it can be found in New York City.

New York became a state July 26, 1788 as the eleventh of the original thirteen states. Prior to that, it had been occupied by various Native American tribes, mainly the Algonquin and the Iroquois.

The state contains 49,108 square miles, with 127 miles of coastline. The highest point is Mt. Marcy at 5,344 feet, located in the Adirondack Upland in northeast New York. There are a large number of lakes and artificial reservoirs, and much of the non-urban areas are forested. The climate is varied with the lowest recorded temperature at -52° at Stillwater Reservoir and the highest at 108° in Troy.

It should come as no surprise that New York has a rich UFO history. The state's first major introduction to UFOs came more than one hundred years ago, during the now-famous 1897 airship wave. Following the dawn of the modern age of UFOs in 1947, New York soon produced a number of significant or high-profile "classic" cases: the Ryan-Neff UFO chase in 1956, the Gary Wilcox UFO landing in 1964, and the Cherry Creek landing in 1965. That same year, the now-famous blackout, caused by a UFO, occurred, plunging nearly one-third of the nation into darkness. This was followed by the 1966 sighting of a UFO hovering over the United Nations building, the revelation of the Robert & Jason Steiner abduction case (one of the first reported cases in the United States), the sighting of a UFO over downtown Manhattan by musical legend John Lennon, several well-known Air Force Project Blue Book cases...and many more.

Then in the mid-1980s, the Hudson Valley area experienced one of the most intense UFO waves in world history, lasting at least four years and involving hundreds of objects and thousands of witnesses. Around the same time, a small town known as Pine Bush began to attract attention as a hotbed of continuing UFO activity.

Also, unknown to many, the UFO abduction movement had much of its origin in New York, spearheaded mainly through the investigative work of New York artist Elliot Budd Hopkins, and by the incredible revelations of novelist Whitley Strieber, whose 1988 book *Communion* about his own abductions by "visitors" from his upstate cabin in New York broke publishing records and remained a *New York Times* bestseller for two years.

In 1999 Budd Hopkins announced the unique Brooklyn Bridge abduction case — one of the very few cases of an observed UFO abduction. The attention of the world became focused on the incident and New York again showed its powerful influence in the UFO movement.

New York also has a surprisingly complex history of UFO/military encounters that illustrate the government's interest in and cover-up of the UFO phenomenon, including several cases of apparent UFO crash/retrievals.

One perhaps unique New York feature is the large number of accounts in which New Yorkers have seen extraterrestrials walking among the urban population; in bookstores, restaurants, hotels, apartment buildings, subways, train-stations, and other seemingly unlikely locations.

These are only a few of the many incredible UFO events that have taken place in New York State. As can be seen, the Empire State has a colorful and unique history of UFO events. In fact, according to the National UFO Reporting Center (NUFORC) based in Washington State, New York ranks fifth against all the other states in terms of the number of reported encounters, with a total of more than 1,760 reports. As we shall see, however, the total number of recorded cases is considerably higher than that.

Because of its prominent position in world society, the history of New York has been exhaustively documented. There have already been a few books written about New York UFO encounters, most notably *Night Siege* by J. Allen Hynek, Philip Imbrogno, and Bob Pratt, which presents the story of the now famous four-year-long Hudson Valley UFO wave, some of which actually took place in Connecticut. Imbrogno also wrote a follow-up book, *Close Encounters of the 5th Kind*, with co-author Marianne Horrigan, which presents more Hudson Valley sightings and several New York abduction cases, though the scope of that book is again not limited to the state. Ellen Crystall's book *Silent Invasion* presents a narrative of her own encounters in California, New Jersey, and most significantly, Pine Bush, New York. Vinny Polise's book, *The Pine Bush Phenomenon*, follows up Crystall's research, again focusing mainly on Pine Bush. Finally Budd Hopkins' book, *Witnessed*, presents the now-famous Brooklyn Bridge abductions. Few other books, however, have focused on New York encounters, and none has done so exclusively.

UFOs over New York: A True History of Extraterrestrial Encounters in the Empire State is the first book to present the complete history of UFOs in New York State—from the first encounters more than 150 years ago to the present day. Cases have been derived from a wide variety of sources including books, magazine and newspaper articles, UFO journals, television and radio programs, websites, UFO organizations, UFO investigators, and firsthand interviews. The book is organized chronologically and topically, starting with a history of simple sightings, then moving on to more extensive cases of UFO landings and humanoids. After that there is a section on abductions and onboard UFO experiences. Finally, there is a chapter on UFO crashes and unique New York conspiracies and cover-ups, and at the very end, a chapter outlining current events. So come along on this fascinating journey as we explore New York's involvement with one of the most persistent and perplexing mysteries of modern times.

Chapter One:
In the Beginning

While the beginning of the modern age of UFOs is said to have begun with the famous sighting of nine silver disks over Mount Rainier, Washington by pilot Kenneth Arnold in 1947, the truth is that UFOs have been seen much earlier than this. New York has produced several very early cases of a variety of types.

Angels or Aliens?

It is not easy to determine the first actual alien encounter in New York. For example, way back in 1820, a fourteen year-old boy from Palmyra, New York had a remarkable experience that, depending on one's cultural point of view, may have been an encounter with angels, spirits, or perhaps aliens. The boy, Joseph Smith, had gone into the woods to pray when he suddenly became paralyzed and unable to speak. Terrified, he watched a brilliant pillar of light approach him. When the light touched him, he lost all fear. He then saw two glowing human-looking figures who urged him not to join the Protestant religion. The beings left and Smith found himself lying on his back, alone in the forest.

Three years later, on September 21, 1823, at age seventeen, Smith was in his bedroom when he was again visited by glowing beings. He was praying when suddenly the room filled with light and he observed a glowing figure floating by his bed. Writes Smith, "He had on a loose robe of most exquisite whiteness. It was a whiteness beyond anything earthly I had ever seen, nor do I believe any earthly thing could be made to appear so exceedingly white and brilliant…not only was his robe exceedingly white, but his whole person was glorious beyond description, and his countenance was truly like lightning… When I first looked upon him, I was afraid; but the fear soon left me."

The *Being* said his name was Moroni, and that he was a messenger from God. He had a mission for Smith, which was to translate a series of religious writings that would be found on gold tablets buried underneath a hill near Manchester, New York. Moroni also told Smith prophecies of an upcoming apocalyptic-type event. Smith later allegedly found the gold tablets and fulfilled his mission, which resulted in the influential *Book of Mormon* and the inception of the Mormon religion.

Today millions of people follow the Mormon faith. A few modern UFO researchers, such as Jerome Clark and Loren Coleman, have identified the above case as containing many of the same elements as today's UFO accounts. If Smith's encounter had occurred 150 years later, it might have been interpreted very differently.[1]

UFO Honeymoons at Niagara Falls

One of the first convincing UFO sightings over New York State occurred November 13, 1833, when an object described as "large, square, and luminous" was seen hovering over Niagara Falls for more than an hour. More than a thousand people on both the American and Canadian sides of Niagara Falls witnessed the spectacle, though no explanation was offered.[2]

A Mothership over New York

Another early report occurred April 12, 1879, when astronomer Harry Harrison of Jersey City, New Jersey observed a glowing circular-shaped object that appeared to be hovering at an extremely high altitude over the New York harbor. What puzzled Harrison was the fact that the object remained in place while the stars continued to rise and set with the Earth's rotation. After three hours, Harrison was even more surprised to watch the object abruptly change direction towards the east. The next day it was gone, ruling out any theories of comets or other large natural astronomical bodies. Harrison reported his sighting to the Naval Observatory in Washington, but received no response. He then contacted the *New York Tribune* and *Scientific American*, who published his account.

At the same time of Harrison's sighting, another astronomer, Spencer J. Devoe of Manhattanville, also observed the same object, which he described as "wonderfully brilliant." Devoe was also astonished by the strange appearance and movement of the object. At one point, he decided to take a short coffee break. When he returned, the mysterious object was gone.

Morris K. Jessup carefully studied the written reports of both astronomers, and after triangulating the numbers, concluded, "Considered from any approach, this object appears to have been organic, intelligently operated and hovering over New York City!…From Devoe's rough description of the size, this object would have been about half a mile in diameter at an altitude of eighty to one hundred miles."[3]

Comet or Flying Saucer?

One year later, on April 11, 1880, Mr. Swift of Rochester, New York reported his observation to the Royal Astronomical Society of what appeared to him to be a "faint comet" located at the constellation Ursa Major. This theory was quickly rejected because, as the report reads, "However, no motion was detected in one hour. It was not a nebula for it could not be found again after a period of bad weather."

With no conception of "extraterrestrial craft," many early UFOs were automatically assumed to be natural astronomical anomalies. Researcher Morris K. Jessup, however, believes that the above case may have been a flying saucer. As he writes, "If a comet, it should have manifest motion in an hour. The fact that it did not, yet moved away later, is indicative of controlled motion. Its stationary position suggests hovering."[4]

A Saturn-Shaped Object

Only a few years later, the UFOs were back. On July 3, 1884, multiple residents of Norwood in St. Lawrence observed an unidentified high-flying "Saturn-shaped" object that cruised at a low speed overhead and then moved away.[5]

The End of the Airships

In late 1896, a wave of weird airships struck the United States, starting in California and eventually sweeping across the nation. On April 30, 1897, (50 years prior to the Kenneth Arnold sighting) three residents of Yonkers, New York were returning to their homes at 3 a.m. when they observed a strange "airship" adorned with a brilliant light. Harry Folkersamb noticed the object first and pointed it out to his two companions. Later, numerous other area residents also reported the strange airship, all of them remarking on the unusually bright lights coming from the object.

As it turns out, this was one of the last sightings of what has come to be known as the Mysterious Airship wave of 1896-1897. For two years, hundreds of reports had poured in across the nation. Today, UFO researchers are at a loss to explain the mystery. There were many rumors that the Air Ship reports were actually the result of early and undisclosed human experiments with dirigibles. For example, one New Yorker, an independently wealthy 25-year-old inventor named Mr. Wilson was credited with having invented and flown a dirigible from New York to Texas in April 1897. However, Wilson never went public with his claims, which remain unproven. Credit for the invention actually went to David Schwarz who, in 1897, flew the first official dirigible in the Austro-Hungarian Empire. The first dirigible flight in the United States took place in 1904 in California by inventor Thomas Scott Baldwin.[6]

The Tilly Foster Mine Spook-Lights

Not all UFOs are necessarily extraterrestrials. Located in the town of Southeast, the Tilly Foster Mine is one of many iron mines located in the Upstate New York area. In 1885, the mine had a maze of passages reaching to a level of six hundred feet, or fifty stories below the ground. The extreme depth, combined with a water seepage problem made the mining operation difficult. This problem was solved by converting the mine to an open pit mine, which worked for another ten years. Then, on November 29, 1895, there was a large cave-in, and thirteen men were killed. Shortly later, the mind flooded and within two years it was shut down.

Sometime after the accident, locals reported seeing "a round, yellow (sometimes white) light the diameter of a basketball." Residents reportedly believed that the lights were the ghosts of the miners who had died in the cave-in. Incredibly, the sightings of the "spook-lights" have continued for more than a century, and have even been photographed as late as 1994. While they are apparently not extraterrestrial in origin, and are allegedly caused by ghosts, they are still technically also UFOs and remain unexplained. And in fact, there are several other cases in which UFOs seem to show interest in mines.[7]

"A Mystery Plane"

In August of 1909, for about a month, a "mystery plane" repeatedly visited Middleton, New York. According to a local newspaper account: "A mysterious airship which flies only at night is causing considerable excitement and keeping the people of Orange County residing between Goshen and Newburg up nights in their efforts to get a look at it. For the past month, persons who have been out late at night have reported seeing an airship, but few believed the stories. For a week or more, the flying machine has not been seen. But at 11 o'clock last night, it made its appearance near Goshen. It was flying high in the air and carried a light which attracted attention. It flew very fast, and was last seen traveling in the direction of Newburg. Those who have seen the machine say it is shaped like a balloon and has wings on each side and a cigar-shaped car underneath. The sound of a motor was distinctly heard."[8]

Was it a bird, a plane...or a UFO?

On December 31, 1908, the Wright Brother's made the first historic airplane flight. Two years later, airplanes were still extremely rare. For example, in 1910 there were only thirty-six known licensed pilots in the entire United States. Which makes it very difficult to explain what happened on the night of August 30, 1910, over Madison Square in New York City.

At 9 p.m. that evening, hundreds of people in Madison Square observed an "object" described as long, black with red and green lights, and an engine noise, which circled around the park and then flew away. The next night the craft returned, again putting on a display for the reporters and crowd of citizens. Many of the witnesses were impressed by the object's dangerous maneuvers among the tall buildings, particularly because it was nighttime.

The press went wild, and newsmen conducted an investigation, checking the location of every known airplane for miles around. They found only one, a plane on Long Island. However, investigators ruled it out as the cause as it had a maximum range of only twenty-five miles, and was very unreliable. The *New York Tribune* published a report of the incident, but was unable to determine the origin of the mystery plane.[9]

UFOs at the World Fair

The New York World Fair is held to exhibit some of the latest developments in innovation and technology. On the evening of April 18, 1933, the fair had attracted thousands of people to New York City to enjoy the various exhibitions. One of these was a complex display involving music, fountains, lights, and gas jets. A large crowd had gathered and was watching the display in action. The display was, of course, meant to attract attention, though perhaps not the kind of attention it was about to get. At some point, a "strange lighted shape" appeared suddenly over the crowd, hovering and apparently watching the exhibition. Writes one witness, "Many people saw it and pointed, including me and my family. It made no noise that could be heard over the music, and suddenly darted straight up and disappeared into the star-lit cloudless sky. I still remember it vividly."[10]

More Cigar-Shaped Crafts

By this time, UFOs began to take on a more modern-type of appearance. A remarkable firsthand account occurred in the summer of 1944 to two witnesses in Queens. Writes one of the gentlemen, "We were riding our bikes on a footpath adjacent to Grand Central Parkway...As we started climbing a hill, we looked up and saw a cigar-shaped object broadside to us...it was longer and slimmer than a blimp; it was of smooth metal construction with no windows or openings in sight. It didn't have a gondola on its underside as normal dirigibles and blimps do."

With the coming of the 1940s, most UFO craft had transformed from cumbersome airships to sleeker, metallic-looking craft. For example, in April of 1946, a motorist was traveling with his friend near the town of Lafayette, New York when a gleam of light in the sky caught his eye. Looking up, he saw that the source of the light was a large, metallic cigar-shaped object, an estimated 300-400 feet in length, hovering silently at about 5,000-10,000 feet in altitude. Each end of the craft came to a sharp point; otherwise there were no marking or protrusions of any kind. The witness observed the object for two minutes when, instead of moving away, it "disappeared instantly."[11]

Astronomer & Students Observe Massive UFO Fleet

While UFOs are often seen traveling alone, it is not uncommon to see them in groups of two, three, four or sometimes even more. It is much more rare to see large groups, involving twenty or more objects. However, it does occasionally happen, as it did over Syracuse on the evening of February 20, 1947.

Two students of Syracuse University were exploring the campus when they came upon the campus astronomical observatory. Inside, they found a gentleman looking through a seven-foot long refractor telescope. When he saw the two students, he turned to them and said, "Thank God, you guys are here. Come and look and tell me I'm not crazy."

The man told the two students that he had seen something strange. He asked each of them to look through the telescope for a full two minutes before making any judgment about what they saw.

Both students looked through the scope and were amazed to see what appeared to be a continuous line of UFOs traveling across the night sky. Says one of the students, "As I began my observation, a moving light entered the field and traversed it completely...Within about 20-30 seconds the next light appeared, and then another and another – until I had seen ten or twelve... There was an unending stream of elliptical or circular objects crossing the heavens, obliterating the stars as they passed at a high rate of speed. They were apparently navigating an unseen highway, because each light followed the same track. The only details visible through that telescope were a gray bottom surface, slightly lighter than the night sky background, and a thin bright yellow-orange trailing edge which seemed to ripple slightly."

The astronomer assured the two students that he had never seen anything like these objects. He then released the lock on the telescope, allowing them to track the objects from the zenith to the horizon, which took about thirty seconds. They watched another thirty objects go by, each following the same exact track. The witness speculated that they were traveling along a magnetic line, heading north. The objects were invisible to the naked eye.

After about an hour of observation, the two students left. Unknown to them, however, the United States was in the middle of a UFO wave of gigantic proportions. At the time, hundreds of people across the United States were sighting the objects. However, it wouldn't be until the month of July that the wave would peak. The month of July 1947 was a pivotal moment in UFO history, including such world-famous cases as the Kenneth Arnold sighting over Mount Rainier in Washington State, and the Roswell UFO crash in New

"Disks Soar Over New York"

"Disks Soar Over New York." So read the July 8, 1947 headline for the *New York Times*. The article, by Murray Schumach, described how people across New York and other states along the East Coast stopped along roadsides or climbed onto rooftops to observe various formations of white and orange-colored, disk-shaped objects swoop across the sky. One married couple from Rochester described their encounter with a "white disk." Also, a resident from Glens Falls, New York claimed he saw a large sphere of light, emitting red fire in front and blue fire in its wake.

Another witness was Anne Faye, a Jackson Heights housewife who lived on 86th Street. In a later interview, Faye said:

> "[It was] a big bright globe…It glowed with light. It seemed as if it were hovering over the houses across the street. There were no little green men dancing or anything. It was circular on the bottom. And I wasn't the least bit afraid. The feeling of peace that came from it was something I will never forget."

The Air Force released an official statement about the rash of sightings, saying only that an investigation was still underway. The New York sightings, again, were only part of a much larger conglomeration of sightings – a massive wave that encompassed much of the United States. Also, it should be noted that the alleged UFO crash in Roswell, New Mexico had occurred only a few days earlier.

Several weeks after the New York wave, another statement was released by officials saying that the UFO may have been a large aluminum balloon used by pilots to determine wind direction. Witness Anne Fay, however, says that explanation is ridiculous. She thinks the object she saw was "extraterrestrial."[13]

Pilots Observe Silver Craft

Pilot sightings of UFOs are not uncommon. More rare, however, are independent reports of the same object. On September 20, 1949, Lieutenant Colonel Phillip Kuhl was flying a C-45 aircraft northeast of Rome, New York when he spotted a "silvery cylindrical-shaped" object descend slowly into a cloud layer at about 7,000 feet.

One hour later another pilot, 1st Lieutenant W. E. Archibold was piloting a C-47 though the same area when he saw an object "similar in size and shape to a fighter fuselage, silver in color, and of an undetermined material." As he watched, the object performed a 45-60 degree dive where it vanished behind the shadow of a cloud.

Over the next week, similar sightings were reported in West Virginia and Massachusetts.[14]

Chapter Two:
Sightings (1950-1959)

The arrival of the 1950s brought a whole new dimension to the UFO phenomenon. Prior to then, most of the cases involved sightings of distant high flying objects that had little or no interaction with the environment or outside observers. The 1950s, however, escalated to the next level of contact. Where before UFOs appeared to be shy and elusive, there was now a flood of a new kind of case. In these cases, UFOs had no fear of being observed. Instead they behaved in a brazen manner, chasing vehicles down highways, hovering at low altitude over sensitive installations and, most prominently, playing cat-and-mouse games with our own military and commercial aircraft.

The UFOs, it appeared, were engaged in a study of our own technological capabilities. In any case, the number of cases rose sharply, and for the first time, people began to investigate and catalogue the many new UFO reports.

Falling Grain from...UFO?

The Empire State Building towers 1,467 feet above the streets on New York. During the summer of 1950, construction employees were working on top of the building to put up a new television mast. Suddenly the workers felt their bodies being pelted by small objects. Looking up, they saw an unbelievable sight: a shower of grain was falling down out of an empty sky. Although the sky was overcast, there was no wind or rain. The grain showered heavily downward, smattering against the windows on the north side of the building.

Mystified and amazed, samples of the grain were collected for scientific analysis. Dr. Michael Lauro, official chemist of the Produce Exchange, identified the grain as barley, and suggested that it may have originated from one of the many breweries in New York. Ernest J. Christie of the Weather Bureau confirmed, however, that there was no wind that day, and certainly not enough to carry several pounds of barley into the sky and then shower it down in a precisely defined area. Speculation ranged from birds and tornados to UFOs. However, as early UFO researcher Morris K. Jessup writes, "Of a reasonably satisfactory explanation, there was none."[15]

Navy Pilot Pursues Flying Disk

Our military is charged with protecting us from foreign invasion. It should therefore come as no surprise that the military has had frequent confrontations with UFOs. For example, on January 21, 1952, an un-named Navy pilot was scrambled from Mitchell Air Force Base on Long Island to pursue a "dome-shaped object" that was hovering over the area. As in most cases of this kind, the pilot was only able to pursue the object for a few moments before he was easily out-distanced. Moments later, the UFO darted away. Blue Book investigator Major Donald Ruppelt admitted that he was unable to explain away the case, though Blue Book personnel declined to classify it as a genuine unknown.[16]

New Yorkers Corroborate the Washington Nationals

On July 22, 1952, the *New York Times* revealed that "two persons on Staten Island reported seeing saucers at about 10:15 p.m. Friday night. The objects, described as silvery in color tinged with red on the rims, were reported flying in a 'V' formation of five, said Mrs. Josephine Hetzel."

Hetzel could barely believe her eyes. "I almost fainted when I looked up in the sky and saw what looked like five large dinner plates flying through the sky."

Frank Gonder also observed the formation of objects, which reminded him of geese. However, the objects, he believed, were definitely artificially constructed. Says Gonder, "They gave off a glow and didn't make a sound."[17]

The above sightings, while dramatic, were completely overshadowed by another incredible case. At the same time that evening, numerous pilots and people on the ground observed – and photographed and tracked on radar – several unknown objects hovering directly over the White House. The Washington National Sightings, as they came to be known, gripped the nation, and became one of the most famous UFO incidents in world history.

Civil Defense Employee Photographs UFO

"I was questioned, badgered, threatened, laughed at, and insulted."

One week after the previous sightings, on July 28, 1952, Civil Defense employee August Roberts was on the roof of the Sixth Precinct Police Station in Jersey City, across the Hudson River. He and two other employees were keeping watch. At exactly 12:11 a.m., the men witnessed a "large ball of light, orange in color, with a dark brownish rim" hovering near the Empire State Building. Even though they were all trained observers and had binoculars, they were still unable to identify the object. Roberts quickly grabbed his camera and snapped a photograph.

Before he could get another, the object turned bright red and darted away. Says Roberts, "Whatever the object was, I'm sure it was not like any type of aircraft I have ever seen."

As per his job duty, Roberts called the local air filter center and air force base. The military and FBI expressed extreme interest in the case and over the next seventy-two hours, Roberts went through an intense and abusive interrogation. Says Roberts:

> "For a combined total of three days, my life was a virtual hell. They just wouldn't let me alone. 'What did you see? How is it possible? What do you think it was?' They just never stopped questioning me. I was so worn out that I had to spend the rest of the week resting up at my sister's home. I was questioned, badgered, threatened, laughed at, and insulted. In the end they accepted my story. I hope I never go through that again!"[18] (See photo section.)

UFO Easily Evades Pilots

On October 29, 1952, two F-94 Interceptor jets were scrambled after a UFO that had been spotted over Hempstead. The pilots attempted to pursue the UFO, however, the object easily evaded the planes using a series of high-speed controlled maneuvers. Researcher Richard L. Thompson pointed to this particular case as a good example of how the Air Force's behavior around UFOs (i.e.: actively pursuing them) lies in direct contradiction to their official position—that UFOs represent no military or national security threat.[19]

UFO Causes Unusual
Plant Growth

On June 24, 1953, an un-named woman was outside her home at Hampton Bay, Long Island when she observed a "large aircraft" moving very slowly at a low altitude directly towards her home. The object maneuvered with a strange oscillating motion, which caught her attention. Looking closer, she saw that the craft was about thirty feet wide and had a red band around the middle, with red lights. She could also see a cabin with portholes. Through one of the portholes she observed some kind of control panel. The craft approached to within seventy-five feet of the witness and stopped, making a low buzzing noise like a swarm of bees. At this point, the object tilted towards the west, rose up into the air, and darted away almost straight up. The entire ordeal lasted about three minutes. However, two days following the event, the witness noticed an unusual yellowish moss in the area where the craft had hovered.[20]

UFO Causes Plane Crash?

Up until this point, New York's UFO history, while interesting, had produced few very high profile cases. This changed when, on July 1, 1954, radar operators at Griffis Air Force Base detected a strange blip approaching the area. A quick check was made for aircraft, but there were no other planes. When the unknown intruder failed to respond to radio inquiries, Base Ground Control quickly scrambled an F-94 Starfire jet and ordered the pilot to vector in on the "unknown."

Immediately after takeoff, the onboard radar operator sitting in the backseat of the F-94 also had the UFO on his own radarscope. Two minutes later, they made visual contact. The object was described as "a gleaming disc-shaped thing…huge and circular" and was now hovering in place a few thousand feet above the jet. The pilot opened the throttle and raced towards the object. At the same time, they turned on the radio and asked the object for identification.

Without warning, the engine of the jet suddenly cut off and the pilot felt a wave of heat "like a blast from a blowtorch" fill the cockpit. The pilot ordered his radar man to bail out, which he did. The pilot followed seconds later. Both men parachuted to safety, however, the fighter plane came crashing down into the town of Walesville, New York, tragically killing two adults and two children in their homes, and injuring five others.

The pilots at first revealed their encounter to citizens, causing a minor media sensation. Later, under Air Force pressure, they recanted their previous statements and told the press that it was only "engine trouble." Major Donald Keyhoe, director of NICAP investigated the incident and learned that in the hours following the crash, a "large silvery UFO" was reported from several communities across New York State, but that the Air Force was afraid to scramble any other jets for fear of a repeat incident. Researcher Kevin Randle later debunked the case, pointing out a confusion in dates and the fact that a balloon was known to be in the area. Still the cause of the accident (other than the UFO) was never found and some researchers remain convinced it was a genuine UFO event.[21]

Near-Miss with a UFO

Similar to the previous case is another UFO-plane encounter that occurred in 1954 (exact date not given) at 8:30 p.m. As investigated by MUFON field investigator Joe Barron, a pilot was flying a Navy AD-4D Skyraider at 7,500 feet when, without warning he was confronted by what appeared to be a row of fifteen to twenty dull-yellow triangular windows heading directly for him. There was no time for evasive maneuvers, and the unknown object passed only a few feet from his right wing. According to the witness, each window was about two or three feet wide, making the entire object at least eighty feet long. After it passed, the pilot turned 180 degrees in an attempt to get a better view, but by then the UFO was long gone.[22]

"A Queer Thing"

The two main "red flags" that often indicate to UFO investigators that they are dealing with a genuine unknown are unusual appearance and unusual movement. When you add a credible witness, you have a strong case for a UFO, such as the following example....At 9:40 p.m. July 30, 1954, science teacher Robert Frenhoff from Yonkers, New York went outside to water his lawn. He describes what happened next:

"I happened to glance up into the evening sky, when I was surprised to see a queer thing like a child's gyroscope or spinning top, whirling along at a great altitude. It was mainly yellow, but had a crimson glow at the edges, which might have been an exhaust. I shouted to my wife and she and our neighbors rushed out to look at it. It moved in a fantastic manner. One moment it would hover near the Great Bear constellation, apparently, and then in a sudden rush, dart away at an angle of ninety degrees; then stop short as if it had hit a brick wall. There was no way of estimating its immense height in the sky. It repeated these hovering and rushing maneuvers until close on midnight."[23]

UFO Wave Jams Telephone Lines Across State

In mid-November 1954, the switchboards of the *Jamestown Post-Journal*, the Buffalo Weather Bureau, the police headquarters in Jamestown and

Dunkirk, and the sheriffs' offices in Little Valley and Mayville, were all jammed by hundreds of calls from frantic residents of Chautauqua and Cattaraugus Counties to report a wave of flying saucers cruising at low altitudes across the countryside.

According to the *Post-Journal*, one witness, James Rowland, said that the saucers were brilliantly lit and covered a large portion of the sky, moving in a back-and-forth pattern over the town. Deputies were dispatched to the location and some reported their observation of strange lights, which they later said were only "reflections of powerful searchlights." While this case remains unsolved, it wouldn't be long before more sightings occurred.[24]

Horsehead Angel Hair

The vast majority of UFO events involve no physical evidence whatsoever. Therefore, when a physical evidence case does arise, it can garner considerable attention. One rare type of evidence is known as angel hair: a sticky, wispy spider web-like substance said to be ejected from UFOs. Only a few dozen well-verified cases have occurred. One of the few recorded New York angel hair cases occurred February 21, 1955 at Horsehead, New York, where a small deposit of the strange stuff was found lying on the ground.

As reported in the *Jamestown Post-Journal* in February of 1955:

"A gray cob-webby substance that fell out of the sky and covered a half-square mile of a residential area in Horsehead, NY two days ago was still a mystery substance today. Scientists who examined the substance reported that it was slightly radioactive but not dangerously so. The substance, which one person described as 'gray, ragged, and nylon-like' covered homes, shrubs, trees, and lay over snow-covered lawns and fields. Area residents said that nothing like it had never happened in the area before."

While in this case no actual UFO was spotted, similar cases point to a strong UFO connection.[25]

UFO Photographed from Manhattan Apartment

"It was eerie, frightening, fascinating."

On May 15, 1955, (according to one source June 14) television technician Warren Seigmond stood with Mademoiselle Jeanine Boullier (from the French Office De Tourisme) on the terrace of his Manhattan apartment that overlooks Union Square. Seigmond was there to photograph Boullier when he realized that she was ignoring him and was instead looking at something in the sky. Her smile froze and she yelled out, "Quick, look at that!"

Turning around, Seigmond saw "an immense ball of fire, glowing like a welder's arc." The object moved silently and quickly, and seemed to be controlled by "a very experienced entity."

Says Seigmond:

> "I had never seen anything like it in my life. It must have been tremendous in size. It looked like a full moon that suddenly appeared. It was eerie, frightening, fascinating. I didn't know what to do. I could feel myself getting tense all over, but I had to watch this thing whatever it was."

Seigmond quickly grabbed his camera and after some effort, succeeded on aiming the lens at the object, and snapped a series of four photographs. He says, "The thing seemed to have an unknown power...giving off that glow and just hanging there in the sky...Then it turned a dull gray and swung lazily over to the right and stopped again, just hovering. Then I noticed another strange thing. Even when it was resting in place, the outline was very blurred, indicating terrific movement. It was of huge size, but who could tell how big? No one else was on the roof, and no one else seemed to see this thing. We were alone. But how could that be in a city of eight million people?"

After hovering for several moments, the object again began to perform amazing maneuvers. Says Seigmond, "Then it moved again, this time to the left to about the original position. It was like a graceful ping-pong ball now. It made a high sweep and settled down at an angle of forty-five degrees. The feeling of dread got worse. Miss Boullier froze the way one does when he sees a beautiful snake. This thing had no wings, tail, insignia or markings of any kind. It left no trail, and above all it made no sound...The object made one more swing to the right. It didn't seem to know what gravity was. If it did, it certainly wasn't respecting it. Then as suddenly as it had appeared, it made a slight turn and simply vanished."

Seigmond is, of course, convinced that he saw something unusual: "It moved like it had intelligence...This was not mass or individual hysteria. It was not an illusion, or a mirage or a light inversion. I believe the pictures prove that."

The photographs were later published in the Swiss magazine, *Le Courrier Interplanetaire*. (See photo section.)[26]

A Perfect Case

"This sighting defies explanation by conventional means."

Investigators are always on the lookout for the "perfect case" — one that has so much corroboration it can't be debunked by skeptics. One such case occurred June 23, 1955, and involved multiple independent witnesses with radar confirmation.

The case began when the co-pilot of a Mohawk Airlines DC-3 (cruising at 3,000 feet about fifteen miles east of Utica) noticed an object a mere five hundred feet above his plane, moving at "great speed." The object was described as oval-shaped, light gray in color, with a line around the perimeter and a row of windows that emitted a bright blue-green light. Both the pilot and the co-pilot then watched the object for several miles, until it moved out of view. They estimated it moved at about 4,500 miles per hour.

Moments later, the crew of two other airliners in the area also observed the object and reported it over their radio. Air traffic controllers at Albany Airport were monitoring the radio transmissions, and were also able to make visual contact as the UFO whizzed through their airspace.

At the same time, radar operators in nearby Boston tracked the object on their scopes. This rare radar-visual sighting report eventually made its way to the controversial "Condon Committee" headed by Dr. Low. The Condon Committee would later be criticized for conducting an unscientific and prejudicial study of UFO reports, including the above case. Incredibly, however, even the skeptical-debunking members of the committee were unable to debunk the Utica case. Gordon Thayer, a radio propagation specialist, was charged with analyzing thirty-five reports. Thayer was skeptical of UFOs and concluded that "there was no case where the meteorological data available tended to negate the anomalous propagation hypothesis," or in other words, all the radar returns from alleged UFOs were "ghost images" caused by weather, birds, insects, and other natural phenomena.

Researcher and physicist James McDonald found many errors in Thayer's reports, however. And when it came to the Utica case, even the skeptical Thayer was at a loss to explain it. He wrote:

> "…a most intriguing report that must certainly be classed as an unknown pending further study, which it certainly deserves. Statements from some of the other witnesses would help in analyzing the event…It does appear that this sighting defies explanation by conventional means."

To James McDonald, this was the perfect case because it fulfilled three qualifications. First, there were multiple, independent and technically trained observers. Second, the object was witnessed from three different airborne locations within the same time period. Finally, the object was also observed from multiple locations on the ground, with radar confirmation.[27]

UFO Emerges from Reservoir

On the evening of September 17, 1955, Mr. and Mrs. Bordes of New York City were fishing in the Bush Pine reservoir when they heard a loud splash and a gurgling sound. Looking towards the source of the noise, they saw a pink, glowing mushroom-shaped object about fifteen feet long rise about five feet above the water, and then sink back down into the reservoir. Several minutes later, the object resurfaced. The water around it became very turbulent. The mysterious object then moved back and forth and finally flew away at high speed.[28]

Plane/UFO Nearly Collide

"Here we were with a load of passengers... What are we going to do?"

One of the biggest and most famous New York sightings of the 1950s occurred April 8, 1956 over Schenectady, New York. On that evening, Captain Raymond Ryan and First Officer William Neff were flying American Airlines Flight 775 at an altitude of 6,000 feet above Schenectady. Without warning they were confronted by "this very brilliant white light, like an approaching aircraft with its landing lights on." The object appeared to be on a direct collision course. Captain Ryan took immediate evasive action and banked his plane to avoid the object. To their shock, the object performed a right-angle turn and moved towards their plane. Seconds later, it zoomed past them at an estimated "800 to 1,000 miles per hour...much faster than a jet."

At this point, the object suddenly decreased in speed and faded in brilliance until it became too dark to see. Still fearing a collision, Captain Ryan flipped on the landing lights. The UFO instantly reappeared in front of them, glowing bright orange.

Says Ryan:

> "It changed color after it got to the west of us...we knew there was something up there, and now here we were with a load of passengers with something on our course up ahead, and what are we going to do? So we watched where this light went out and this orange object came on."

The crew of Flight 775 radioed Griffis Air Force Base near Rome, New York. The officers on the base reported that they had visual contact with the airplane and requested that the crew extinguish the airplane's landing lights. Captain Ryan complied.

According to Ryan, the Griffis base officers confirmed that they could see "an orange object" ahead of the aircraft, and had a "definite silhouette in sight south of the field." They were unable to confirm the object on their radarscopes, as the instruments [they said] were not in operation. However, they did ask the crew to keep the object in sight while the base scrambled two jet fighters to intercept the object. At this point, stewardess Phyllis Reynolds entered the flight cabin where she also observed the object. The Air Force Base then "ordered" Flight 775 to deviate from their flight plan and to pursue the UFO. Ryan and Neff were surprised to find their commercial aircraft suddenly under military control, but because of the urgency displayed by the officers at Griffis Base, they obeyed the command.

More than twenty minutes passed as they pursued the orange UFO northwards and still there was no sign of the promised fighter jets from Griffis Base. Captain Ryan now had a decision to make. He was already in violation of normal safety rules and he would soon be out of radio distance from Griffis Base. He had already chased the object a distance of 150 miles. He could either increase his speed and continue to pursue the UFO, or he could cut off the chase and return.

Realizing that he could not jeopardize the safety of his passengers, he chose to return to his normal flight plan. The UFO continued to move north towards Canada at increasing speed until it was out of sight.

Ryan is convinced that the object was a genuine UFO. As he said in a public interview following the incident, "This was absolutely real. I am convinced there was something fantastic up there."

Afterwards, when questions arose as to why a commercial airliner was ordered to pursue a UFO by a military base, the Civil Aeronautics Board released a statement denying that Captain Ryan was requested to change his course, though they did admit that an unidentified object was seen. Arch skeptic and alleged MJ-12 member, Donald Menzel, however, concluded that the crew had seen only "the planet Venus." The entire case was thoroughly investigated by Major Donald Keyhoe who was stonewalled by Air Force officials and became convinced that they were lying about their version of events.[29]

UFO Evades Aircraft

On July 30, 1956, an un-named resident of Utica, New York had a fifteen-minute observation of a round, black object with an estimated diameter of twenty-five yards. As he watched, the object maneuvered up and down like a yo-yo through the clouds, appearing to hover at one point. The witness noticed a curious detail: whenever any other planes came into view, the object rose rapidly and disappeared into the clouds. Then when the sky was clear, the UFO again descended. The Air Force later investigated the incident and determined that the UFO would move away whenever any other aircraft approached to within a range of four miles.[30]

Another Angel Hair Case

Many people who see UFOs are not excellent witnesses simply because they are not formally trained to recognize the various aircraft in the sky. However, Richard Holsapple was a member of the Ground Observer Corps, and therefore a trained and experienced aircraft observer. In September 1957, Holsapple and his father saw three "strange objects" in the sky that were "flying faster than any jet I ever saw. Two were silver and another was somewhat darker."

As Holsapple and his father watched, the objects ejected several long strings of "flimsy material" that drifted slowly down to the south, too far away to attempt to locate. Holsapple called the *New Yorker* in Poughkeepsie, which printed a short account of his sighting.[31]

That's Not a UFO!

As any UFO investigator will tell you, many UFO reports turn out to have conventional explanations. It is the difficult job of the UFO investigator to sift the few valid cases from the mountain of bogus and conventional reports. Some cases may seem very strange at first, but then further investigation reveals the shocking truth. For example, during the year of 1957, a sizeable UFO wave swept across the United States, producing many genuine reports. However, not everything is what it seems....

At 9:30 p.m. November 3, 1957, residents of Long Beach, New York reported their sighting of a UFO, described as a round, hovering object, that appeared to pulsate in size and brightness, from a pin-prick of light to about the size of dime. Some witnesses also reported seeing "beams of light" from the object. Sounds like a great case, right? The only problem was, a quick investigation revealed that the location of the UFO coincided exactly with the appearance of Venus.

An equally enigmatic case occurred three days later, from 10:10 to 10:30 p.m., on November 6, 1957. On this occasion, residents of Buffalo observed an object described as pear-shaped, metallic, and the size of a B-52 bomber. The object was seen through binoculars. It hovered low in the southwest sky for about twenty minutes before fading out. Again, sounds like it might be a good case. However, investigators quickly discovered the culprit: Venus! The planet of Venus remains the number one guilty party for masquerading as a UFO.[32]

Flying Saucers on Broadway

One of the prominent themes of this book is that UFOs can be seen in places one would least expect, such as downtown New York City. On November 5, 1957, a UFO hovered only a few feet over Van Cortlandt Park, which is bordered on its western edge by Broadway. At 4:30 a.m., New York City garbage-man Frank C. was talking to a Broadway bus driver when he saw something strange over the park. About a quarter mile away, both men observed a "classical" silver flying saucer, complete with dome and portholes hovering fifty feet in the air over the playing fields in the center of the park. The base of the saucer appeared to be rotating, and the object emitted a low humming noise. There were no lights on the object, but it was illuminated by the street-lamps from Broadway.

The bus driver and the garbage man watched the disk for about thirty seconds, neither daring to move closer. Suddenly, the object shot forth a brilliant yellow light, illuminating the park like daylight. It then took off "just like a shooting star" and disappeared into the sky. The account was never publicized and only reached UFO investigator Aime Michel by coincidence. One month later, Frank C. was still shaken by the ordeal and told Michel, "I stay far away from that park now."[33]

UFOs Tease Jet Fighters

"We don't like to chase these damn saucers, because we don't know what they can do."

Only a few days after the Van Cortlandt Park sighting, the UFOs were back, this time over Sloanville in central New York. At around 2 a.m. November 8, 1957, an anonymous truck driver observed a "200-foot-long cigar-shaped object hovering about 200 feet off the ground." He was so impressed by his sighting that he called the *Albany Times Union* newspaper and reported his sighting.

However, the story was just beginning. Later that morning, Plattsburg Air Force Base was overwhelmed by a wave of "round silvery objects" that were maneuvering over the base. According to UFO researcher A. G. Dittmar, witnesses in the area watched as the base scrambled jets after the UFO. Instead of evading the jets, however, the UFOs appeared to tease their pursuers by waiting until the jets approached, then outrunning them with a burst of speed, only to wait again. Afterwards, some of the Plattsburg pilots revealed that they were frustrated by the strange behavior of the UFOs, telling the local state troopers, "We're just as glad we couldn't catch up with them. We don't like to chase these damn saucers, because we don't know what they can do."[34]

A Baseball Bat-Shaped UFO

One of the curious facts about UFOs is that appear in a wide variety of shapes. The vast majority of UFOs are described as saucer-shaped, spherical-shaped, egg-shaped, cigar-shaped and triangular-shaped. Some UFOs, however, arrive in shapes that are frustratingly unique. For example, on July

21, 1959, witnesses observed a white object described as a cylinder, "like a baseball bat." It hung vertically in the sky, reflecting the sun, for a period of about forty-five minutes. The case was investigated by the Aerospace Technical Intelligence Center (ATIC).[35]

Blue Book Case #6446

One of the few New York cases that the United States Air Force officially declared "unidentified" occurred at 1:30 p.m. July 25, 1959 over Irondequoit, New York. The un-named witness – a technical machine illustrator and private pilot, age 28 – was at home when he heard the noise of a jet. He grabbed a pair of 6-X power binoculars and went outside to locate and observe the plane. Instead, however, he was surprised to see a UFO. The object was described as crescent-shaped, about fifty feet across, brown-black in color with a white bubble or cupola in the center. The object appeared to hover motionless and totally silent, at an estimated distance of 6,000 feet from the witness just above treetop level. Seconds after he saw the object, it suddenly accelerated to a speed of about eight hundred miles per hour, banked in a swing to the east and disappeared behind some trees. In the distance, the witness could also see the jet that had originally drawn him outside.

Because of the reliability of the witness and the strangeness of his observation, Air Force Blue Book Officers had no choice but to label the case "unidentified."[36]

UFO over Mitchell AFB

One of the most common places to see a UFO is over any large military or technological installation, such as an air force base. Mrs. N. of Long Island makes her residence just six miles south of Mitchell Air Force Base. At precisely 6:55 p.m. August 19, 1959, Mrs. N. reported her sighting of a "vertical, luminous red object" that moved very fast in a straight line at a high altitude over the base and to the southeast. While the sighting was brief, the observation was actually part of a conglomeration of sightings that began earlier that day in Washington, DC, then moved to New York, then appeared in Trenton, New Jersey, flew back to Elburn, Illinois, and made a final appearance in Shelton, Connecticut![37]

UFO over Olean

One evening in December 1959, Duane F. Rarey was outside his home in Olean when he saw a glowing Saturn-shaped object hovering at a very low altitude over the house across the street. He grabbed his camera and snapped a photograph of the object, which almost seemed to pose for him. The photograph clearly shows what appears to be a solid glowing object with a strange ring around its circumference.[38] (See photo section.)

Chapter Three:

The Great New York Black Out

With the arrival of the 1960s, the UFO phenomenon continued its pattern of escalating encounters. By this time, beyond interactive sightings, numerous cases of landings and humanoids had been reported. The 1960s also brought the first cases of reported UFO abductions, though these types of cases stretch back much earlier, with several New York cases occurring prior to the 1960s. Again, these cases shall be covered in later chapters. The history of sightings in the 1960s – like the 1950s – shows an even greater tendency for UFOs to put on displays, often very dramatic – and in at least one case – undeniable. Clearly, the UFOs were making a great effort to be noticed.

UFO over Nantucket

It was 3 a.m. on January 5, 1963, and Mr. Cherrington was working the nightshift at the train station at Nantucket Point, Long Island. He was out-side filling the tanks when he observed a classical metallic flying disk about seventy-five feet in diameter hovering silently about 1,000 feet above him. A bright blue shaft of light beamed out of the top of the object. As he watched, the UFO began to execute a series of incredible maneuvers, including runs and flips, darting in all different directions, and swooping low as five-hundred feet above the ground. The display continued for about an hour until a large plane approached. Suddenly, the disk zoomed rapidly straight up towards the plane, which was flying at an estimated 15,000 feet, obscuring the plane's running lights from Cherrington's view. Cherrington assumed the disk was about to strike the plane, but at the last second it swerved around the plane and soared up into the sky where it assumed a star-like appearance. At this point, Cherrington's co-worker came out of the train and observed the object before it moved away. Cherrington was shaken by the encounter. As he says, "If something like this has to happen, let it be on someone else's shift."

Cherrington reported his sighting to authorities. Blue Book Intelligence officers conducted an interview and then made the following absurd conclu-sion: "Air Force evaluation: Star and planet. Object has characteristics of astronomical object with distortion due to the atmospheric conditions present and the interpretations of the object's behavior by the witness under these unusual conditions."

J. Allen Hynek, astronomical consultant to Blue Book, disagreed with the conclusion and emphasized this particular case (among others), as he says, "to illustrate the lackadaisical and irresponsible manner in which many of the UFO reports were treated by Blue Book. 'Get rid of the report quickly, no matter how' seems to have been the operative principle."[39]

UFO over U.N. & Empire State Building

One afternoon in June 1963, Milton B. was in a high-rise building in downtown New York City when he saw a strange object scooting across the sky beneath a low cloud layer. He grabbed his camera and began snapping photographs. He managed to catch two clear photographs of the UFO. One shows the object as it hovers over the United Nations Building. The other shows the object right next to the Empire State Building. Milton later turned his photographs over to UFO researchers who could find no evidence of trickery.[40] (See photo section.)

Blue Book Case #8739

"I have observed a phenomenon which is beyond my comprehension."

Blue Book officers were not always able to easily dismiss UFO reports. At 6:30 p.m. April 11, 1964, physiotherapist Warren B. Ochsner, his wife, and their two children were enjoying a picnic on a hillside ten miles northwest of Homer, New York. Looking up, they noticed an unusually wide white contrail in the sky, the tip of which was black. When the contrail drifted away, but the black part remained, the witness used a pair of binoculars to observe the dark area. He was shocked to see an object that "resembled a smoking plane slowly falling from the sky, at the same time assuming a shape not unlike a banana."

As the family watched, the object suddenly stopped moving, hovered in place, then faded away. Three minutes later, however, another object appeared. Says the witness, "It appeared as a horizontal pencil-shaped object. It was impossible to determine the length, but it could have been as large as a submarine...As I was observing it with my binoculars, there was a flash of white light from the rear of it and it shot forward for a distance about five times its length and as suddenly stopped, still maintaining the pencil shape, apparently hovering."

As they watched, the object changed into the shape of a saucer, then into a sphere. At this point, it divided into two parts. The top part sped away, while the bottom part moved downward, and divided again into two pieces. One piece sped quickly away while the other one slowly faded from sight. The entire sighting lasted for forty-five minutes. The witnesses found it hard to believe their eyes and said, "If it were not for the fact that all four of us observed this event I would hesitate to bring this to your attention... During World War II, I was a pilot in the U.S. Air Force. In all that time I never once, day or night, observed anything unusual in the skies. Now at age 43, I have observed a phenomenon which is beyond my comprehension and which taxes my sense of reasoning and credulity."

Fortunately, the witness did report the sighting, which was promptly investigated by Air Force Intelligence Officers from Project Blue Book. Not surprisingly, the officers were unable to account for the sighting, and it became one of only sixteen cases in New York that was officially labeled: unidentified.[41]

The UFO Beams

On July 27, 1964, an un-named engineer was driving through Sherburne when he slammed his car to a stop and stared upwards in amazement. Hanging motionless in the sky about forty-five feet above the ground was a large metallic-looking craft. The edge of the object glowed with a strange fluorescence. Suddenly, the craft emitted three powerful beams of bright light and took off at high speeds. The incident was reported to the Aerospace Technical Intelligence Center (ATIC) and Project Blue Book, who declared it officially "unidentified." (Blue Book Case #8969)[42]

Astronomer Chases Flying Saucer

Just after sunset August 9, 1965, an anonymous astronomer, his wife, her friend, and two children were driving east at about thirty miles per hour through Long Island. Suddenly, they all noticed "a silvery, disc-shaped object" with a "ring of bluish-white lights." The object moved slowly southward, then turned and accelerated rapidly in an east-northeast direction. The astronomer turned onto the main highway and also accelerated his vehicle up to eighty miles per hour in pursuit. However, in a matter of seconds, the disk dwindled in size until it became a star-like light high in the sky. It then moved up and down several times before darting to the south over the Atlantic.[43]

Dozens Observe UFOs

According to the *Niagara Gazette*, shortly after sunset September 22, 1965, dozens of residents from Buffalo, Lewiston, Clarence, Niagara Falls, North Tonawanda, and other cities reported seeing two brightly lit objects which changed colors and moved at a low altitude across upstate New York.

The first reports came from Lewiston, with witnesses reporting bright objects over the river. Shortly later, Roselle Simon, Leonard Butler, and other residents of Alden spotted the UFOs flying over Blossom Lee Drive. Next, State

Trooper John Riel spotted the object, which he described as globe-shaped, reflective, and metallic. Riel watched as the object swerved first northwest and then veered southwest.

Around this time, a reporter for the *Niagara Gazette* and his two children observed the UFOs cruise over the town of Niagara Falls. Shortly later, V. D. Price and his foreman, Raymond Bright, at American Standard Division, watched the object for nearly a half-hour as it passed over North Tonawanda. Said Bright, "This was not a satellite...This hung around the sky for about half an hour. It would move off in one direction and then stop. Then it would change direction and move off again. It was heading generally towards Cheektowaga, I'd say."

Other witnesses reported watching the objects cavort and dance around each other over Buffalo.

Reporters contacted local authorities, but were unable to obtain much additional information. The Niagara Falls Air Force Base denied any knowledge of UFOs in the area on that night. The Federal Aviation Agency at Niagara Falls International Airport was contacted, but said that the night crew had not received any UFO reports that evening. However, one of the controllers did admit that he had spotted a UFO the night before.[44]

The Great New York Black Out

"I'll swear on a Bible that I saw them out there and that they talked to me."

A month and a half later, on the evening of November 9, 1965, New York City experienced one of the largest blackouts in United States history, covering an area of 80,000 square miles, affecting more than five million homes and businesses, and 36,000,000 people — fully one-fifth of the nation's population. At first the blackout was a mystery, and no damage could be found. Later an official investigation finally concluded that a faulty relay break at the Sir Adam Beck Plant #2 in Clay, New York, was allegedly responsible. It apparently became overloaded and when the power trippers failed to function, it set off a domino effect that couldn't be stopped. At least, that is the official explanation.

However, there is considerable evidence that the blackout may have been caused by UFOs. Certainly UFOs have been known to affect electromagnetic devices and had already been associated with other widespread power outages. The New York Blackout, however, turned out to be the clincher that cemented the connection between UFOs and power failures.

One night before the blackout, a group of teenagers were on a Syracuse hilltop when they observed a "reddish ball" of light moving over the local dormitory.

The next evening, on November 9, 1965, Robert C. Walsh, then the Deputy City Aviation Commissioner for Syracuse, was flying at about 1,500 feet above Syracuse when the blackout struck. As all the lights disappeared, he became disoriented and decided to land at the nearest airport. He successfully landed and was discussing the blackout with others when they all observed an enormous "ball of fiery light" fifty feet in diameter flying upwards overhead at an altitude of one hundred feet.

Meanwhile, Flight Instructor Weldon Ross and his student James Brooking were flying over the airport when they too observed a large "glowing ball-shaped body" traveling over the power-lines leading to the Niagara Falls power plant. They later signed statements for NICAP investigators.

At the same time, William Stilwell, sexton of St. Paul's Episcopal Church, had a 117-power telescope set up next to the window on his third story room in the cathedral. When he saw several glowing objects outside, he aimed his 117-power telescope on one of the objects. He could see that the center of the glowing object was rotating. He snapped several photographs, two of which were later published in the *New York Herald Journal* under the headline, "Flying Fireball Photographed." One of the objects remained in place for up to two hours before finally streaking away.

He later revealed to investigators that he had seen the strange "fireballs" at least twelve times prior to mid-August. Sometimes the balls of light would dart around quickly and disappear. On other occasions, they would "hang there for a couple of hours." Stilwell didn't report his sightings because he was afraid how people might react. He had actually photographed several of them prior to the night of the black out. The photographs show small white objects in the night sky. Later, Stilwell would have a much closer encounter (described later).

Another witness who managed to capture a photograph was *Life* photographer, Arthur Rickerby. Immediately following the blackout, Rickerby whipped out his camera and began snapping photographs. He and numerous other witnesses in the building observed an unexplained bright light in the sky. One of his photos shows the New York City skyline just after the blackout. In the western portion of the sky, the photograph shows a "brilliant, silvery object." The photo appeared in the November 19, 1965 issue of *Time*, and has never been satisfactorily explained.

Yet another photograph was taken during the blackout by an anonymous photographer. Writes Antonio Huneeus, "Many [UFO photos] were taken around the period of the great blackout of 1965, including one that shows a totally black, saucer-shaped figure flying very close to the Empire State Building, precisely at the point of the huge antenna at the top. I have been unable so far, however, to obtain any reliable data that can back up this picture, such as the name of the photographer, the type of camera and film used, the exact date and time of the event, etc. Until such data can be produced the photo remains in a 'maybe' category."

Meanwhile, six people (including Renato Pacini, the Assistant Conductor of the Indianapolis Symphony Orchestra) were driving from Syracuse to Rochester and observed a "peculiarly brilliant light in the sky." Everyone in the car watched the glowing object as it descended from the sky and moved towards Syracuse. Shortly after it disappeared from sight, an announcement came over the car radio that the blackout had struck.

Mrs. Gerry Falk was driving along Prospect Avenue at the time the blackout struck. Looking up, she saw a strange red streak of light ahead of her in the sky. As she crested the hill, she got a closer look. Says Falk, "It was shaped rather like a half-moon, with two tips facing up. It was pale red, not like a flame, and there appeared to be something at the tip. It was very high in the air…it was different from anything I had ever seen."

Mrs. Sol Kaplan was watching television in the bedroom of her Central Park West apartment. When the power suddenly went out, she walked over to her window and looked outside. Says Kaplan, "There were a number of planes in the sky…As I kept looking I saw a big circular dome — it was not flying, but going up and down and sideways. It was silvery looking, no lights like an airplane. I was looking through binoculars."

In the nearby town of Camillus, the Boshers family all observed a "huge dome-shaped" object hovering still in the sky for about ten minutes. Suddenly it rose upwards. At that moment, the blackout occurred and the UFO darted away in a flash.

Nearby resident Tom Doxsee, of Manlius, and his neighbor went outside after the blackout had occurred and observed a large, yellow, glowing object that hovered in the sky for "sometime within an hour of the time the lights went out."

During the blackout, an un-named resident of Mattydale said that he was driving near Hancock field when he saw a large "egg-shaped" object hovering at a low altitude.

In the days that followed, the *Syracuse-Herald Journal* received more than one hundred reports of "strange glowing objects in and around Syracuse" since the night of the blackout. Dozens of other accounts came from surrounding areas including as far away as Pennsylvania, Massachusetts, Rhode Island, and New Jersey.

One of the most amazing and revealing testimonies from this incredible night comes from actor Stuart Whitman who was in his twelfth-floor New York City hotel room when he was woken up by a loud siren-like sound. Seconds later, he heard his last name being called "as though the voice was being projected by a loudspeaker." Looking outside his window, he observed two large, glowing egg-shaped objects hovering in place, one blue and one orange. Says Whitman, "They gave off a strange luminescent light. So I couldn't see if there were portholes or who was in them."

Speaking perfect English, the voice said he had been contacted because he held no malice or hatred. They then proceeded to give him a message, says Whitman:

> "They were concerned about our continued use of uncontrolled nuclear weapons, and about the chaos and lack of morality now in existence on our planet... They informed me that they will definitely interfere if we go too far in our war-like attitudes. They claimed that they are able to stop all electrical apparatus from functioning and could put a halt to our normal everyday activities any time they wanted to!"

The voice said that they had contacted several other people and that they wanted Whitman to tell their message "to all those with ears that will hear." They told him that the blackout had been a "demonstration," but that their only concern was the welfare of humanity. Says Whitman, "They requested that I attempt to assist in any possible manner, their campaign to wipe out racial prejudice, hatred, bigotry, and war from our planet."

During the encounter, Whitman felt no fear. Rather, he felt as if he were in the presence of friends. Says Whitman, "I was not frightened, but strangely elated. I had no fear, as I somehow knew they would do me no harm."

Following his encounter, Whitman bravely told his account to reporters, and spread the message of the ETs as they had instructed him to do. Says Whitman, "I don't know why they picked me as a contact. But I'll swear on a Bible that I saw them out there and that they talked to me."

Even one week later, UFOs were still being reported over Syracuse. A group of teenagers who had seen UFOs the night before the blackout observed a repeat performance involving a mysterious reddish ball of light. Fortunately, there were no further blackouts.

Pioneering researchers Ralph and Judy Blum investigated the blackout and learned from an inside source that the incident caused major concern at high levels of government. An Air Force intelligence officer told them, "My boss suggested that the UFOs were showing off — making it plain what they could do. I think he expected us to laugh. Nobody laughed."

Three years later, Congress held open hearings on the subject of UFOs. Atmospheric scientist and UFO researcher Dr. James McDonald was asked to testify. He told Congress that in his opinion, UFOs may have been responsible for the New York Blackout. Said McDonald, "Dr. Hynek probably would be the most appropriate man to describe the Manhattan sighting, since he interviewed several witnesses involved. I interviewed a woman in Seacliff, New York. She saw a disk hovering and going up and down and then shooting away from New York just after the power failure. I went to the Federal Power Commission for data. They didn't take them seriously although they had many dozens of sighting reports for that famous evening. There were reports all over New England in the midst of that blackout, and five witnesses near Syracuse saw a glowing object ascending within about a minute of the blackout."

McDonald then quoted a few other known cases and concluded, "Just how a UFO could trigger an outage on a large power network is, however, not yet clear. But this is a disturbing series of coincidences that I think warrant much more attention than they have so far received."

Congressman William Ryan asked McDonald if any agency had investigated the New York blackout in relation to UFOs.

McDonald: "None at all…There is no one looking at this relation between UFOs and outages."

Congressman Ryan: "One final question. Do you think it is imperative that the Federal Power Commission, or Federal Communications Commission investigate the relationship between the sightings and the blackout?"

McDonald: "My position would call for a somewhat weaker adjective. I'd say extremely desirable."[45]

Crowd Surprised by UFO

While UFOs are normally evasive, they do occasionally exhibit behavior that can only be described as playful. A good example occurred March 3, 1966 over Oswego. On that day, a group of "several civilians" saw an unidentified object that was flying southwards in a straight line. However, as it approached the witnesses, the UFO stopped, hovered in place, then swooped down towards the witnesses—approaching within fifty feet of the stunned crowd. It then immediately darted away towards the southwest.[46]

UFO Stalls Truck

On the evening of March 30, 1966, truck driver Bruce Field was on his way home to East Hampton from Montauk. Somewhere in the vicinity of Napeague, not far from the coast, his truck engine suddenly stalled and the car lights blinked off. Field just had time to pull off the road and roll to a stop. He tried his horn, but it wouldn't work either. After trying the ignition a few more times, he got out of his vehicle and checked under the hood. He fiddled with the wires when, suddenly, the car lights came back on.

He climbed back into his truck and turned the ignition. The engine started with no problem. He continued driving down the road. Around this time he noticed a bright light down by the shoreline. He assumed it was a beach buggy and paid it little attention, other than to notice that it seemed to be pacing his vehicle.

Field drove no more than a block when his truck engine suddenly quit again. It was a new truck, and he was at a complete loss to explain the engine failure. Again he got outside and opened the hood. As he was examining it, his attention became drawn to the light by the shoreline. Suddenly it became apparent that it was not a beach buggy. The light now suddenly veered inshore and moved directly toward the truck driver.

Seconds later, the object was directly over Field, casting down a brilliant white light. He could just make out a torpedo-shape behind the blindingly bright light. At this point the object darted away "faster than a jet." Said Field, "It was out of my sight in a second, and it didn't make a sound."

Field's truck lights suddenly flashed on. He scrambled back into his vehicle, which started normally. He wasted no time and drove directly to the local police station to report his encounter.

Officers at the station were stunned to hear Field's testimony. Only five minutes earlier they had received another UFO report from local resident Dallas Spicer, who lived off Three Mile Harbor Road. At around 9 p.m., the radio in Spicer's home became filled with static. He went outside to get something out of the garage when he saw a "very funny light" hovering over the telephone pole down the street. At the same time, all the neighborhood dogs began barking and Spicer's pony became restless and nervous. Spicer got into his car and drove down the street to investigate. As he approached the location, he discerned a bulky, black object hanging in the sky. Suddenly, the object flashed brightly and swooped down towards Spicer's vehicle, then turned and circled over the ocean, and headed towards East Hampton. Spicer went home and called the police.[47]

Woken Up by a UFO

About one week after the East Hampton encounter, on April 5, 1966, a resident of Durhamville, New York was awakened by an intense bright light that illuminated the entire interior of her trailer home. After a second, the flash of light disappeared. Thinking her heater had exploded, she got up to inspect it, but was unable to find anything out of order.

The next day, however, she was approached by her neighbors who told her that in the middle of the night, a "pulsating, luminous object" flew at a very low altitude directly over her trailer, circled it once, and then left. The three witnesses all reported hearing a low buzzing noise coming from the craft. No explanation could be found for the UFO's apparent interest in the trailer.

What may have been the same UFO was seen on the same night over Lycoming. A civilian woman, age 42, was getting a glass of water in her kitchen when she saw a nine-foot-wide object that was spinning and hovering about fifteen feet above her home. After a few moments, it darted quickly away, leaving a luminescent trail. This case eventually made its way into the Air Force's Project Blue Book where it was labeled unidentified. (See Blue Book Case #13085.)[48]

UFO Hospitalizes Woman

On April 24, 1966, Viola Swartwood was admitted to Auburn Memorial Hospital in Auburn, New York following an encounter in which a UFO swooped down over her automobile, apparently sending down some kind of electrical shock. Hospital physicians said it that it appeared as if the right side of Swartwood's body had been subjected to an electrical shock. There were no signs of any burns or other damage.[49]

UFO over United Nations Building... Again

One sighting that should have made front-page news across the world was fated to receive almost no publicity whatsoever. At 4:20 p.m. November 22, 1966, eight employees of the American Newspaper Publishers Association (ANPA) were in their offices on the seventeenth floor of 750 Third Avenue in New York City when, looking out the window, they observed a large "rectangular cushion-shaped object" heading southwards over the East River. When it reached the United Nations Building, the object stopped and hovered, fluttering and bobbing like a ship in rough seas. The metallic surface of the object glinted a bright gold color in the afternoon sun. After several moments, the object rose rapidly in altitude, then accelerated eastward at high speed.

The witnesses were all professionals and, as newspapermen, knew that what they had seen was significant. One of them, W. H. Lieck, called the Air Force, who promised to send an officer over for an interview, but never did. The witnesses tried calling various newspapers, but incredibly, they were not interested. Unable to generate interest in their report, the witnesses finally turned to NICAP. Dr. James McDonald, senior physicist with the Institute of Atmospheric Physics and the University of Arizona, interviewed the witnesses and became convinced that the case was legitimate. As McDonald wrote in an official statement that he prepared for the 1968 Congressional Hearings on UFOs: "I accept this as a quite real sighting, made by reliable observers under viewing conditions that would seem to rule out obvious conventional explanations."[50]

UFO over Bear Mountain

The year of 1966 turned out to be very busy. At 4:30 p.m. December 18, 1966, 23-year-old construction worker Vincent Perna was fishing with his brother and a friend on Lake Tiorati, a finger-shaped reservoir located on the west side of the Hudson River, near Pearl River, New York, when the three men observed a dull copper-colored, disk-shaped object emerge from behind a nearby ridge and hover over the lake. The object was silent and appeared to be about eighteen feet in diameter. It maneuvered with ease and quickly darted away, but not before Perna grabbed his small, plastic Brownie Starflash camera and snapped four quick photographs. (See photo section.)

Excited, Perna and the others decided to contact authorities. Little did they know what they were in for.

Park patrol officers were impressed and told Perna to call Stewart Air Force Base and make a report. Perna called the base and was surprised to find that they were interested in his sighting and even requested the negatives and prints of the UFO for examination. Perna complied.

The case was routed to the office of Blue Book. The officers conducted a detailed interview. They then returned his photos and prints with the conclusion that Perna had photographed a three to four foot diameter object that was close to the camera: in other words, a hoax. Perna and the others, however, denied any hoax and insisted that the object was much larger and distant from the camera.

J. Allen Hynek was shocked at the official conclusion of hoax. He wrote a lengthy letter to Major Hector Quintanilla, then head of Blue Book, saying in part, "I find no substantiation for the evaluation of hoax, particularly in view of the photo analysis report...Mr. Beckman, a qualified photoanalyst, disagrees with the photo analysis presented in the report as to the distance of the object. He points out the that depth of field extends much farther than indicated in the report...Consequently no judgment can be made as to the real size of the object...My recommendation is, therefore, that the evaluation be changed from hoax to unidentified."

Says Hynek, "Blue Book ignored my recommendation and maintained a file on the Bear Mountain photograph with the "Hoax" label intact; not really fair to either the scientific method or the character of the witness."

While Blue Book attempted to downplay the report, the story was not over yet. Later reporters from the *Rockland News* got hold of the story. Their reporters called up Stewart Air Force Base and asked for confirmation. They were told that officials had examined the photos and believed they showed a "blob of developing fluid."

At this point, NICAP investigators entered the scene. Two photographic experts examined the negatives and photos and declared them genuine. Perna was interviewed extensively, and later underwent an interrogation using sodium pentathol, which is normally reserved for use as a "truth serum," by military interrogators. No inconsistencies in his story were found. Leading UFO researcher Frank Edwards was also convinced that the case was genuine. Writes Edwards, "Because of the apparent authenticity of the pictures, they could conceivably become among the most important civilian photos ever taken." The photos are impressive. One of the photos clearly shows a large metallic object at some distance from the camera, hovering at an angle, and glinting in the afternoon sun.[51]

State Police Officers Encounter UFO

On February 17, 1967, the police station in Massena in northern New York received a call from an excited resident who said she had just observed a bright, orange-red object that was floating slowly across town. Two state troopers were sent to investigate. Moments later, they reported back to the station that they had the object in view and were unable to identify it. The object moved away.

Meanwhile, a third state trooper from Norfolk, New York (ten miles south of Massena) came upon the UFO as it hovered low over a local residence. After the object left, he approached the home and questioned the occupants. They told him that they had also observed the UFO and had become frightened when it hovered low over their house and sent down a brilliant orange-red illumination.[52]

UFO Hovers over Downtown Syracuse

William Stillwell's most famous UFO encounter occurred during the Great New York Blackout of November 9, 1965. Stillwell, a church sexton located in St. Paul's Episcopal Cathedral in downtown Syracuse, was able to capture photographs of the UFOs on the night of the blackout that were later published in the *Herald Journal*. However, Stillwell says that he has had many other encounters.

They began in the 1960s. He was standing on the roof of the rectory looking at the twinkling stars when some of the apparent stars started to move. Suddenly, a few of them swooped down out of the sky. Within seconds they were hovering right over the history museum and the Chimes Building across Montgomery Street. Since then, he has observed the star-like UFOs hiding by pretending to be stars as they hover above Syracuse.

As we have seen, Stillwell also saw unexplained fireballs on a dozen occasions leading up to the New York black out. However, he says that his most dramatic encounter occurred about six months later, in May of 1967. Says Stillwell, "It was about 10 at night. I saw a light diving over by the Chimes Building. Then it got closer. It was a craft, gray-colored, with the portholes glowing orange. I was dumbfounded. It was only 30 to 40 feet away. I felt like I was on a wharf standing next to the Queen Mary. It was a big steel wall."

Stillwell was so stunned, he was unable to move. The object came forward, then backed up and faded away. He told few people about his experience, and by the 1960s, stopped attempting to photograph the UFOs. However, he says, "They're up there."[53]

Steamship Crew Sees Darting Lights

In the summer of 1967, Gerald Mastropaolo (currently of Schenectady) was employed as assistant purser on the Hudson River Day Line's excursion steamer, Alexander Hamilton.

On July 17, they had chartered a cruise and had about 2,000 passengers on board. They left Pier 81 in New York City at about 9 p.m., heading north. As they sailed past Yonkers, several officers in the wheelhouse saw three (possibly four) brightly lit objects moving a "tremendous speed" towards the west.

Mastropaolo also saw the lights, as did Captain Edward Grady, Pilot George Carroll, Chief Purser Plotzky and the quartermaster. Says Mastropaolo,

"These 'lights' were hundreds of miles out and looked like stars except that they were brighter and moving. Within two or three minutes they had crisscrossed the horizon, changed directions and gone the opposite way, zigzagging each other as they went."

The crew of the Alexander Hamilton watched for the next ten minutes as the three lights performed dazzling maneuvers. According to Mastropaolo, they were all convinced that the lights were not any kind of conventional aircraft, as they moved too fast and could turn at sharp, right angles.

After ten minutes, the objects dispersed in three different directions. Mastropaolo wrote of his experience in a letter to *UFO Universe* magazine, concluding with, "I have never forgotten this experience and have often wondered if others elsewhere had observed these UFOs as had many from the decks of the Alexander Hamilton. What were they?"[54]

UFO Causes Temporary Paralysis

While UFO sightings are admittedly rare, even more rare are cases that involve physiological effects. On March 3, 1968, Nick Sgouris of Syracuse was driving to his place of employment when he was confronted by a sixty-foot-long, glowing cigar-shaped object covered with multi-colored lights, hovering ahead of him on the highway. The object quickly moved directly over his car. At that point, the engine began to fail and the car came to a slow crawl. At the same time, the witness felt "briefly paralyzed." After the object moved away, both the witness and the car recovered fully.[55]

Struck by a UFO Beam

UFOs seem to have a penchant for hovering over cars, sending down beams of light and chasing them down the road. A typical case occurred one evening in July 1968. Harold "Butch" Hunt, a musician/barber who lives in Pine Bush, and two friends were driving across the Red Mills Bridge in Crawford when a UFO showed up without warning and hovered directly over their car. The object appeared to be metallic, about one hundred feet in diameter, with a row of lights around its perimeter. Seconds after it appeared over the car, the object sent down three beams of light, which engulfed the car and the interior in blazing illumination. The three men wasted no time. Says Hunt, "I stepped on the gas and got the hell out of there as fast as I could."

As the men raced away, the UFO followed them for a short distance, however, after a few miles, they suddenly lost sight of it. However, a few weeks later, Hunt was driving through the same area during the day when he saw a huge cigar-shaped object floating slowly through the sky. He pulled over and exited his car to observe. The object appeared to be about a half mile away. A row of round windows was clearly visible around the perimeter of the craft, which made no sound. After a few moments, the object made a sharp turn and accelerated out of sight. Hunt reports that several of his friends and neighbors had seen UFOs in the area over the past several years.[56]

Men in Black Silence UFO Investigator

While UFO investigations can be time consuming, exciting and even unnerving, in some cases it can even be dangerous. An example is the unfortunate events that allegedly befell Jennifer Stevens of Schenectady. Before 1968 Stevens was an active UFO researcher. That year, however, she suffered a large number of crank calls and had bizarre phone problems that the telephone company could not explain, especially since her number was unlisted. During this time, her husband Peter was approached by a strange-looking man who warned him about his wife's UFO investigations. Peter drew a sketch of the man. UFO researcher John Keel saw the sketch and recognized the man as a typical Man-in-Black. Not long after Peter gave Keel a copy of his sketch, tragedy struck and Peter died suddenly and unexpectedly. Mrs. Jennifer Stevens was convinced that her husband's death was somehow linked to the Men-in-Black encounter, and she promptly abandoned UFO research.[57]

The Great New York Blackout – Not Again!

The 1965 Great New York Blackout remains one of the most important UFO events not only in New York history, but in the world. The fact that UFOs could so easily paralyze nearly one-third of the nation in a matter of seconds was cause for grave concern. The 1965 blackout was also followed by a series of similar UFO-related blackouts across the country. To UFO investigators it looked as if the UFOs were testing their abilities to disable Earth's power sources.

The 1965 blackout was eventually traced to the Sir Adam Beck power plant, and linked to the appearance of one or more UFOs in the area. So when, four years later, on November 9, 1969, UFOs were again seen hovering over the same Sir Adam Beck power plant, reporters at the *Niagara Gazette* took immediate notice. On this occasion, the report was made by three Niagara Falls police officers, each of who said that they watched four pulsating lights for nearly an hour starting at 2:15 a.m. November 9.

Patrolman Thomas Shumway watched the objects from the intersection of Lewiston Road and Hyde Park Boulevard. The objects appeared to pulsate red, white, and blue colors. Says Shumway, "They were like something I have never seen before. They were in formation and they were pulsating."

With him was patrolman Richard Wells, and later patrolman Richard Atkins. All three observed strange red streaks of lights pass between the objects. Atkins estimated that the objects were about 1,000 feet high. At one point, Shumway observed a single bright light shoot over the Niagara River at "a tremendous rate of speed."

They contacted the guards for the State Power Authority [SPA], who told them that they "have been seeing lights over the reservoir all week." The SPA was contacted, but a spokesman denied any knowledge of UFO activity over the power facility. A Hydro spokesman also denied that anything out of the ordinary took place, saying enigmatically that on that evening, "There were not any unusual operating conditions."

Thankfully on this occasion, there was no power blackout.[58]

Chapter Four:

Sightings (1970-1979)

The arrival of the 1970s brought a continuing series of UFO events over New York. The activity seemed to be spread equally throughout the state, with the majority of reports coming from the highly populated suburban areas. The most prominent patterns of UFO behavior continued to include dramatic displays, UFO-car chases, military confrontations, and of course, a growing list of landings and abductions. Again, the UFO occupants behaved as if they wanted to be noticed, though apparently only to a certain extent.

"It Wasn't Swamp Gas"

In 1971, police officer Robert Comeau had been a member of the Crawford Police Department for about four years. On January 4, 1971, Comeau was awakened by a strange whirring sound coming from outside his Crawford home. Looking out the window, he was amazed to see a silver disk-shaped craft about one hundred feet in diameter with a row of windows around the circumference and a dome top. Red and green colored lights pulsated at regular intervals. The object hovered in the sky at a low altitude, remaining in place for more than forty minutes.

He dutifully reported the sighting to his senior officer. When word got out about his sighting, Comeau's fellow officers reacted in various ways. Said Comeau, "Half the police department has seen them, and the other half thinks those who've seen them are crazy."

Years later in 1985 Comeau reported his sighting to the Middleton Record. He is, of course, convinced that he saw an extraterrestrial craft. As he told reporters, "It made the hair on my neck stand up. It wasn't swamp gas."[59]

The Flying Iron

On the evening of October 9, 1972, an anonymous couple was driving between Smithtown and Coram on Long Island when they both observed "a bright, white light, similar to the bright landing light of an airplane, low in the sky to the east and just slightly to the left."

According to the witnesses: "Its brightness considerably exceeded that of a star...so much brighter, so much bigger." As they drove, the glowing light seemed to pace their car. When they approached Seldon, the UFO disappeared and then reappeared shortly later. This time, they could see the shape of the object clearly. It had the appearance of a "pressing iron," with a rectangular shield at one end. The entire object was lined with strangely shaped bright lights. After a few moments, it darted away.[60]

The Communicating Lights

During the summer of 1973, scores of low-level sightings swept across the United States. One interesting New York case comes from Pat X. of Brooklyn. On May 31, 1973, Pat and eleven other adults were at a friend's apartment, looking out the window and commenting on the thunderstorm. Says Pat, "At about 9 p.m., we began to notice what I can best describe as weird lights floating outside. To get a better view, we left the apartment and went up to the roof since we realized right away that what we were seeing was not any form of lightning. We looked up and there in the cloud-covered sky were two bright lights shining from behind some dark clouds spaced a good distance apartment. The lights were flashing on and off, as if responding to each other."

The display continued for about an hour and a half, during which time, about seven or eight planes also flew by the lights, as if, thought Pat, to observe the phenomenon. The witness contacted UFO researcher Timothy Green Beckley, who himself contacted local newspapers and discovered that there had been another sighting in the area one week earlier.

One month after that case, sometime during the midnight hours of June 28, 1973, the same (or similar) strange blinking lights returned. On this occasion, more than a dozen residents of New York City reported their observation of a pair of bright red lights that appeared to be pulsating with "deliberate communication." The lights moved in a strange circular pattern for more than an hour before moving away.[61]

Rotating Object Observed

On the evening of October 17, 1973, sixteen witnesses, including a police officer, gathered outside in Gloverville to watch an unidentified object described as rotating with alternate colored lights. The object remained in view for approximately forty minutes, at which time it suddenly darted away.[62]

New York City Columnist Healed by UFO

At 10:15 p.m. July 8, 1974 numerous witnesses observed a glowing object hovering over Prospect Park in Brooklyn. One of the witnesses was Claudia Monteleone, the editor of a well-known financial magazine. She looked up and saw a strange glow hover over an apartment building on Caton Avenue. Monteleone quickly got another witness. She pointed out the object to Brandon Blackman, who was himself a successful New York City syndicated columnist. Blackman watched as the object performed a "wobbling in a falling leaf motion," rising up and down repeatedly.

Suddenly the object zoomed closer, so that Blackman could clearly see an "illuminated compartment" beneath the craft. Eventually the craft left and Brandon returned home. To his dismay, he couldn't find his keys and had to call the building superintendent to be admitted into his own apartment. Once inside, he came upon a bizarre mystery. Says Blackman, "I was dumbfounded to find the set of keys lying smack in the middle of the bed after entering the apartment."

There was no way the keys could have been there as he had locked the apartment when he left. Then came the final shocker. Earlier that day Brandon had slashed his finger, which he quickly bandaged. That evening before going to bed, he removed the bandage to be confronted by another mystery. Says Blackman, "When I removed the wrapping, I discovered much to my amazement that the wound was completely healed, as though absolutely nothing at all had happened."[63]

UFO Display over Glen Falls

On the evening of August 19-20, 1974, an extremely intense wave of sightings struck the town of Glen Falls and the surrounding areas. The first reports came from residents in the Malta and Round Lake areas of Saratoga County who called the police to report sightings of multiple large, blimp-like objects covered with colored lights. The objects were seen to hover in place and maneuver in various directions at high speed.

Meanwhile, police stations at Loudonville, Saratoga, Warren, Washington, and Glen Falls were fielding hundreds of calls from concerned residents.

By midnight, more than one hundred people had gathered along Dix Avenue in Glen Falls to watch several objects that were putting on a dramatic display for the growing crowd. Radio stations were alerted to the activity along Dix Avenue and broadcast the sightings as they occurred. By this time, numerous police officers had been called to the scene and also observed the objects. State police from Saratoga watched as one giant blimp-like object descended down over Saratoga Lake, drew water out of it, and then accelerated off to the south at an extremely high rate of speed.

The scene at Dix Avenue was now becoming out of control. By 1 a.m. more than four hundred people had gathered, completely blocking all traffic. State and local police were forced to move the huge crowd to East Field along Dix Avenue.

Meanwhile, the Civil Air Patrol at Albany sent units to investigate. One pilot reported that he was flying over Albany at 8,000 feet when a silent object flew over his plane at "a tremendous rate of speed." The Albany County Airport and Federal Aviation Authority tracked the speed of the object at 3,000 miles per hour.

Plattsburgh Air Force Base was notified, however, the public information officer said that they had no explanation for or information about the sightings, and denied that there were any UFO sightings over the base itself.

One Glen Falls resident didn't only see the UFO, but was apparently knocked unconscious by it. Joann Warren woke up on the evening prior to the wave of sightings to find a large object hovering in the sky outside her window. Looking up, she saw "a very strange object, like two diamonds connected by a bar."

While Warren gazed out the window, her thirteen-year-old son, Larry, (who had been sleeping in the same room because of a nightmare earlier in the evening) also woke up. He saw his mother looking out the window and she was speaking to him excitedly, telling him to look out the window. Says Larry, "I tried to see what was at the window, but couldn't. Everything occurred in slow motion, and when I finally succeeded in focusing on the window, my vision went black. My last recollection was of moving slowly back to the floor."

Joanne Warren confirms her son's account, and also reports that she was unable to wake up her daughter either. Her last memory was of going to sleep while the object was still there. The next day, the wave of sightings hit Glen Falls. Hearing about the sightings on the radio, Joanne Warren stepped outside to check the sky. Says Joanne Warren, "We saw them, the neighbors saw them. You could go out, right in the front here where the parking lot is and could see these things zooming all over the place and stopping, zoom here and zoom there, and you could see them...It was not just I that saw it or Larry, or my friend next door — half the town saw that."

Incidentally, Larry Warren would later become one of the primary witnesses involved in the famous 1981 Rendlesham Forest UFO incident in which a UFO apparently landed on a U.S. Air Force Base in Bentwaters, England.[64]

Craft over Staten Island

In late 1974, Staten Island residents Daniel and Margaret Kish were returning home from shopping when they saw a large cigar-shaped craft cross the road in front of them. Says Kish, "The object had a clearly visible row of lighted windows. It was down real close, so that we had no trouble making out the details."

Over the next few months, Margaret Kish claims to have seen the same UFO on several different occasions. She says, "If you ask me, I think they are probably from outer space."[65]

UFO Descends into Harbor

In 1975, the small weekly community newspaper, *The Brooklyn Home Reporter*, published a report from a local resident who said that she was at the Verrazano Narrows Bridge, which connects Staten Island to Brooklyn, when she saw a strange object descend into the lower harbor. Described as a "brilliant ball of fire," the UFO glided over the bridge and then landed on the surface of the water, where it quickly submerged, never to be seen again.[66]

UFO Follows Woman Home

"From the moment I passed under it, it followed me...bathing the area all around me with such bright light."

Fifteen minutes before midnight February 12, 1976, Sandra Maldonado and her husband Edward, owners of a boutique-beauty parlor in Catskill, were on their way home from visiting friends. Sandra was driving and Edward was asleep in the front seat. She had the radio playing as she drove along Vosenkill Road, which is full of hills, turns, and dips.

Sandra was just coming over a rise when she saw a flashing red light ahead of her. She first thought a disabled plane was making an emergency landing. As the object seemed to hang in space, she wondered instead if it might be a helicopter.

Says Sandra, "As I got near it, I realized (with some developing fright) that it was neither a plane nor a 'copter. I slammed on my brakes, turned off my radio, and stared, unbelieving, for a moment or so. There the 'thing' was, hovering motionless directly over the road, just above the utility poles and the trees. It was as wide as the road, but was distinguished by a tall mast like structure on top of a rounded dome which made it seem out of proportion to its width. At the top of this skeleton-like mast, was a square 'box' (with transparent sides) in which a red light revolves, like our fire-trucks.

"This was the only light source I saw at any time. This light, as it streamed out of the box in all directions, became a soft, but very bright white light. The object was low enough in my headlights for me to make out a metallic hull similar in appearance to pewter. The configuration was like an inverted bowl on a plate. I saw no openings, hatches, trapdoors, ports...I did notice, however, two concentric half circles of a very intricate design on the side facing me. It stood out in bold relief."

At this point, a wave of fear swept over the witness. She jammed on the gas pedal and raced home. However, to her shock, the object began to chase her. Says Sandra, "From the moment I passed under it, it followed me, staying directly overhead, and bathing the area all around me with such bright light that I really did not need my headlights. Just before I reached my driveway, the object seemed to be gone."

Sandra screamed at her husband to wake up, but he wouldn't react. All attempts to wake him failed. She got out of the car and ran inside, leaving her husband in the car. Looking outside her window, she saw that the object had reappeared, and was continuing to drift up and down Vosenkill Road, as if waiting for another carload of innocent witnesses to scare. The object didn't approach her home, but for the next half-hour it remained in view.

Finally an airplane flew overhead and the object promptly extinguished its lights. After the plane passed, the UFO lit up again. Shortly later, it moved south and appeared to settle down in a swampy area. The next day she called the police in Leeds, but they denied receiving any reports. They referred her to UFO researchers Gary Levine and Harold Bates, who investigated the case. Said Bates, "I think we can say that we believe the story."[67]

A UFO/Police Chase

On November 19, 1977, Diane Diaz and Toni Corbo, both student nurses in their twenties, were driving home from a Staten Island diner when they saw what appeared to be a bright orange saucer-shaped object glide over Hylan Boulevard. The object was "bobbing up and down," said Diaz. "My girlfriend almost drove off the road. It was bright yellowy-orange, and it glowed so much we couldn't look at it. Terrified is not the word."

However, instead of fleeing, Diaz and Corbo decided to take action. They flagged down a passing patrol car and pointed out the UFO to the two incredulous officers. When the UFO started to move away, the police officers took off chasing it, reportedly all the way to the border of New Jersey.

The police officers issued a report. This was followed by an official Air Force investigation. Before they knew it, the nurses were besieged by the media, quickly conducting more than two dozen media interviews. The reaction shocked the witnesses. Said Diaz, "My family thought I was crazy. My brothers tortured me."

However, all the publicity also brought more than a hundred calls from other New Yorkers expressing support or relating their own encounters. Said Diaz, "People understood what we were going through. They had seen the same thing."[68]

A Thunderous UFO

Four days after the previous sighting, on November 23, 1977, six people in Plymouth Township reported a large triangular object that hovered overhead. While most UFOs are described as silent, one farm couple reported that as it passed overhead, it stopped and hovered, emitting a thunderous noise that made their entire house vibrate.[69]

Another UFO-Caused Blackout

The UFO connection to power blackouts should now be obvious. However, as if to remind humanity of their ability to paralyze large power grids, UFO-related blackouts (although rare) seem to occur regularly, as in the following alarming case.

On April 6, 1978, a police officer and his family reported seeing a large oval object hover near their home in Baldwinsville, in Onondaga County. Ten minutes later, there was a bright flash of light, and power was cut off to 3,000 homes. Looking outside, the family saw a helicopter appear and the UFO flew away. Later, investigators researched the incident and uncovered two separate groups of independent witnesses who reported similar sightings in the same county, though on the following evening.[70]

UFOs over Niagara Falls AFB

As reported to MUFON, in 1979, an un-named family – including a father, brother, sister, and cousin – who lives adjacent to the Niagara Falls Air Force Base was driving near their home when they sighted a "glowing orb-like orange light" streak across the sky. The witnesses were convinced that the object was unusual because one minute afterwards, two military jets took off from the Niagara AFB in pursuit of the object. The father, who was driving, also attempted to pursue the object and the jets by car, but was unsuccessful. The witness writes that even twenty-eight years later, the event still comes up in family discussions about UFOs.[71]

Chapter Five:

The Hudson Valley UFO Wave

UFO waves, also known as flaps, can be defined as a period of time during which a geographically defined area experiences a disproportional large amount of UFO activity. These waves can last for a few days or weeks, or in some cases months or even years. Some investigators feel that waves are, in effect, publicity campaigns designed by the UFO occupants to attract attention.

By the time the 1980s rolled around, New York had already experienced several intense UFO waves, though most of these were short-lived. However, in 1982, a monumental wave would sweep across the upstate New York area. Within the space of four years, the wave would produce hundreds of sightings and involve literally thousands of witnesses. It would become New York's single largest UFO wave and would send shockwaves throughout the community and beyond for years to come.

Although the wave is said to have began in 1982 following one particularly dramatic and widely viewed event, there are indications that it began earlier than that. In any case, the high level of activity was unprecedented, and a certain area of New York would soon be permanently placed on the map as a UFO hotspot.

Airport Employees See UFOs

The upstate New York area has apparently always been a hotbed of activity. However, a small town known as Pine Bush had earned a reputation among the local population for having an abnormally large number of encounters.

One of the closest major airports to Pine Bush is Stewart International Airport, about fifteen miles southeast. One evening in early 1980, air controller Tom Vicarro was on duty in the control tower when he received a call from the airport's operation supervisor. The local newspaper had just called. Apparently they were being flooded with calls reporting a UFO in the area. The newspaper editor wanted to know if any strange aircraft were visible from the tower. Vicarro scanned the skies around the airport and saw nothing. He told the operations supervisor that the skies were clear.

A half hour later, the operations supervisor called again saying that they were now receiving direct reports from witnesses who were seeing UFOs in the area. Says Vicarro, "When I was notified of this, I decided to go over to the other side of the tower to take another look. What I saw was a very bright light hovering in the sky. It was much too intense and enormous in size to have been a star or a planet."

Later, *Omni* columnist Harry Lebelson, interviewed Vicarro and learned further interesting information. The Pine Bush UFO activity, according to Vicarro, was nothing new. He said that the pilots and airport personnel saw the UFOs "frequently." He also pointed out that by a coincidence of its location, Pine Bush is a "border area" and is not covered by radar. Therefore, it would make an ideal location for UFOs to hide.[72]

Crystall Visits Pine Bush

In 1980, researcher Ellen Crystall was searching for a UFO hotspot where she might see UFOs firsthand. When she read a UFO column by Harry Lebelson in *Omni* magazine, she called him up and asked him if he knew of any areas of high activity. Lebelson mentioned Pine Bush, and told her about a couple he knew, "Bruce and Wendy," that claimed to be having close-up UFO sightings on a regular basis.

In July of 1980, Crystall and Lebelson drove to Pine Bush to begin a firsthand field investigation. They soon learned that activity in the area had been fairly regular since at least 1969, and had been reported by a wide variety of Pine Bush and nearby Crawford residents, including a policeman, a barber, store clerks, laborers and others. Business owners and downtown employees had allegedly seen UFOs directly over their stores and offices. Crystall and Lebelson interviewed Bruce and Wendy, and learned that they had been seeing the craft for several years, including several close-up sightings and landings. They said the craft showed on a nearly nightly basis, and that they could see them practically anytime.

They promised to show Crystall and Lebelson where the UFOs were appearing. It was around 10 p.m. July 18, 1980, as Crystall, Lebelson, and her new friends drove east on Hill Avenue and parked next to a certain remote farm pasture. Bruce assured her that the UFOs would soon arrive.

To Crystall's shock, the UFOs showed up right on schedule. Writes Crystall, "We got out of the car and looked up. Almost immediately we were surrounded by about a dozen large triangular craft with amber-yellow lights in the form of a 'plus sign' on their front. The plus-sign-shaped lighting panels divided four window panels that made up most of the front of the ships...When the intensity of the lights was raised to full bore, the entire sky lit up. The ships also had multicolored blinking lights all over them...The ships were filling the sky around us and landing in the field. It seemed like Grand Central Station at rush hour. Some flew as close as fifty feet, but none of them were close enough for us to see the occupants. They made no sound. The sky was too dark to make out other details."

During this time, they used up more than two rolls of film taking photographs. They tried to walk through the field to get closer, but the terrain was too rough. They drove around to another area. Moments later, a ship rose up from another field, approached them and passed directly over their car only a few feet above their heads.

The four witnesses watched various craft until 3 a.m., then finally returned to home. The next morning they returned to the site and found areas of crushed vegetation, which they photographed. The photographs of the landing marks came out clear, however, every single one of the UFO photos showed only bursts and sprays of multicolored lights, and not what they had actually seen. Crystall later concluded (after taking many more photographs) that the film was being intentionally altered or tampered with by radiation (possibly short-wave) from the UFOs.

The next night, on July 19, Crystall and Lebelson went out again in search of UFOs. They saw more craft, though this time from a greater distance than the previous night. Again, the objects were totally silent. They also saw some of the craft send down beams of light to the ground.

Crystall and Lebelson were hooked. Over the next month, they returned several times each week for more UFO hunting. On each night, they saw what appeared to be UFOs skirting at low altitude through the forested fields.

On July 26, 1980, Crystall, Lebelson, Bruce and Wendy, and three other people pulled over along Hill Avenue outside of town to wait for the UFOs. It was twilight when a craft suddenly appeared and moved directly overhead. Writes Crystall, "We held our breath, transfixed by the spectacular sight. The craft could be seen clearly in detail, right down to the seams in the metal...We could see the bulky curvature of its sides. It seemed to be about sixty feet in length...Our mouths hung open as we watches this silent beauty move across the sky at about fifteen miles per hour. What a sight!"

The above sighting was unusual. Most of the sightings were from a distance and not nearly as impressive. On one such occasion, Crystall and Lebelson were watching what appeared to be one of the crafts in the distance when a plane approached the UFO. Suddenly the object turned off its lights and dropped in altitude. The pilot of the plane turned and left the area. As soon as it was gone, the UFO turned its lights back on.

Lebelson and Crystall drove around to see if they could get closer to the object. They began discussing if they could communicate with the UFO by flashing their car lights. Suddenly the object approached, faced directly towards them and flashed its lights off and on three times in a row. Crystall and Lebelson looked at each other in shock. Had the UFO been listening to their conversation?

By mid-August, Crystall and Lebelson had made nearly twenty field trips to Pine Bush, seeing groups of anywhere from one or two triangular-shaped craft to about thirty, on dozens of occasions. They also began to bring other people to also witness the craft. On several occasions, Crystall says that the UFOs not only approached closely, they were occasionally struck by powerful and focused light beams from the craft.

By now she realized that she had developed some kind of weird ability to sense where they would appear. She also felt an emotional connection to the occupants. On August 7, Crystall also had a face-to-face encounter with one of the occupants of the craft, the details of which are presented in a later chapter. On one occasion, as they were walking through a field, a large ship silently lifted up only a few yards away and disappeared into the distance. By this time, Crystall had also concluded that the craft had the ability to turn completely invisible at will.

Crystall and Lebelson continued their treks through August, September, and October. However, by mid-October, they noticed a sudden and dramatic drop in the number of sightings. All they could see were one or two lights off in the distance. By November 1980, the Pine Bush wave appeared to be over.

In 1981, she made several trips and saw only a few lights from a distance. In the summer of 1982, Pine Bush resident Bob Lloyd told her that the UFOs had come around for the past two weeks. Unfortunately, she missed the mini-wave. Crystal continued to visit regularly, but somehow the UFOs eluded her. She was determined to continue, however, and would later return to Pine Bush for more research. Meanwhile, however, upstate New York was about to be thrust into the one of the most intense UFO super-waves in UFO history.[73]

The Hudson Valley Wave Officially Begins

"It was so huge, it filled up the entire sky."

By 1983, Philip Imbrogno, an astronomer, science teacher, and chairman of the Science Department at Windward School in White Plaines, was already quite familiar with UFOs. Ten years earlier in 1973, he joined the Mutual UFO Network, and then one year later, joined the Center for UFO Studies (CUFOS). As a field investigator for CUFOS he had researched many local cases.

In early 1983, Imbrogno received a report from a retired police officer who insisted upon anonymity. The officer said that around midnight on New Year's Eve 1982, he stepped outside his home in Kent and saw a slow moving object with bright white, green and red lights approaching their home. Moments later, it was five hundred feet overhead. The officer said it was boomerang-shaped, and silent except for a deep hum. Suddenly, all the colored lights turned off and three white lights appeared in a triangular pattern, illuminating the ground like daylight. Five seconds later, the white lights went out and about fifteen colored lights turned on. The object moved slowly away towards Interstate 84. Said the officer, "I never saw anything like this before, but I can tell you this was not any type of aircraft that I know of."

The officer managed to videotape the object, but unfortunately, the UFO didn't register well on the tape.

Meanwhile, Imbrogno received another call from Edwin Hansen who said he was driving along Interstate 84 just after midnight when he saw an object circling at a low altitude above the highway, sending down powerful beams of light. Several other cars had also pulled over to watch it. Hansen wished for the UFO to come closer, at which point it immediately began to approach his car.

Says Hansen, "It was so huge, it filled up the entire sky." The object came right over his car, sending down a powerful beam of light. Hansen honked his horn in terror, and pleaded for the object to go away. However, in his mind he said, "I felt thoughts that weren't my own, but a kind of voice telling me not to be afraid."

Imbrogno reports that this sort of telepathic message would appear in several other future close-up sightings. At this point, however, there was no indication of the upcoming activity. It wasn't until two months later, on February 26, 1983, when another dramatic series of sightings occurred that Imbrogno and other local investigators began to suspect that they might be dealing with a wave of epic proportions.[74]

UFO over White Pond Lake

At around 8 p.m. February 26, 1983 Monique O'Driscoll was driving with her daughter near their home in Kent when the radio began to static. Looking up and to their left, they saw an enormous flying boomerang-shaped craft pacing their car. The object appeared to have an estimated fifty lights across its surface. It moved right over the car and stopped to hover over White Pond Lake, where it started flashing its lights furiously. As it moved away, O'Driscoll thought to herself, "Don't go." The object immediately responded. Says O'Driscoll, "At that split second, it stopped, made a complete turn, and then it was facing toward me. Then it started moving toward me very slowly." Her daughter began screaming and the object stopped and began to move away.

Meanwhile, at the same time Rita Rivera was driving by and also saw the object as it hovered over the pond. Nearby residents Mr. and Mrs. Donald Nandick saw the lights from their home, but were afraid to go outside. They called the police who told them that they were receiving many calls from other people reporting UFOs. The wave had begun.[75]

The Wave Continues...

Three weeks later, the UFOs were back. As evening fell March 17, 1983, the sheriff's office in Brewster began receiving calls from frightened residents reporting a large object over the highway. Imbrogno and his team (including Fred Dennis, Sheila Sabo, Chris Clark, and George Lesnick) also received several calls from witnesses who described seeing an object in the same area.

On that evening, Linda Nicoletti of Brewster looked out the window of her home towards Interstate 84 when she saw what looked like a jet about to crash. Then she realized it was moving too slowly and was totally silent. At the same time, several cars pulled over and stopped to watch the object, and several neighbors exited their homes and also stared upwards. Says Nicoletti, "It was V-shaped and had rows of bright lights along its wings. So many lights it was impossible to count them. They were all colors of the rainbow, with one much larger and brighter in the center underneath."

Around the same time, Dennis Sant was driving home with his children when they saw the object hovering about fifty feet over their home. Says Sant, "It was a very large V-object, a very massive size...it illuminated the whole area...It seemed to be about the width of a football field and was a dark, very gray metal. It was so close you could hit it with a baseball."

Sant actually walked directly underneath it, and was able to hear a very low humming sound before the object moved away.

Imbrogno and his team received several other reports from people who were driving along I-84 that evening. Most described how traffic came to a screeching halt as frightened drivers stopped to gaze at the gigantic boomerang-shaped object. One gentleman, William Durkin, had pulled over to watch when the object came right over a nearby truck, flashing it with a brilliant beam of light. The anonymous truck driver accelerated away in fear.

Meanwhile, the UFOs moved to the east, towards Danbury, Connecticut where it made several more dramatic appearances.[76]

"Hundreds Claim to Have Seen UFO"

"Hundreds Claim to Have Seen UFO," so read the headline for the front-page story of the *Westchester-Rockland Daily Item*. Imbrogno looked at the headline in shock. The article described how on March 24, 1983, between 8:20 and 9:30 p.m., the Yorktown Police Station switchboard was jammed with hundreds of calls from residents reporting a low-flying boomerang-shaped UFO covered with multi-colored lights. Imbrogno quickly scrambled his team together and began an immediate investigation.

They soon learned that the newspaper article had seriously underestimated the situation. Their investigation revealed that police stations in at least fifteen communities throughout Westchester and Putnam Counties were flooded with calls. Imbrogno set up a hotline and within one day had received more than one hundred calls. Hundreds more would come in the days and weeks that followed. Writes Imbrogno:

> "Just how many people actually saw the large, boomerang-shaped object as it drifted over the valley during a two-and-a-half hour period that evening will probably never be known... It is likely that several thousand people saw this strange phenomenon that night."

By this point, there were so many cases that the investigators were overwhelmed. Writes Imbrogno, "There were so many reports that investigators had to ignore the many 'routine' sightings in order to concentrate on those that involved 'close encounters' or sightings in which the object came within five hundred feet of the witnesses." Although they didn't know it at the time, this would remain a problem for the next three years of the investigation.

The night of March 24, 1983 was unique in New York history. Never before had a UFO appeared to so many people for so long a period of time. Writes Imbrogno, "Eighty-five percent of all the sightings reported that night came from an area of Westchester and Putnam Counties only three miles wide and twelve miles long. The Taconic Parkway runs through the center of this area, and the object appeared to have been meandering back and forth across that roadway."

At 7:30 p.m., business executive Hunt Middleton saw a group of colored lights connected to a strange craft hovering outside his home in Bedford. One hour later in Carmel, computer consultant Steve Wittles and three friends watched a large object with colored lights hovering for a minute outside their home. A few minutes later, Dr. Lawrence Greenman and his family (also in Carmel) saw the same object, which they described as V-shaped. As they watched, it sent down a beam of white light, and in the beam of light, a smaller red sphere descended and then darted away.

A half-hour later, the object descended over Millwood and Yorktown. Joan Lindauer was driving through Millwood when she was followed by the UFO, which she described as "the size of a large jet with brilliant white lights in the shape of a V." The object continued north and appeared over the Taconic highway where it hovered over cars, engulfing them with beams of light. Traffic on both sides of the highway came to a halt as numerous drivers stopped to watch.

Computer programmer Ed Burns was also followed by the object as he drove through Millwood. He pulled over with a group of about a dozen other cars and watched as the object hovered. It appeared to be triangular in shape and covered with forty colored lights. Said Burns, "This was a flying city. It was not a small craft. It was huge."

The object then moved over downtown Yorktown. The police station was flooded with calls. Police Officer Kevin Soravilla was on patrol when he saw the object make a slow 180-degree turn. He called the station and was told that the switchboard was jammed with calls. By now, traffic along several highways was coming to a standstill.

Bill Hele, chief meteorologist for the National Weather Corporation, stopped his car along the Taconic Parkway and exited his vehicle to better observe the object. As he watched, the giant V-shaped craft descended from 2,000 to 1,000 feet and slowed down to only a few miles per hour. It then turned off its lights and became totally invisible. A few seconds later, the object turned its lights back on and moved directly over his vehicle. It then moved northward along the highway. Seconds later, two men drove up and told him that they had been chasing the craft through the city.

Another witness was Dennis Fleming. He was first alerted to the object when the cars around him began weaving and reducing their speed. Finally, he pulled over with another group of cars and watched the large craft. He could also hear a faint hum.

At around 8:15 p.m., the object appeared over the Ossining Reservoir. David Scarpino witnessed the object close-up hovering at treetop level and estimated that it was easily the size of a 747 jet. It was covered with colored lights. However, at one point it turned off its lights and turned completely invisible.

At around 8:30, the Holtsman family of Kent was driving along Route 301 when they saw the object three hundred feet ahead of them, hovering above the road. The light from the craft was so bright...it illuminated the treetops. A car coming from the other direction stopped underneath the object. Suddenly it began to flash its lights brightly. The car sped away and the Holtsman family quickly drove underneath the object and then back to their home.

At the same time, John Miller was driving north through Brewster when he saw a large V-shaped object descend to about 120 feet above a small pond of water. It then sent down searchlights as if looking for something. Meanwhile, a dozen people in a restaurant in Stormville watched a large boomerang-shaped object hovering over a utility pole only two hundred yards away. Unknown to the witnesses, this UFO was apparently in the process of abducting an entire family (an account that's presented in a later chapter).

At 8:45 p.m. John Piccone and his family watched the UFO from their home in Yorktown. The object made a faint humming noise as it passed overhead at about 1,500 feet. Suddenly one of the lights separated from the craft and approached the family. Says Piccone, "It almost seemed as if it was observing us. Ten or twenty seconds later, it pulled back into formation."

A half-mile from the Piccone's home, the Karp family also observed the object as it passed overhead, badly frightening their cat.

The object then moved over Putnam Valley, where a seventeen-year-old snapped a photograph of the object. Imbrogno later learned that dozens of people had tried to photograph the object, but every single photographer said that the film failed to register any object.

Joe Trongone was in his home in Putnam Valley when his neighbor began screaming that a UFO was hovering overhead. He ran outside and saw the object suddenly move and descend towards him. As he says, "This is what scared the hell out of me. It came down like something out of the movie 'Close Encounters.'"

At around 9 p.m., the police station in New Castle was flooded with calls from residents. Police officer Andy Sadoff was on patrol when she saw the object, which she estimated at three hundred feet in size, pass back and forth overhead, finally hovering directly over her car. She reported her sighting to her sergeant. Says Sadoff, "He said the entire area was spotting it. We called Yorktown, and their officers had seen it and didn't know what it was."

Also around 9 p.m., Gloria Scalzo was driving along the Taconic Parkway near Ossining when she saw the object pacing the highway. As she drove past it, she realized it was a UFO. She turned around and chased the object, watching it for several minutes.

At 9:15 p.m., Herbert and Elaine Keuchen watched the object as they left

Briarcliff. As they drove along the Taconic Parkway, they sighted the object again. They estimated that it was at least six stories in height. They reported their sighting to the New Castle police, who admitted that they had already received many reports.

At 9:30 p.m., Tom Richman and his daughter watched a boomerang-shaped object hover three hundred feet over Kirk Lake near Mahopac. A few minutes later, Mark Galli saw the object in Carmel south of Interstate 54, and then later over Stormville. At this point, the object moved over Connecticut, leaving another trail of bewildered people.[77]

UFOs Spooks Physicist

Two days after the mass sighting, on March 26, 1983, physicist Dr. Albert Silbert of White Plains was driving home with his wife and two children when they saw a V-formation of lights hovering over their street. Silbert stopped the car and exited to get a closer look. Says Silbert, "This craft came straight for me. It came over the trees, just clearing them. It seemed to be about twenty-five feet above the trees and moving at a speed of about forty miles an hour. As it approached, it started to drop even lower, about another ten feet, and was still coming straight at me. At this point, I realized that this was something highly unusual, and I started to get spooked about the whole thing."

Silbert became frightened and retreated back into the car. He looked away for only a second when the craft made a sharp turn. His family was screaming wildly. Silbert raced to their home. They found the entire neighborhood outside watching the object. Says Silbert, "I saw the movie 'Close Encounters,' and it looked like something right out of the movie."

Silbert is still not convinced that the object was necessarily extraterrestrial, and yet, he admits that it was a very scary experience. "I must say, there was a feeling of almost terror, since no matter how sure I was that this was not some spaceship, there is always doubt in my mind. The object was very strange looking."[78]

The Mystery Fliers

Following the intense wave of sightings, the Yorktown Police released an official statement saying that it was their assessment that the UFO sightings were caused by a group of private pilots who were flying ultra-light craft in close formation in a deliberate effort to make people believe they were seeing UFOs. An investigation was allegedly in progress to determine the identity of the mystery flyers.

Shortly following the wave, numerous residents across Hudson Valley did, in fact, report seeing groups of planes flying in close formations. Many, however, had already seen the Hudson Valley UFO and easily recognized the difference. Some witnesses believed that the planes were in fact being purposefully flown over the Hudson Valley to confuse the issue, and basically cover-up the real UFO events.

Imbrogno and others contacted several police stations, each of whom repeated the ultralight aircraft theory, although it is illegal to fly ultralights at night. Other police stations said that they had been informed that the UFO was actually a military craft that was following the Taconic Parkway because they didn't want to get lost.

Later, after subsequent sightings, witnesses would continue to report seeing the mystery fliers. Imbrogno again became convinced there was a cover-up and that "someone in a very powerful position was spending a great deal of money and resources to keep a lid on the situation."

While the FAA, police and airport officials all denied any knowledge of the identity of the mystery flyers, they were eventually tracked to International Stewart Airport, now officially owned by the New York Air National Guard and the Marine Corps.

In 1992, Imbrogno actually received a letter from one of the pilots who helped to perpetrate the cover-up. He wrote that the CIA contacted him and five other pilots to fly in 0-2A aircraft, which have muffled engines, long range capabilities and are very stable. He said that each of their planes were equipped with additional unconventional multicolored lights. They were instructed to fly at low altitude over most of southern New York state and parts of Connecticut, flashing the colored lights on and off.

Whatever the explanation, the Hudson Valley UFO wave suddenly slowed down. While there were a few more sightings through March and April, by August the activity had come to a virtual stop. The wave, it seemed, was over. In reality, however, the UFOs were gearing up for next year.[79]

UFO over Croton Falls Reservoir

One of the most interesting encounters that happened in 1983 occurred October 28, at the tail end of the first wave of sightings. Biomedical engineer Jim Cooke was driving home at around 2:15 a.m. when he saw a strange object swoop down out of the sky and hover at a very low altitude over the Croton Falls Reservoir. He stopped his car and walked out to the shoreline. The object was hovering about fifteen feet above the water. It sent down a red beam of light and seemed to be probing the water. It moved to several different locations, projecting the same red beam. At some point, it also projected what looked like a glowing screen of light. Whenever a car passed by, the lights on the object winked off, and would come back on when the car left. Cooke watched the object for an undetermined period of time, at which point it suddenly rose up and darted away.[80]

"Whoever Was in the Ship... Was Looking At Me"

The line between sighting and close encounter is often hard to draw. Many people have very close up sightings and feel a strong telepathic connection to the occupants, or that they are being closely observed.

At 8 p.m. March 21, 1984, truck driver Gordon Gebert was driving south on Highway 87 near Woodbury when he saw a very bright light approaching him from the rear. It disappeared, but then reappeared five minutes later. This time, it was about one hundred yards away and was heading directly for his truck, losing altitude as it approached. The radio filled with static and Gebert slowed his truck down as the object moved overhead. The object appeared flat black and about the size of a 747. It gave off brilliant colored lights. Says Gebert, "The colors were the purest colors I have ever seen in my life."

At this point, Gebert realized that he was in a vulnerable position, especially if the beings were hostile. Says Gebert, "I felt like whoever was in the ship was looking at me since it seemed to follow my truck." As he continued driving, the object suddenly disappeared.[81]

UFO returns to Valley

Three days later, on March 25, 1984, exactly one year and one day after the most widely viewed UFO event in New York history, the Hudson Valley UFO returned for a repeat performance. Imbrogno estimates that on this occasion there were about two hundred to three hundred witnesses.

At around 8:20 p.m., calls poured into the Peekskill police station. Shortly later, the Bedford police received about forty calls. Later, the Carmel police received about twenty calls. After learning this and talking with other witnesses, investigators were able to track the path of the object as it moved across Upstate New York.

Events actually began at around 8 p.m. Bobby Boulanger was driving with his family along Interstate 84 when they saw ten red and white lights hanging stationary over the highway, brightly illuminating the roadway. They pulled over to watch. One by one, the object turned its lights off. When the last light winked out, the object was no longer visible, and seemed to have completely disappeared.

At 8:20, Armand Favilla was driving along the Taconic Parkway near Yorktown when he saw a boomerang-shaped object hovering six hundred feet above his car. It moved slowly away towards the east.

Shortly later, Michael Piazza watched the object as it passed over Bedford. He had heard about the Hudson Valley UFO and the ultralight aircraft explanation. After watching the object maneuver and turn, he concluded, "There was no way this thing could have been a group of individual objects flying in formation."

At this point, the Carmel police began receiving calls and actually viewed the object from their station. One of the officers was dispatched to the scene and reportedly chased the object to the Connecticut border.

Around this time, bus driver Mark Galli was driving along the Taconic Parkway when he saw the giant V-shaped craft approach. He instantly recognized the object as the same UFO he had observed one year earlier in nearly the same location.

At 8:45 p.m., professional photographer Jack Grimsley was driving home along Route 6 when he saw a strange group of lights heading towards the Croton Falls Reservoir. Says Grimsley, "I saw some type of dark structure connecting the lights. It could not have been more than 500 feet in the air. It was huge! It was going about as fast as my car, and that was about thirty miles an hour at the time. I was able to stay right under it."

The object suddenly slowed down, descended and hovered directly over the reservoir. Grimsley estimates that it was three hundred feet long. As a photographer, he was ready to film. He grabbed a video camera and filmed about ten minutes of footage. Suddenly, the object left. Grimsley admits that he lost track of time, and was surprised to find that it was suddenly so late. Upon returning home, he played the tape and was disappointed to find that it was totally blank.

At 9:30 p.m. Christine Fisher was in her home in Kent when she saw the object pass directly overhead. She said it was so large that it dwarfed the size of her home.

Again the sightings caused a local media sensation. The *Reporter Dispatch* ran an article saying: "The UFOs Are Back and They're Right On Schedule." Imbrogno and his team dutifully collected the reports and continued their investigation into the wave.[82]

UFOs Near the Empire State Building

During this time, the UFOs were by no means confined to upstate New York. On May 9, 1984, Chilean professional photographer Felipe Orrego was in Hoboken, New Jersey, taking photographs of the Manhattan skyline from across the Hudson River. He was working on an audio-visual project for Bowery Savings Bank, and needed some good photographs of New York City. He took several photographs with a Nikon F-2 camera, and satisfied that he got some good shots, he put the camera away.

Later, when he had the photos developed, Orrego was shocked to see that one of them showed what appeared to be three glowing objects hovering in a triangular formation near the Empire State Building. Orrego did not notice the objects when he took the picture. He was skeptical of UFOs, but he had the picture enlarged. Seeing that they were actual objects, he sent the photos to his friend and UFO researcher, Antonio Huneeus, who in turn sent them to be professionally analyzed.

William Sherwood, a senior photo technician with Eastman Kodak writes, "I have studied the slide of three lights over New York City very carefully and decided it cannot be explained as a result of flare or stars...by a process of elimination, they must be UFOs. At least that seems a likely possibility to those of us who are knowledgeable in that discipline."

UFO photo expert Colman von Keviczky analyzed the photograph and discovered that there were actually four lights, three up close, and one dimmer and more distant.[83]

The Hudson Valley Triangle Returns

Another highly visible UFO event attributed to the famous Hudson Valley Triangle occurred May 31, 1984. Again, the object was seen up and down the Taconic Parkway, hovering over cars, and stopping traffic. Imbrogno and his team located more than a dozen witnesses, though they discovered that there were many more.

Arthur Matiello was driving south on the Taconic that evening when he noticed several cars pulled over, and people exiting to look at the sky. He also stopped his car and got out. Says Matiello, "I saw this big V-shaped thing come right over."

He lived nearby, so he rushed home and got his wife. Together, they watched the object move towards them. Says Matiello, "It went overhead, very quiet, very slow and steady, and then it just disappeared in the trees." Matiello later learned that more than 260 people called the local radio station to report the object.

Two or three miles south of Matiello, Joseph Marks witnessed the object over the Croton Falls Reservoir. Says Marks, "It didn't have any tail section. It was just a big V-shape, a wedge-shaped thing."

At the same time, David Boyd observed the lights from Yorktown. He called the police who told him it was just ultralight aircraft. Boyd, however, disagrees and believes that he saw one large aircraft.[84]

The Sizzling Summer of 1984

The Hudson Valley UFO wave came to a climax in the summer of 1984. From the beginning of June 1984 to the end of August, scarcely a week went by without a major cluster of sightings.

On June 11, a flurry of sightings struck the New Castle area. Several New Castle police officers witnessed the object. Lieutenant George Lowery was called outside by another officer to see the object. Says Lowery, "So I ran outside, and I looked up, and I saw approximately six lights in a V-formation — a wide V, not a narrow V."

Lieutenant Herbert Peterson also viewed the objects. He says, "What we saw was not planes." Peterson called the control tower at Westchester Airport and learned that controllers had tracked the object on radar; though this was later denied.

Meanwhile, numerous other residents also reported seeing the craft as it moved over various neighborhoods, apparently with no fear of being seen.

Ralph Troccoli viewed the object from Peekskill and was amazed to watch it actually change size. Says Troccoli, "One minute it was small, and the next it was gigantic. I couldn't tell how high up it was, but it looked as big as a four-story building."

More sightings were reported throughout June, however on July 12, Hudson Valley experienced what Imbrogno calls "its biggest night of sightings yet."

Most of the sightings occurred over Danbury, Connecticut, with several involving police officers. Mark Purdy, a resident of Brewster, New York, says that he was driving along Interstate 84 when a large disk-shaped craft approached the road. He and several other drivers stopped their cars to watch. Purdy exited his car and was amazed to see the object approach his vehicle. Scared, he was about to jump back inside his car when the object sent down an extremely bright beam of light. Says Purdy, "It was so bright that it was a white-out…it was like snow blindness." The light winked out and Purdy, still dazzled by the light, drove slowly to his brother's house. His brother also saw the object. He got in his car and chased it up Route 684. He watched it hover in place for fifteen minutes when it finally moved away.

On July 12, John Dorazio and his brother-in-law Richard Glick chased the Hudson Valley UFO along Interstate 684. They also saw several other people in their cars watching the object. On the same day, Bill Sockey and his wife saw the object hovering over the Yorktown reservoir along the Taconic Parkway. They followed the object for several minutes, until they were convinced that it was a genuine UFO. Sockey was amazed by the way the craft hovered in place, but he was mostly impressed by the almost total silence of the object.

While many people attempted to photograph the Hudson Valley UFOs, very few were successful. In each case, the photos seem to have been affected by the presence of the UFO. However, for each case there are exceptions. Bob Pozzuoli, the vice president of a major electronics firm in New York City, phoned Imbrogno to tell him that he had videotaped a UFO from his home in Brewster on July 24. Imbrogno viewed the videotape and was impressed. He says, "What we saw was a disc-like object with a string of six bright lights around it moving across the sky. It then moved behind a pine tree and was lost to sight for three seconds. As it emerged from behind the tree, the object was different. We now saw a string of multicolored lights in the shape of a disc with a red light flashing behind it. The lights appeared to be rotating. Then they went behind some houses low on the horizon and vanished. We were impressed." The videotape was later analyzed in detail. The conclusion was that the videotape showed some type of large unidentified object flying at a distance from the camera.

In early August, Carol Scampoli watched the UFO move directly over their home at only fifty feet in height. Her son took several photographs, but they all came out blank.

On August 7, Terry Johnson of Ossining saw the object fly by as she took out the trash.

On August 13, John De Aguirre Sr. and his wife joined a group of about one hundred people to watch a formation of nine lights pass over the town of Kisco. At the same time, Michael Miller and Jerry Sweeny of Brewster watched an object "larger than a football field" pass about five hundred feet overhead. Also on this date, witnesses in Peekskill saw a triangular formation of a dozen red and yellow lights pass overhead.

On August 25, numerous people throughout Kingston reported seeing the low-flying UFO. Following this event, however, the sightings dropped dramatically. While Imbrogno's team still received scattered reports, the intensity of the summer months had passed. Never again would they experience anything equal to what happened in the summer of 1984. Again, the book *Night Siege* remains essential reading for anyone who wants to truly understand the size and scope of this enormous UFO super-wave.[85]

Crystall Returns to Pine Bush

In the summer of 1980, researcher Ellen Crystall arrived in Pine Bush where she experienced and documented an intense wave of UFO activity as it occurred. Over the next three years she returned to the same area without success. Then, in June 1984, during the peak of the Hudson Valley wave, Crystall returned to the area to "find the sky filled with lighted ships."

This time, Crystall was determined to better document the incidents. She not only continued to take hundreds of photographs, she brought along anybody that she could convince to come with her, including a series of scientists, researchers and media representatives.

One evening in June 1984, Crystall brought her friend Ellen Motichka to one of the fields where the ships seemed to hang out. They stayed in the field until suddenly, they heard a rock being thrown at them. Then they heard sticks cracking. They jumped up and ran back into their car. Crystall suspected that it was a ploy by the aliens to get them to leave. She shined the car headlights into the field. Writes Crystall, "Suddenly, all the lights of a triangle craft came on as it lifted up out of a small clearing between the trees."

Another evening, she brought three other people to one of the fields only to find that the UFOs were already there. Writes Crystall, "When we arrived there, lights were flying all around the area. A large lit object came up from the trees towards us...the entire lighting system changed, and a hulk of a triangle ship came...entirely lit and completely silent. It was about sixty feet on each side, with antenna-like projections bobbing from it. I could clearly see every seam and detail."

Crystall was close enough to notice a faint electrical discharge or mist that surrounded the craft. At this point, the object reversed direction and moved away. They examined the field and found "a perfectly oval depression, about three feet across and eight inches deep, exactly like the ones Harry [Lebelson] and I had found the day after out first sighting in 1980. The ground was pressed inward from something that was obviously heavy and shaped like a giant egg." Further examination revealed a total of four identical "pod marks" in the field.

Crystall continued her fieldwork throughout the summer, bringing carloads of people to view the UFOs. While most of the encounters were distant sightings, on many occasions, the UFOs approached to within five hundred feet. They also found other apparent landing traces in various fields where they had seen the craft.

On October 21, 1984, she brought her friend Ellen Motichka for another stakeout. On this occasion, they had just entered one of the fields when a UFO lit up right next to them. As Motichka wrote in a signed statement, "We didn't take ten steps when dual headlights lifted off the back corner of the field, maybe six hundred feet from us, and came towards us. The craft came to about mid-field and turned to move across the field going north. The rectangle shape was completely lit up with seams in the metal. It had a flat back with a tiny red light hanging from a wire like a wagging tail. Four yellow lights were in each corner of the craft, which may have been thirty feet off the ground if that."

The craft moved towards them and then shut off its light, turning invisible. Again, as summer ended, the sightings seemed to slow down. However, Crystall was determined to return next year with more witnesses, and somehow try to solve the mystery of what was happening in Pine Bush.[86]

UFO Hovers over Indian Point Nuclear Power Plant

"It seemed very brazen. It acted like it didn't care who saw it."

Of all the encounters during the Hudson Valley UFO wave, the one that occurred July 24, 1984 may be the most important and controversial. Imbrogno and his team had received several reports from the Peekskill area reporting UFOs on this evening. They then learned that local police also received a series of calls. Several of the witnesses told Imbrogno that Indian Point Nuclear Power Plant was located nearby, and that the UFOs seemed to show a particular interest in the installation.

Imbrogno knew that UFOs often appeared over sensitive installations, so he wasn't surprised when he was contacted by one of the power plant employees who told him of an incredible encounter that had occurred July 24, 1984. On that evening, said the employee, a giant UFO had hovered three hundred feet over the exhaust tower at reactor number three for a period of more than ten minutes.

Imbrogno asked for a formal interview. The employee, "Carl," said he had to ask his supervisor for approval. The supervisor agreed and the meeting was arranged. However, at the last minute, the meeting was cancelled, and the guards were forbidden to reveal any details. Imbrogno, however, decided to use stronger tactics. He contacted officials at the base and told them that they were going to reveal the story to the local television stations unless they allowed the security officers who witnessed the UFO to be interviewed.

The officials relented and granted an interview, though taping and photographing was not allowed. It turned out that there had been two recent sightings over the reactor. On June 14, Carl was outside on guard patrol when he saw a group of lights approaching. Carl called for assistance. Two other guards arrived, and together they watched the lights hover in place for a period of fifteen minutes. Finally, to the great relief of the officers, the object moved away.

Ten days later, however, the object was back. One of the outside security guards announced over the radio, "Hey, here comes that UFO again."

On this occasion, numerous employees ran outside to see the object. Said Carl, "It looked like an ice cream cone. You could see it was a solid body about the size of three football fields."

At the time, only one of the three reactors was in operation. The object moved directly over the active reactor, hovering within thirty feet. The officers had their shotguns aimed and ready, waiting for the order from their supervisor to shoot.

Another officer, "Milton," was ordered by his superiors to turn one of the security cameras located on the base onto the object, which he did. Milton said that the object was so large that he had to pan the camera nearly 180 degrees to capture the image. Said Milton, "It was one solid structure, and very large. We had it on camera for about fifteen minutes…It seemed very brazen. It acted like it didn't care who saw it."

Another officer, who also insisted upon anonymity, told the investigators, "It was so close I actually got scared looking at it."

After interviewing the officers extensively, Imbrogno learned several alarming facts. The moment the object appeared over reactor three, the nuclear power plant's security system allegedly failed completely. All motion sensors went offline and the entire alarm system shut down. Inside the security console, the computer that controls security and communications also failed. Helicopters equipped with rocket launchers were scrambled and surrounded the UFO, which finally moved away over the Hudson, heading north. There were an estimated seventy witnesses to the event.

The next day, all the employees were told not to discuss the incident. A few days later, officials from the United States Nuclear Regulatory Commission visited the plant, and there was a "shakeup" of the entire security system. Imbrogno later learned that after the incident, plant officials discovered an "irregularity" in reactor number three.

Imbrogno reports that his insistence on investigating and publicizing the incident was not without repercussion. The New York Power Authority (NYPA) pressured him repeatedly not to reveal the incident. The IRS audited him four times. Writes Imbrogno, "It is hard to believe that people like John Lear and Bill Cooper are revealing 'top secret' information with little or no repercussions. I just poked my nose a little too deep into an area of national security and I got my ears pinned back for it."

The Indian Point Nuclear power plant, according to Imbrogno, has experienced much more than simple sightings. Unfortunately, the case is so sensitive that Imbrogno hesitates to become too deeply involved. Says Imbrogno:

> "If I really wanted to go into this, with no fear of what would happen to me, I'm sure there's an incredible story here. I am still being given information about certain things going on there — In the nighttime, people seeing little creatures coming through the walls of the casing on the reactor, and military personnel indicating 'we're aware of these creatures and we don't care if they're from outer space — shoot 'em!'"[87]

The Mt. Kisko Sightings

At around 9:15 p.m. October 30, 1984 Imbrogno and his team were alerted to sightings taking place at Mt. Kisko. At the same time, they heard the Bedford police over their scanners discussing their sighting of a large triangular-shaped object the size of a football field.

Gerry Culliton, the night news editor at WVIP radio station in Mt. Kisco, said that their station had received a series of calls reporting a UFO in the area. Culliton ran outside and saw the object as it came over the trees. Says Culliton:

> *"It was something I had never seen before, and it shocked me enough to scream, 'There's a UFO coming!'"*

Four other station employees rushed out of the building and also observed the strange craft, which circled the area for the next twenty-five minutes.

At the same time as Culliton and his co-workers were watching the object, reporter Betty Ballantoni had just stepped out of the Mt. Kisco Police Station when she saw cars stopping on the street and a crowd gathering in the parking lot. Looking up, she saw a dozen very bright lights attached to a massive dark structure the size of a jet. She later called the police who confirmed that they had received a great number of calls.

At 9:30 p.m., more information came from the police scanner saying that the UFO had moved towards Stormville. Several newspapers printed articles about the sightings, again blaming ultralight aircraft.[88]

A Fourth-Dimensional UFO?

While UFOs are often thought of as coming from outer space, the truth may be quite different. The many reports of objects that appear and disappear out of thin air point toward the possibility that these craft are inter-dimensional as well as extraterrestrial.

During the Hudson Valley wave of 1984, Hynek was particularly intrigued by one report involving the pilot of a small twin-engine plane. It was 2 p.m. in the afternoon. The anonymous pilot was flying over New York City at about 8,000 feet when he saw a jet-black object about a half-mile ahead of him approaching his plane. Growing concerned, he radioed the FAA radar control tower in Islip, Long Island and asked for identification of the craft. The tower personnel told the pilot that there was no other known traffic in his area.

The pilot became increasingly concerned and fearing that his small plane would be struck by the larger plane, he altered his course to avoid it. He was still unable to identify the approaching object which looked like "a black rip in the sky." In a few moments, despite his course change, the object came much closer, and the pilot could make out a dark boomerang-shaped object. He estimated that it was about the size of a 747. He changed course again, but still the object got closer.

Minutes later, his concern grew to worry and then fear as it became apparent that the object was determined to remain on a collision course with the pilot. As the pilot said in a recorded interview with Hynek, "I thought for sure it was going to hit me when all of a sudden the thing just folded in on itself and turned into a thick, dark line, then vanished with a flash…When my plane passed through the area where the UFO had been, there was quite a bit of turbulence for about two or three seconds."

Moments later, the pilot saw four F-14 fly by at around 15,000 feet and circle the area twice. Shortly later he landed at Westchester County Airport, where he expected to be greeted by officials to discuss what he had seen. Instead, nobody came, so the pilot parked his plane and kept his sighting a secret. The pilot later reluctantly allowed Hynek to interview him. Hynek used the case as an example of a UFO that is traveling interdimensionally rather than spatially.[89]

More Proof of Media Cover-up

Unknown to many people, UFO researchers have learned on numerous occasions that there is, in fact, a media blackout on many UFO stories. While a few accounts do leak out into the mainstream press, most do not. Many of these reports are of extremely high quality, and yet, the large newspaper conglomerates not only ignore the stories, they actively suppress them. A good example is the clearly unconstitutional violations suffered by Greg Boone, a reporter then employed by *The Poughkeepsie Journal*.

On August 25, 1985, Boone and ten other journalists were in their newspaper office on the third floor when a call came in from one of their photographers in the field that a UFO was heading directly for their building. The group of journalists ran to the windows and observed a large boomerang-shaped object with red and amber lights approach at an altitude of one hundred feet. Says Boone, "This thing got huge and believe it or not flew right over top of us by about 40 feet. It had to be 200 feet wide and was jet black."

The reporters were amazed and began to put together what they were sure would be the story of the century: proof of the Hudson Valley Triangle. Said Boone, "We had access to AP, Gannett, etc., and *USA Today*, which we mainly put out. Nope. Word came down from up high that not one word was to be mentioned. Solid object, hovered, maneuvered, seen by tens of thousands, pictures taken, and no mention anywhere."

This was not the end of the story. Says Boone, "The next day some 'menacing' chaps showed up in our editorial office. I got in trouble for staring back just as menacingly. That night at the local watering hole where I could sit and do sketches after work another big menacing fellow waltzes in with a stack of papers and pictures eight inches high. Slams them on the bar and bellows a threat: 'So! Somebody in here wanted to talk about UFOs?'"

"He made a big mistake," says Boone. "My high school and college chums were at the bar that night and were just as big and menacing. He was ceremoniously ushered out of the bar by about 3,000 pounds of very angry citizens."

Determined to have his story told, Boone later recounted his ordeal in an article titled, "More Proof of Media UFO Coverup."[90]

An Underground Alien Base?

"The ships were always in the woods, in exactly the same place month after month, year after year..."

In the summer of 1985, Ellen Crystall returned to Pine Bush to continue her research. By this time, she had begun to wonder why this particular area of upstate New York seemed singled out from other areas to have so much activity. Why were the UFOs continually landing and rising up from these fields? What could they be doing and why here?

Imbrogno and his team had wondered the same thing and had already noticed what appeared to be a higher number of sightings over the areas known for mining. At one point during their investigation, they were contacted by a man who claimed to be a CIA agent. The agent told them that the aliens have, in fact, established several underground bases in the area, including in Orange, Putnam, and Ulster Counties.

Consider the following letter that was published in the *New York Post* in July 1984:

"Why are people seeing all these UFOs all of a sudden in the Hudson River Valley area? The answer is simple: there seems to be some kind of underground activity in the Brewster area in the old abandoned iron ore mines. Some years ago the government went out of its way to purchase the land that the mines are located on and people who live in the area, including myself, have seen military vehicles entering the dirt roads. They never come out."

The writer goes on to describe UFO sightings, helicopter encounters, hearing strange noises at night, and more. He speculates that the government or the aliens have "established an underground base in which some type of experimental aircraft is being kept."

Imbrogno confirmed that in 1967, the government did, in fact, purchase property around the mines in Brewster and nearby Putnam Valley and Lake Carmel. Crystall has also concluded that the ETs were conducting some type of mining operation. She had already interviewed many local residents who told her that they believed the aliens were mining the area. She did some research and discovered an amazing fact: Orange County in upstate New York, which includes Pine Bush, is one of the few locations on Earth to find several rare metals including beryllium, zirconium, and titanium.

During the summer of 1985, Crystall not only continued to see multitudes of ships hovering in the skies of Pine Bush, she also noticed another strange phenomenon. On numerous occasions, she and other witnesses observed what appeared to be "arc lights" coming from the ground itself. Each time they approached the area, the lights would stop.

On another occasion, Crystall was in a field with two other people when a strong blast of warm air came from below, through the ground. Around this same time, she had interviewed numerous residents who heard drilling noises at night and found evidence of strange digging on their property. These and other incidents brought Crystall to a startling conclusion. She writes, "In time, however, we were staggered by the realization that the aliens were constructing underground installations...Everything fell into place. Until then, I hadn't figured out why the ships were landing in the same fields and forest areas night after night. The ships were always in the woods, in exactly the same place month after month, year after year, but we couldn't get to them. The terrain was too rough. The drilling in the woods – in the middle of the night, no less. I'd been there with other people, and we'd heard it. But we couldn't find its source. The noise seemed to be everywhere we walked. Now the reason was clear: it was coming from under us."

Similar claims have been made of numerous areas across the United States and the world. What are the reasons for these bases? Writes Crystall, "Laboratories? Some abductees have described being led into large areas with many rooms: that would fit the bill exactly. We also believe that aircraft are being housed in these installations. On many occasions we have seen ships come down to ground level and not rise for the rest of the night. On other occasions, at dusk we have seen ships ascending from the ground in areas we suspect have been entrances."

Regarding the Pine Bush area, Imbrogno has come to the same conclusions, though he remains unsure if the bases are government, extraterrestrial, or perhaps a mixture of both. Writes Imbrogno, "In regard to the underground operations in that area, we do believe that some type of installation exists. Perhaps it is UFO-related, but we don't know for sure since most of our data from that area come from secondary sources. We did, however, interview several people who independently claim that they were abducted and taken into an underground complex. There they saw beings who had very long faces with white skin."[91]

400 See UFO

On November 21, 1985 one of the last major mass sightings of the year took place. At around 8 p.m., the Hudson Valley team began receiving calls from witnesses in Peekskill, Yorktown and Port Chester. Most of the witnesses described a large circular object with colored lights. The investigators spoke with more than twenty-five witnesses, though calls to police stations and radio stations revealed that at least four hundred people saw the strange object.

The FAA was contacted. An official media representative said that the FAA believed helicopters caused the sightings.[92]

"It Was Not of the Earth!"

One person's most amazing UFO sighting can be another person's most terrifying abduction. In other words, while somebody is seeing a UFO, another person may have been inside it.

For example, on the evening of December 26, 1985, numerous people in the town of Ellenville witnessed a "flying saucer" moving at a very low altitude overhead. At 9 p.m., the Jones family received a call from their nephew to go outside and look for the UFO. Five members of the family ran outside and were amazed to see the object hovering below treetop level. Says one of the witnesses, Chester Jones, "There in the sky was this thing that was just stopped in mid-air...when we saw the object there were two trees in front of it. This thing was so big that its size overlapped the nearby trees. The object stayed there and moved slowly for a good twenty minutes. The lights on the bottom were blinking bright and dull, one after the other. Then the UFO suddenly shot up at an angle, and was gone."

All the witnesses were deeply impressed that they saw a genuine UFO. Says Chester, "I served over thirteen years in the Army. I am now in the Reserves. I know what we saw was not a military aircraft. It was not of the earth! I now know that there is something out there. I wish we could get our government to tell the truth about this matter."

Unknown to the Jones family, numerous other people throughout Ellenville and beyond also saw the UFO that night. Incredibly, only one night earlier, author Whitley Strieber (who lived nearby) experienced one of the most dramatic UFO abductions in his life. Could it be that the UFO sighted by the residents of Ellenville was the same one that abducted Whitley Strieber?[93]

The Wave Ends

After approximately four years of nearly constant UFO activity involving an unprecedented number of witnesses viewing what appeared to be a large group of the same type of triangular-shaped craft, the Hudson Valley UFO wave came to a sudden end.

On June 21, 1986 another rash of sightings struck central Westchester County. Three weeks later, on July 10, a wave swept across southwestern Westchester County moving down to Queens and south-central Long Island. These sightings failed to generate much publicity. While sightings continued to be reported after this, they fell back down to normal levels. If the wave was a publicity stunt, then it seems to have had its desired effect. The Hudson Valley wave got the attention of the entire world, convincing thousands, if not millions, that UFOs are real. In 1998, *Omni* Magazine released a list of what they considered to be the top fifty most significant UFO sightings in history. The Hudson Valley UFO wave topped the list at number one.[94]

Air Traffic Controller & Wife Spot UFOs

According to Penfield-based investigator Dana Schmidt, his biggest case for 1986 involved an anonymous air traffic controller from Rochester who claimed to notice unusual lights in the sky, while at the same time blips on the radar screen started to jump around erratically. Meanwhile, his wife who was a few miles away, was gazing out at the night sky when she saw the same unexplained lights moving about. Schmidt investigated the case and registered in the files of MUFON National.[95]

More on Pine Bush

"It was so near I could have touched it."

In early 1986, Crystall returned to Pine Bush for more UFO hunting. The Hudson Valley wave may have been over, but Pine Bush continued to be a hotbed of activity. She and several other people saw craft in the distance, but the cold weather made close observation very difficult. Then one evening in May 1986, Crystall had one of her closest sightings to date. She was alone, standing beside her car watching several lights in the distance when a craft suddenly came scooting over the field directly towards her. Writes Crystall, "The first craft stopped about thirty feet away…It slowly moved towards me. I was determined not to flee. It came directly over the car and stopped about eight feet or so above it. There was only a slight buzzing sound…It was so near I could have touched it."

Crystall was amazed at the way the metal was dark and non-reflective, and turned almost invisible when there was no light source.

Throughout the summer of 1986, she continued to bring carloads of people to view the objects. Sometimes, skeptics would come along and declare that the objects were planes. However, these usually involved distant sightings. When the ships came close, says Crystall, witnesses were usually convinced. On more than one occasion, she brought her karate teacher, Rich Rohrman and several of his students. They had many sightings and on one occasion, saw a craft landed in a nearby field. On another, a craft approached them, scaring the group and causing them to retreat.

On August 30, 1986, Crystall brought a group of people, one of who was Edward Moret. She was explaining the geography of the area when a brilliant red light appeared at a distance of about a half-mile. Moments later, another light appeared. Moret was impressed. As the sighting occurred, Crystall recorded his reaction. Said Moret, "I can't believe this. This is incredible. The one we're spotting right now is spectacular. Oh, my God! There's another one. There's two huge ships out here! They're phenomenal in size."

After putting out in ad in the *Middleton Record*, Crystall found many others who were willing to join her on her expeditions. One was MUFON field investigator Robert Toto of Montgomery, New York. He joined her team in October 1986. Writes Crystall, "We were out in the fields several times a week and had many incredible sightings in which we both took many photographs."

Some of Crystall's most spectacular encounters have occurred when she was alone. In the end of the December 1986, she was standing beside her car along a dirt road outside of Pine Bush watching the ships fly up and down the tree line at the edge of the fields in the distance. She wanted to get closer, but knowing the roughness of the terrain, she remained by the road.

Her patience was rewarded with an incredible sighting. Writes Crystall, "Suddenly an absolutely monstrous-sized craft lifted above the trees and came toward me from the field on the other side. It was enormous. It seemed as wide as the field itself."

Most of the other craft she had seen seemed to be about three hundred feet across. This one was so large, it made the others look "like mosquitoes." The craft ascended as it approached, making the ground vibrate. It then moved up and off into the distance. It was the largest craft Crystall had seen and she was determined to see it again.

She returned over the next few months and into 1987. Again, the winter months made close-up viewing impossible. However, one early February evening in 1987, she and Robert Toto stopped the car along the roadside when suddenly the same gigantic craft Crystall had seen earlier rose up from behind the trees, moved towards them and passed overhead. It made only a slight rumbling sound as it passed overhead. Crystall and Toto both agreed that the object was "beautiful."

Throughout February, Crystall and Toto had several more sightings of the "Big One" as they called it. As always, they were impressed not only by the size of the craft, but by its silence. Writes Crystall, "There in the Pine Bush area, ships were flying with no noise. It was like watching a movie without the speaker on. Surreal, perhaps, but not unreal."

She continued to photograph the objects, but again, no matter how close the objects were, the film usually showed no evidence of the craft other than strange sprays of light coming off the edges of where the craft should be. Sometimes, the craft were invisible to the naked eye, but appeared on photographs.

In April 1987, Crystall brought a group of people – all engineers, physicists, and scientists – when they saw "a ship" rise and descend in field about a half mile away. They tried to hike towards it, but as they approached, the lights turned off. Crystall took a photograph anyway. Later, she was surprised to see that a row of lights appeared dead center in the photograph, though at the time, nothing had been visible.

John White was along on this trip. He had heard of Crystall's research and had joined her on earlier stakeouts, but saw nothing he could conclusively say was extraterrestrial. On this evening, however, he became convinced. Writes White, "We saw many aircraft that evening, but as we scanned the sky, we saw something different. A brilliant red light rose slowly from behind the tree line and hovered slightly above the trees. Its appearance lasted no longer than perhaps fifteen seconds before it sank below the trees again and was lost to sight...I'm sure the light was not an aircraft navigational light. It was rectangular, with its length about twice as long as its height."

White observed the light/object through binoculars and was amazed to see it change shape and rearrange the placement of its lights. White fell short of calling the object an alien craft, but as he says, "I can call it a UFO because it was an unidentified nocturnal light and an unidentified aerial phenomenon... I'm left with an experience that is, by definition, a UFO sighting."

By now, Crystall was getting increasing publicity. She also began to receive criticism from skeptics who believed that she was calling any light in the sky a UFO. In May, the ships were back in large numbers, and throughout the summer of 1987, Crystall continued to bring small groups of people to Pine Bush. On October 9, 1987, Crystall took Arlene Clifford to the area. Clifford parked her trailer alongside the road and spent the night watching UFO activity. Writes Clifford, "We enjoyed seeing the lights...An object all lit up came over and they put a spotlight on us."[96]

"UFOs Are Not our Jurisdiction"

On the evening of July 12, 1987, Sue and her friend, Kris, drove down Fairfield Drive near Putnam Lake in Brewster when they observed what they first thought was a blimp hovering about twenty feet above the lake. They stopped the car and walked to the edge. From this location they could see that a weird disturbance like "heat waves" was coming from beneath the craft and entering the lake. The object then sent a bright beam of light into the water. At the same time it emitted a buzzing noise that was so loud, both Sue and Kris clamped their hands over their ears. At that point, the object suddenly vanished.

Excited by their encounter, the witnesses drove directly to the State Police on Route 22 and told the officer on duty what they had just seen. He told the frightened witnesses, "UFOs are not our jurisdiction. You are going to have to call the Air Force or NASA."

He then told them that it was probably just pilots flying ultra-light aircraft pretending to be UFOs.

The witnesses left the police station feeling disappointed and foolish. Says Sue, "We left and decided not to tell anyone again." Fortunately, they later revealed their encounter to Philip Imbrogno.[97]

Couple Chases Saucer

It may seem hard to believe that a UFO could fly at low levels over downtown city streets, but as we have seen, New York UFOs seem to be particularly unafraid of being seen. For example, one evening in late 1987 a young couple was driving down Sunrise Highway in Valley Stream (a very densely-populated Five Towns area) when they saw a very large, oval-shaped object with white flashing lights around it hovering and gliding just above the street. They instantly recognized the object as a classic UFO, and took off chasing it. They followed the object into Gibson, until it suddenly accelerated and disappeared into the night sky. The couple told their sighting to reporters, but insisted upon anonymity, for fear that their peers would call them "weird, strange or even crazy."[98]

A Predicted Sighting

While the Hudson Valley UFO wave winded to a close, investigators pondered the data to search for patterns. At first the sightings seemed to be largely random. However, after looking over the data, they had noticed several important correlations. Most of the low-level sightings took place around magnetic anomalies, often over reservoirs. Sightings seemed to peak just after a new or full moon. Most sightings took place between 8 and 11 p.m. Finally, the sightings seemed to spread across the upstate area, hitting one area, then moving to the next and then to another.

Armed with this knowledge, the team decided to predict where the next sighting would occur. The data showed that there was a forty-two percent chance that the next sighting would be within two miles of the Stormville area. Imbrogno came up with his prediction: 8:20 p.m. October 29, in Kent Cliffs or Brewster. They sent out the team, equipped with photographic equipment and two-way radios.

They arrived at the location at 8:10 p.m. However, before they even arrived, one of the vehicles pulled over to look at some strange lights in the sky. UFO researcher Chris Clark saw it first, a group of white lights about one mile away. Said Clark, "They just appeared out of nowhere! They did a sort of dance in the sky, and joined together."

The object then approached the group, which was stretched along the highway at various locations. Writes Marianne Horrigan, "The object moved much too slowly to be a plane. It was huge and there was no sound at all… Phil later calculated that, at its closest point to us, the UFO was less than 800 feet above the ground as its size was at least that of a 747!"

As they watched, the object turned and moved east. They could discern a distinct boomerang-shaped, covered with multi-colored lights. Writes Horrigan, "We counted at least eighteen various colors. The object displayed the purest reds, greens, blues and yellows that we had over seen…it was such a beautiful sight that it looked like a Christmas tree in the sky."

The UFO had showed up right on schedule. The group was amazed. As the object moved off, they chased it down the highway. It disappeared, but reappeared later, as if playing a cat and mouse game. For the next forty minutes they followed the object, also watching as numerous other people pulled over along the roadsides to gaze at the amazing sight. Of course they took numerous photographs. Unfortunately, all the photographs showed were fuzzy blurs of light.

Following this amazing incident, the team was unable to successfully predict any future sightings. The Hudson Valley wave, for whatever reason, was over.[99]

The Long Island UFO Network

In 1988, South Shore, Long Island residents John Ford and Richard Stout heard rumors about UFO sightings in the area. They decided to look for themselves and were amazed to encounter apparent UFOs. Says Ford, "We were going out at night just to see if we could see something, and we started to observe things which we kept to ourselves."

At 9:55 p.m. April 16, 1988, Ford and Stout observed an object in the sky off Moriches Bay. At one point, the object flashed a light which was so bright it "turned the night sky to pure daylight."

Amazed, the two men teamed with other individuals and formed the Long Island UFO Network, Inc. (LIUFON). The set up a hotline and began to advertise for UFO information from local residents. The response shocked the members of LIUFON. By the end of 1988, they had recorded 161 case histories, and by March of 1989, they already had fourteen new UFO events. A few weeks later, the number had grown to thirty. Before long they had more than one hundred active members. Almost immediately, the organization uncovered several significant cases, and became a powerful force in New York UFO investigations. Says Ford, "There is not a town or an area on Long Island that we did not get news of a sighting from credible people…Something's definitely going on, on Long Island."[100]

Pine Bush Produces More UFO Witnesses

Thanks primarily to the research of Ellen Crystall, the area of Pine Bush has been documented as one of the most active UFO spots in New York State.

For nearly a decade Crystall conducted live fieldwork, viewing UFOs on an estimated 1,000 occasions, and taking several hundred photographs. She documented her research in her controversial 1991 book, *Silent Invasion*.

After seeing the UFOs on so many occasions, Crystall began to direct her efforts to getting other people out to Pine Bush to see the activity. While people weren't always convinced, others were.

On May 29, 1988, Renee Petrella traveled to Pine Bush and saw a formation of colored lights "move in the sky like nothing I have ever seen, treetop high, no noise...It was a night that we talked about for a long time." Petrella's sister, Luanna, also came along and was similarly impressed.

At 10:30 p.m. June 30, 1988, David DeLia joined the group and had an incredible sighting. As he says, "A large light came down the tree line, put on more lights and stopped in midair...It was stationary and then started to rotate a bit, still hovering." The object appeared to be about a quarter mile away. They tried to drive around to see if they could get closer but lost sight of the object.[101]

UFO Videotaped from Empire State Building

The Empire State Building has played a prominent role in several New York UFO encounters. One of its most interesting events occurred on the afternoon of June 18, 1988 when the Fernandez family was taking a tour of the famous building. Manuel Fernandez, his wife, Mirna, and their son and three nephews climbed up to the eighty-sixth floor and were enjoying the view of the Hudson River looking towards New Jersey. Fernandez had a Zenith 8mm Camcorder, which he had purchased a year earlier. He had never had any problems with it, but as he was trying to film in the Empire State building, the camera seemed to be experiencing strange interference. He continued filming anyway, taking some footage from the terrace on the eighty-sixth floor. He wanted to capture the stunning sunset that was taking place. At no point did he or anyone in his family notice anything unusual.

When he viewed the tape afterwards, the definition of most of the footage was so poor that he was going to erase it. It was sheer luck that he happened to glance at the tape and see what appeared to be a UFO, a metallic saucer-shaped craft, hovering over the Hudson River glinting in the afternoon sun.

Says Fernandez, "I was rewinding it to use the tape again when I saw it." By a strange coincidence, Fernandez was put in touch with several UFO researchers. He offered them the videotape for analysis, insisting that there was no trickery involved. Von Keviczky viewed the footage and said that it "seems genuine."

He also remarked that it is not unusual for photographers not to see the UFO until after the film is developed. He speculates that either the photographers weren't paying attention, or that the camera is quicker than the eye.

After learning of this and other encounters near the Empire State Building, Antonio Huneeus wrote, "There is good reason to believe that we haven't seen the last of UFOs hovering near one of the tallest buildings in the world, attracting the attention of other-worldly intelligence who may be just as curious about this structure as any out-of-town visitor might be."[102]

"It Can't be a UFO!"

As investigated by LIUFON, Cheryl Estler encountered a UFO while driving along Middle Road in Bayport. It was 8:30 p.m. September 5, 1988. Estler was driving. With her in the car were her two daughters and their two friends. Suddenly Estler noticed two lights "brighter but about the same size as head lights" cruising through the air on the left side, pacing their car. Estler first wondered if it was a plane coming in for a landing at MacArthur, but the craft remained just above treetop level, and continued to pace their car. At this point, they noticed a weird time distortion. Says Estler, "The time seemed to go so slow, like it took us forever to go down the road. Every time I looked, that thing was right there."

Estler thought the craft was rectangular-shaped, though her daughters both recalled seeing a dome. One saw a pulsating red light beneath the craft. Estler couldn't believe her eyes. "I tried to stop myself from thinking what I was thinking," said Estler. "I said, 'Come on, Cheryl, it can't be a UFO,' but I was mesmerized by it."

As they approached their home, the strange craft suddenly disappeared. While her daughters and their friends scrambled onto the deck hollering for the UFO to "come back," Estler called MacArthur Airport. Unfortunately, there was no answer, and Estler was forced to look elsewhere for help. Later she discovered LIUFON and was able to report her encounter. Says Estler, "A lot of people say I'm crazy, but I know what I saw."

LIUFON also investigated another case that occurred a few days later on September 8 and 9, involving three "very large objects" viewed by multiple witnesses over the Rockaways. An additional case from this date involved a witness from Queens who observed a disk that dropped down out of the sky, hovered for a few moments, then took off at tremendous speed.[103]

UFO Buzzes Postal Worker

Another dramatic case investigated by LIUFON occurred at 4:30 p.m. October 18, 1988 over Port Jefferson. A postal worker driving at the intersection of Hallock and Columbia said that a "large object" swooped down out of the sky and buzzed his vehicle. Frightened, he reported his encounter to the police.

According to researcher John Ford, five police officers from the sixth precinct responded. Arriving at the scene, they observed a "round domed aircraft." When the UFO began to swoop over the officers, a few of them drew their guns and prepared to fire.

Ford says that following the incident, three of the five police officers involved were transferred out of the precinct. Ford says that federal agents have threatened at least three witnesses to the incident.

Despite Ford's claims, Sixth Precinct Commanding Officer Russell Brown denies any record of UFO sightings involving police officers, and also denies that any unusual transfers have taken place. Ford, however, claims to have spoken with firsthand witnesses, each of who remains afraid to go public.[104]

Disk Hovers over Shoreham Power Plant

One 1988 Long Island case cited by researcher Bill Knell comes from two security guards employed at LILCO's Shoreham plant. The two guards say that one evening they saw a huge circular craft come in over the Sound. Says Knell, "It stopped in mid-air beside the plant, and a substantial power loss was noted at the time."[105]

UFO Jams Radar

While UFOs are often caught on radar, in the following case, a UFO is credited with jamming a radarscope. On January 30, 1989, Captain David Gaviola and two other crewmembers were on their thirty-foot fishing boat off of Montauk Point when they saw a strange glow in the sea. Captain Gaviola changed course and headed towards the glow, which seemed to be coming from an object in the sky. Looking up, they saw a strange 150-foot-long diamond-shaped craft. It quickly approached and sent down a powerful beam of light into the sea. At that exact moment, the boat's onboard radar quit, and other electrical equipment failed. The object made a low humming noise. It then started to move back and forth, edging closer and closer towards the boat. Captain Gaviola told reporters of the *East Hampton Star*, "I really thought seriously about jumping. I really thought it was going to stop right over us."

Instead, the strange craft appeared to "turn belly up." It then cruised west, then south and climbed out of sight. As soon as it moved away, the boat's radar started again.[106]

Hundreds of Long Island Cases Documented

There are many influential investigators that have contributed their research skills into New York cases. The year 1989 was very active and kept more than one investigator very busy. A good example is Jean Mundy who uncovered and documented a wide variety of cases, from sightings to abductions. On April 24, 1989, Mundy wrote in a letter to the *East Hampton Star*:

> "There have been over thirty sightings of UFOs over Long Island in the past five years, unexplainable by natural or man-made events. The *East Hampton Star* reported two different sightings, one on April 16, 1987, and another on July 23, 1987. Anyone interested in the complete list should contact me."

Another prominent New York investigator is security consultant, Bill Knell, from Flushing. In 1989, Knell's home-based UFO hotline received an average of five to twenty calls per week reporting UFOs. Says Knell:

> "A lot of them are crazy stories that if I hadn't heard them from the person, I wouldn't believe it, but credible scientists are telling me these things. I've gotten really concerned about the level of activity around here, and I feel people have a right to know...Long Island is, without a doubt, the hottest spot for UFOs in the country."[107]

3,000 See UFO

As we have seen, UFOs in New York State seem to have a certain penchant for appearing to very large numbers of people. While the Hudson Valley wave may have officially ended, the UFOs continued to put on occasional appearances for very large audiences. A perfect example occurred in the summer of 1989 in Ithaca. On the evening of May 18 more than seventy-five phone calls describing brightly lit UFOs were received by local police agencies across Ithaca. The big incident, however, was still to come.

Eight weeks later, at around 10 p.m. July 16, hundreds of calls came pouring in again. The Tompkins County Sheriff's Department alone admitted to having received about eighty calls from people who were seeing a brightly lit object in the sky that they could not identify. About two-dozen calls also came into the office of John MacLean, a maintenance supervisor at Tompkins

County Airport. He went outside and observed a formation of six aircraft. He didn't think they were helicopters, but he discounted the UFO possibility. He said he could hear some engine noise, and concluded they were planes.

Michael Holdridge, a pilot, however, disagrees. He observed the lights from his home on Coddington Road, and was unable to hear any sound. "I listened," he said. "I listened hard. I heard nothing."

Dick Shulman observed the object through binoculars from his boat in Cayuga Lake, south of Taughannock State Park. Says Shulman, "It was truly strange because it was huge." Shulman also said he was unable to hear any noise coming from the object, which he felt was moving too slowly to be a plane.

The police frequencies buzzed about the sightings, and according to State Police Sergeant Robert Parlett, a spokesman called from the Seneca Army Depot to say that the objects were only helicopters on maneuvers.

Witnesses, however, disagree. James Dryden witnessed the sight and doesn't believe that helicopters are able to perform the precise circular, triangular and horizontal patterns he observed, especially in complete silence. And he should know. Dryden served in an Army infantry unit for four years that used helicopters almost exclusively. Says Dryden, "I've never seen helicopters do that."

According to WBNG News, more than 3,000 racetrack spectators in Whitney Point saw the object pass overhead at around 10:40 p.m.

In the days following the incident, a spokesman from the Fort Drum military base near Watertown said that their post doesn't track the exact route of all the aircraft they oversee, and couldn't confirm if there were any aircraft in the area. Tony Struzic, an executive assistant at the Seneca Army Depot attempted to confirm if there were helicopter maneuvers as claimed earlier by a spokesperson. However, Struzic checked the records and says that there were no maneuvers scheduled for that evening as claimed.

One witness to the July wave of sightings was Larry Warren (of the Rendlesham Forest Incident). On the Fourth of July evening, Warren was working in downtown Glen Falls. As he stood outside along Glen Street with a co-worker, he thought he heard somebody call his name. Looking up, a flash of light caught his eye. Says Warren, "There above the First National Bank was a large cylinder — spinning on its axis and surrounded by a black Saturn-like ring. Watching it was difficult because its surface was highly reflective. The sight was amazing. Even time seemed to stand still at one point."

Nobody else seemed to notice the object, which shocked Warren as the object was very apparent. He pointed the object out to his co-worker who was suitably impressed. Writes Warren, "He had never seen anything like it before." They watched the object for a few minutes until a cloudbank suddenly obscured the object. Moments later, two Air Force F-16s made a grid search over the Glen Falls area. Warren learned later that the FAA at Warren County Airport had tracked the object, and that the interceptors had been scrambled from Pease Air Force Base in New Hampshire.[108]

Chapter Six:
Sightings (1990-1999)

By now, many patterns of UFO behavior should be clear, probably the most prominent being their tendency to put on displays. Despite this, the displays rarely last more than a few hours, and seem to be orchestrated in a way as to cause attention but not panic. While the UFOs seem to want to be noticed, they still remain elusive, providing just enough evidence of their existence to convince people, without actually landing and demonstrating open and official contact.

The main difference between the 1990s and the earlier decades of UFO history is again an apparent escalation of contact. By this time, UFOs had become well publicized with numerous discussions of the subject in the popular media. This heightened awareness of the phenomenon may be responsible for the increased number of reports of sightings, landings and onboard experiences.

In any case, the 1990s brought more stunning interactive encounters, including underwater UFOs, military confrontations, low-level flyovers, UFO-car chases, UFO-related blackouts, several photographic cases and more.

The Novotny Photographs

In 1990, the office of *UFO Universe* magazine received a series of fourteen color photographs of a metallic disk-shaped object hovering over Van Cortlandt Park, between Yonkers and Bronx. The photos were taken by New York City resident George Novotny using a Minolta Freedom Zoom 90.

Novotny often used Van Cortlandt Park to walk his dog. On October 22, 1989 at around 2 p.m., he was walking his dog in the area when he saw "an unusual-shaped object resembling a balloon."

Novotny kept his eyes glued to the object. At first all he could see was a bright metallic reflection. "Suddenly, the object headed closer at high speed, about three times faster than the planes passing overhead. I realized immediately that there was no balloon capable of such acceleration. The outline of the object also became shaper and appeared to be more oval-shaped, somewhat like a plane without wings."

Novotny had his camera, which he habitually brought to the park to take pictures of his dog. He quickly started snapping photographs. Says Novotny, "The object moved its position in kind of 'leaps and bounds,' always remaining motionless for a few seconds. In spite of the distance, I judged it to be approximately comparable in size to a large commercial aircraft."

The object appeared to pose while he snapped his photographs. However, it remained in view for only about three minutes before darting away. Novotny developed his photographs and was surprised to see that they clearly showed a large, metallic disk-shaped object hovering in the clear blue sky.

Not a believer in UFOs, Novotny assumed at first that they were experimental government craft. However, as he says, "I find it very unlikely that such testing would be conducted within New York airspace."

After enlarging one of the best of his photos, Novotny became convinced that the object was "a real mystery." He sent the photographs to UFO Universe in the hopes that there were other witnesses or that somebody might be able to explain what he saw and photographed on that Autumn afternoon in 1989.[109]

UFO Drains Powerlines?

On January 13, 1990 at around 9 p.m. a Syracuse real-estate investor was showing his friends a newly renovated house when they observed a bright orange-white sphere of light about the size of a full moon. Looking in the opposite direction, they saw another very bright object floating at a low elevation, illuminating the countryside at least a quarter mile in each direction. Suddenly the object faded into darkness and hundreds of tiny flashes of light appeared running in a horizontal line off either side of the object. The flashes then died down going from the ends inward. Then a bright red vertical streak was seen where the ball of light had been. The sighting was reported to MUFON. Investigators surveyed the site and discovered that there was an electrical transformer exactly where the object had been hovering. They speculated that the white flashes may have been arcing between the power lines that ran east-west.[110]

Another UFO-related Black-out?

Possibly related to the previous incident, on March 24, 1990, a minor power outage struck the Queens and Brooklyn area. According to researcher Bill Knell, UFOs may have been responsible. Says Knell, "Weather balloons, helicopters, atmospheric anomalies and mass hallucinations just don't explain the minor blackout in Queens and Brooklyn two weeks ago. It happened just about the same time some unusual craft was seen by dozens of witnesses hovering over the Con Edison plant in Manhattan."[111]

The Jumping Triangle

On May 21, 1990, a family of four from Trenton contacted MUFON field investigator Keith Conroy and described their sighting of a large triangular-shaped object the size of a house that hovered about sixty feet above their home. The objects had three round white lights on the bottom corners, and one large light on top. The witnesses also watched weird "swirling streams" of light emitted from the bottom center of the craft. They could all hear a faint humming or rushing sound. The object cruised at about two miles per hour, and would sometimes appear to "jump from one place to another." The witnesses watched the object for a period of two hours, until it finally left.[112]

Police Chase UFO

As investigated by MUFON field investigator Keith Conroy, one evening in October 1990, two young boys, ages 11 and 9, were playing in the parking lot of a bowling alley in Little Falls when they saw a large triangular-shaped object approach from a high altitude and descend over them at tree-top level. The witnesses estimated that the object was about six car-lengths long. It had a dark, reflective surface and a circular window or opening on the bottom from which light poured out. One of the boys became frightened and hid under the nearest car. After thirty seconds, the object made a whistling noise, rose in elevation and continued on its way.

Moments later, a patrol car from the Little Falls Police station arrived on the scene. They questioned the boys and asked if they had "seen anything unusual in the sky." The boys said yes and described what happened. The officers jumped in their car and sped after the object.[113]

Witnesses Suffer Side-Effects

As investigated by MUFON Field investigator Hal Haglund, at 10:20 p.m. March 3, 1991, four ladies, all employees of Cornell University, were driving about twelve miles west of Ithaca when they observed a low-flying triangular shaped object. The object glowed red and had three lights, two green and one red. As they watched, the object crossed the road in front of them, then appeared to make a vertical descent behind a wooded hill less than a mile away. The witnesses exited the car to watch the craft, which they observed for ten minutes as it scooted behind the trees. Afterwards, the driver reported feeling disoriented, one witness felt a strange warmth that persisted for two hours, and another suffered eye irritation for a full day.[114]

Two Low Flying Disks

At 9:30 a.m. June 8, 1991, a 26-year-old resident of Port Crane received quite a shock when she encountered a white domed disk-shaped craft that crossed the road in front of her at a distance of about 1,500 feet. The object was at least four times the apparent size of a full moon. Shortly after she saw it, the UFO traveled to the northeast and flew out of sight. The case was investigated by MUFON field investigator Douglas K. Dains.

Meanwhile, a mere two days later, MUFON field investigator Tom Nesser had his hands full with another case. At 2 a.m. June 10, 1991, a 33-year-old computer programmer from Honeoye Falls had a brief sighting of an elliptical white light which moved across the sky at about forty degrees per second. Most unusual, however, was the fact that the object made an instant change of direction before it was lost behind view behind some distant trees.[115]

A Baseball Cap-Shaped UFO

Some UFO researchers have pointed out that UFOs don't actually fly, at least not in the traditional sense. They have no indication of propellants as we know them, and they often arrive in shapes that are not aerodynamically suited for flight. They can stop instantly, turn at sharp angles, hover perfectly still in space, and go from zero to thousands of miles per hour without any intervening acceleration. They can even travel in and out of water (and in some cases Earth) without any apparent force of impact. Clearly, these crafts are not using transportation as we conceive of it.

A good example of a UFO using inter-dimensional locomotion occurred at 11:35 a.m. July 24, 1991 near Port Crane. As documented by MUFON field investigator Ronald V. Hamilton, a 49-year-old housewife was driving near her home when she saw an object shaped like "a baseball cap without a visor." It was stationary, about the size of a full moon, and had a brushed aluminum surface that reflected the sunlight. As she watched it, the object departed in a very unusual way. It first appeared to shrink its vertical dimension until it appeared as a horizontal line. At that point, the horizontal line itself shrunk down and disappeared.[116]

UFO over Staten Island

On the evening of December 19, 1991, Staten Island resident Randy Duke looked out his bathroom window and saw a large metallic saucer-shaped object. Later, Duke was shocked to find that somebody else had photographed a UFO that looked exactly like the one he had seen. The photograph, he learned, had been taken by a man named Ed Walters of Gulf Breeze, Florida. Duke references Ed Walters' photograph #23, as it appears in his book, *UFOs over Gulf Breeze*. Writes Duke, "It looked just like that UFO. I couldn't get a picture of it because I didn't have a camera. I wish to God that I did. This is 100% true!"[117]

UFOs in the East River

The East River runs straight through the heart of New York City. One afternoon at 1:20 p.m. April 12, 1993, an anonymous landscape photographer was taking photos of New York City landmarks from across the river when he heard his coworkers shouting. They were all pointing at a certain area of the river where the water was bubbling furiously. Suddenly, a metallic saucer-shaped craft rose up out of the water and darted away. The landscape photographer was ready, however, and snapped no less than five consecutive photos. Unfortunately, two of the photographs missed the object completely. In two other photographs, the object was too small. However, one of the photographs clearly shows a shiny silver metallic craft soaring upwards from the river.

The witness says that he and two co-workers observed the entire incident. Afterwards, they each told other co-workers about the sighting. At first they were skeptical, until they saw the photograph.

The witness wrote a short statement about his sighting and sent the photos to investigators, but has insisted on remaining anonymous. As he says, "I am very sorry, but I do not want to get involved with newspapers or other people asking me about the photography. Everything happened very fast, and this is all that I know." (See photo section.)[118]

Summer Lights over Ilion

Throughout June and July of 1993, the area around Ilion was visited by UFOs described only as "hovering lights." MUFON field investigator Jim Cormia uncovered four cases.

At 8:45 p.m. June 10, a boy returning home with his mother from a concert saw an unusual bright light in the sky. A few minutes later, as the mother drove the babysitter home, the babysitter saw the same bright light hovering overhead. The mother looked up and both women watched the light. The mother had a video camera with freshly charged batteries that she had gotten ready for her son's concert. She attempted to film the object, but strangely, the camera malfunctioned. After about three minutes, the light suddenly dimmed and disappeared.

A short time later at 11:15 p.m., a college student was returning home from a friend's house in the same area when he saw a "stationary bright light emanating from a flat, round object at tree-top level." After watching the object for less than a minute, the witness became frightened and drove away.

Two weeks later, on July 23, in the same area, a man was returning home from work at 1:20 a.m. when he saw a craft with a bright light hovering low overhead.

One week later, at 3 a.m. on July 30, a resident from nearby West Winfield saw an object pass silently over his field.

Cormia was impressed by the cluster of sightings. He says, "Things are going on big-time. These kinds of activities have really been progressing in the last fifteen years."[119]

Object Emerges from Carmel Lake

During the full lunar eclipse of November 29-30, 1993, prominent upstate New York researcher Philip Imbrogno, received a flood of calls from local citizens reporting yet more UFOs. Writes Imbrogno, "The number of overall UFO reports that came to my attention have been very numerous." The bulk of the sightings took place a day before the lunar eclipse and the sightings continued until seventy-two hours after the eclipse. Imbrogno speculates the reason for the sudden jump of sightings during the eclipse is because, as he says, "The moon might, in act, enhance a magnetic anomaly to cause a disturbance in the space-time continuum that allows a window to open up to the fourth dimension."

Whatever the reason, Imbrogno and others have recorded apparent correlations in the cycles of the moon and UFO sightings.

One particularly fascinating case occurred to a father and his two sons, ages twelve and fifteen. On November 30, "Dan" and his sons drove along Route 301 and parked along Carmel Lake in the Hudson Valley area to view the eclipse. They brought a small telescope, binoculars, and a camera to take pictures.

At around 1 a.m., when the moon was deep in shadow, a UFO emerged from the lake. Says Dan, "I heard some type of bubbling sound from the reservoir, and about one hundred yards from the shore a very large light came out of the water."

Dan grabbed his binoculars and looked at the object. "It seemed to be bright yellow in color, and surrounding it was this red glow. I could see that the light was illuminating a darker structure around it — a structure that was very large. It seemed that this object was at least 150 feet across, but the light was only about five to seven feet in diameter."

Dan's sons began screaming that it was "a UFO" and to grab the camera and take a picture. At this point, the object approached the witnesses, passing in complete silence overhead at an altitude of about three hundred feet. Both sons described feeling a wave of heat. Dan, however, was too busy snapping photographs to notice. The object continued moving overhead, then moved off over the forest where it couldn't be followed.

Of the several photographs Dan took, only one clearly showed a strangely shaped illuminated object in the night sky.

At the same time as this encounter, several others also saw what appeared to be the same UFO. Writes Imbrogno, "The sighting was verified by residents of the area, and a number of reports were made to the Carmel police."

From November 30 to December 9, another series of sightings struck the Glen Falls area. The many reports all agreed that the unknown lights were totally silent and behaved unlike conventional aircraft.[120]

UFO Flap over Stillwater

In 1993 and 1994, MUFON field investigators Raymond Cecot and Jim Bouck found themselves embroiled in investigating a series of UFO sightings over Stillwater in Saratoga County and Cairo in Greene County. Says Cecot, "There were many sightings of moving lights in the sky over Stillwater and in Greene County around that time."

One particular 1993 case involved a man who, while walking his dog, saw what he first thought was a plane. The object then turned and approached to within one hundred feet away and about twenty-five feet off the ground. At this point, it appeared to explode, illuminating the entire area with a brilliant light. Terrified, the witness ran home and reported his sighting to MUFON. Cecot arrived to find that the witnesses had left the area. He was unable to find any landing trace evidence, however, he was able to interview the witnesses the following day. One witness was so upset by the encounter that he sold his home and moved away.

Another case occurred October 7, 1994 when residents of Stillwater reported seeing as many as twelve UFOs hovering in the sky. Cecot and Bouck hurried to the site and found a crowd of people staring into the sky. The UFOs, they were told, appeared to be star-like objects that danced across the sky and moved into triangular formations. By the time Cecot and Bouck arrived, however, the objects had just left.[121]

Motorists See Daylight Disk

It was a bitter cold, but sunny morning at about 8 a.m. February 6, 1994 when two separate motorists driving along Route 219 and Irish Hill Road in Ellicottville both observed "an odd, silent, gliding, then hovering object."

Reporter Carol Fisher decided to research the incident. She soon began receiving calls from other local residents reporting similar recent incidents involving large, silent V-shaped crafts that cruised through the area at low altitude late at night. Fisher began driving around late at night and paying closer attention to the skies above her head. She saw many planes, and on a few occasions, perhaps a UFO.

On August 12, 1994, she heard a plane flying overhead. Looking out the window, she was startled to also see "a huge bright red flashing light to the left, slightly ahead of a very large carrier type plane, flying at an extremely low altitude over the house and then veering off up Bryant Hill towards Franklinville."

Fisher called the police and asked if they were conducting searches using infrared photography. The officer denied any such activity.

On August 14, 1994 at 7:22 p.m., while driving through the winding tree-lined mountain roads, she saw "something so large above my head it caught my attention."

Was it a plane? Fisher isn't sure. "Since it was traveling rather slowly, I could see it had no markings, no lights, and made no sound! I saw it. I didn't hear it! Further, I was sure it was coming in for a crash landing since I felt it would possibly not clear the trees on the next hill which was mere yards away. I caught glimpses of it through the trees and watched it bank to the right, barely clearing the top of the trees. It had to go straight up 242 towards Machias. I never heard a sound, even though my window was open, and the air conditioning and radio off. I raced to the corner, turned left and searched the skies, but it was gone...What did I see?"

On August 18, she had another sighting of a red ball of light. Says Fisher, "I heard the same loud sound of the previous week. Looking out the same window, I saw, and heard a repeat of the Wednesday before. A bright red flashing light followed by a loud, large low-flying plane." Fisher wondered if perhaps the aircraft were secret government crafts, but Ellicottville hardly seemed the place to test such advanced technology.[122]

Hovering Bright Lights

Starting in mid-November 1994, a wave of UFO activity involving unusual hovering lights swept across several New York cities including Rome, Point Rock, Utica, and Black River. Utica resident Keith Conroy, an electrical engineer, has investigated many local encounters. Within a period of a few weeks, he received ten different calls reporting close encounters.

On December 13, he received a call from a Point Rock resident reporting bright lights hovering in the sky. The next day, at 5:45 p.m., two witnesses were driving in the area when they saw three lights as bright as RFA stadium lights, hanging in a row "lower than an airplane should be." As they watched, the lights changed position and color, blinking red, white, and green in sequence.

As they drove closer to investigate, the object moved to the east.

Fifteen minutes later, a resident of Stanwix reported also seeing unusual lights.

Two days later, on December 16, there were two additional sightings; one at 9 p.m. near Lake Delta, the other at 4 a.m. over Black River. A Black River resident attempted to videotape the object, but all the tape showed was a dim circle of light.

Conroy has been unable to find any conventional explanation for the weird lights. Says Conroy, "At this point, it warrants further investigation. I would like to speak with the other people."[123]

UFO over Mohegan Lake

When it comes to UFOs, a picture is not always worth a thousands words. On August 20, 1995, John Jordan of Mohegan Lake observed a glowing white sphere hovering outside his home. He quickly grabbed a camera and snapped two photographs. However, according to reporter Phil Reisman from the *Yonkers Journal News*, "To me the image looked like a harmless pale moon suspended against a deep blue sky, but who knows? Sometimes pictures don't do justice to UFOs, or so I've been told." Jordan, however, is convinced that he photographed an actual UFO.[124]

An Air Force Cover-up?

That the Air Force is still actively covering up UFO activity is perhaps illustrated by the following recent case. On the evening of May 4, 1997, Andrew Cavaseno and his girlfriend used binoculars to observe three metallic UFOs that were hovering at an estimated altitude of 30,000 feet over Nassau, New York. The objects glowed with an orange hue, and sometimes appeared to change shape. Suddenly, the witnesses noticed two F-16 Air Force jets approach the objects from the southwest. The UFOs promptly disappeared and the jets departed. Fifteen minutes later, the witnesses were shocked to see two unmarked black helicopters arrive in the area. As they watched, the helicopters released "a large quantity of (white) balloons" in three separate groups. Could the balloons be meant to confuse any UFO reports that might be generated by the original appearance of the objects?[125]

The End of Pine Bush?

Throughout the 1990s, Pine Bush's reputation as a UFO hotspot continued to grow. Ellen Crystall had investigated the area for a decade. Her book, *Silent Invasion*, painted Pine Bush as a sort of "UFO grand central station." After the book's publication, a number of vocal skeptics began to complain about what they perceived as shoddy research, saying that Crystall's claims were exaggerated and that most people were mistaking plane-lights landing at nearby airports for UFOs. Nevertheless, the area continued to attract growing crowds of people.

Crystall's own investigation into the area was winding down. However, she had achieved one of her primary goals, which was to bring the attention of the world to the weird happenings at Pine Bush. By this time, numerous other people, like Crystall, became dedicated Pine Bush field researchers, experiencing and cataloguing the ongoing activity. Prominent among these was a young New Jersey-based researcher, Vincent Polise.

Back in 1991, Polise, then a teenager, was shocked to hear his brother come home and talk about how "UFOs had taken over the state of New York." His brother held up Crystall's book *Silent Invasion*, and announced that he was going to venture to the town of Pine Bush to hunt for UFOs. Polise was intrigued, but skeptical. He decided to remain at home and wait to see what his brother found out.

Two nights later, Polise's brother reported excitedly how he and a small group of observers had watched a small golden ball of light play a "cat and mouse" game with them as it darted over the fields, trying to avoid them as they approached.

Polise was impressed by his brother's report and agreed to accompany him on the next trip. On his first night in Pine Bush, Polise saw nothing but a few planes. He wondered if the stories about the area were being exaggerated. However, on his next trip, he was more successful.

His first sighting involved unexplained "pulsing white lights" about a half-mile into the fields. He and a small group of people watched the lights for twenty minutes before the display suddenly ended. Polise was impressed, but skeptical and a little confused. He agreed that the lights were unusual, but wondered if the locals were just having fun with gullible Pine Bush UFO hunters.

He returned home and pondered the experience. Had he just seen UFOs? Writes Polise, "This strange sighting triggered something in my consciousness. I became extremely curious with the area and felt the need to go back, again and again, to see if something else would happen."

Polise did return. Like Crystall, his first sighting was only the beginning of a series of sightings that would soon escalate into interactive/telepathic encounters and culminating in an apparent face-to-face contact with the ETs and an actual abduction.

For the next five years, Polise returned to Pine Bush frequently; on many occasions, having unusual and profound experiences with UFOs.

For the first few years, most of these experiences involved sightings of anomalous lights in the distance. Of course, he also saw what appeared to be solid V-shaped craft hovering at low altitudes in complete silence.

Gradually, however, the phenomenon began to move in closer. On several occasions, he would be driving in the area or standing around when suddenly he would have an experience he called "scanning." Writes Polise, "I would just be talking or walking and then poof, hit on the head or the face with a sudden flash of white light."

Polise was not alone in his attraction to Pine Bush. The area was becoming increasingly popular. Writes Polise, "In the latter months of 1994, West Searsville Road became incredibly crowded. It became increasingly difficult to park and this small country road was where people came hoping for a glimpse into the supernatural."

By this time, Polise had noticed that some of his closest and most profound encounters occurred when he was alone or with only a small group of people. Like Crystall, he felt that he had developed a kind of relationship with the ETs, and could sense when and where they would appear. He would communicate with them both verbally and telepathically, and sometimes thereby initiate an encounter. Writes Polise:

"It seemed 'we' had developed a rapport. It became almost uncanny how I could go into an area around Pine Bush and telepathically ask for activity or an experience and then see flashes, lights, or take photos where strange images would appear on my film, or experience a host of other strange phenomenon."

By the time the next year rolled around, Pine Bush had reached what appeared to be the peak of its popularity. Researcher Scott Carr writes that by 1995, there was "a line of cars parked along West Searsville Road on virtually any night, weather permitting."

By this time, after more than five years of field research, Polise experienced a dramatic new level of contact. Like Crystall, Polise became convinced that the ETs were not only aware of him, but were playing strange cat-and-mouse games. Like Crystall, he was shocked to find that suddenly he had become a UFO contactee.

On July 30, 1995 he and a friend were parked along West Searsville Road watching the skies when suddenly a small white sphere appeared. Polise had seen these on countless occasions, however, this time it was literally "in his face." Writes Polise, "I was sitting on the hood of my car talking when my left eye was blinded by a golf ball-sized white light...This little sphere danced on my face for about five seconds before moving to my chest. It then moved to the bushes next to me and disappeared."

Polise initially thought that someone was shining a flashlight in his face, until the sphere finally darted away. His friend had observed the entire incident. Writes Polise, "She said that the sphere was about the size of a tennis ball and had a dull white glow to it…She told me its movement was very erratic but seemed to start at the forehead and work its way all over my face. She said it moved to the top of the chest before moving to the bushes and disappearing."

Throughout 1995, Polise had numerous interactions with the Pine Bush UFOs. These included close-up sightings of strobes, colored lights, various-sized orbs of light, small craft that appeared to be mimicking planes, large metallic V-shaped craft that would take off, land, hover, and maneuver unconventionally, and also a wide variety of telepathic encounters, weird knockings, and other unexplained noises.

Again, Polise was not alone during many of these encounters, and he also maintained a fairly consistent photographic record of these events.

In August 1997, he had one of his most profound encounters. He was meditating with a group of people along West Searsville Road when he had what appears to be a face-to-face encounter with a possible ET. Writes Polise, "I looked to my left and to my surprise there was a white being standing there, looking at me! This being was female in form and wearing a flowing white gown. The gown seemed to be flowing in the wind but the air was still. She reached out to me and placed her hand on the left side of my face. I could feel her touch, but I wasn't scared or startled. I felt safe and began to suspect I was still in meditation. This 'being' continued to stare at me with white eyes and the darkest black pupils I have ever seen."

Finally, Polise broke his stare to look at the others in his group. They all still had their eyes closed in meditation. When he looked back at the *Being*, it was gone. Writes Polise, "It became clear to me that this was a contact experience that I had opened myself up to during meditation. It was one of the best nights I had experienced; maybe it was their turn to watch us!"

Pine Bush had been a famous hotbed of UFO activity for decades. However, the last ten years had brought unprecedented large crowds of outsiders to the area. While the majority of local residents didn't seem to mind, some researchers were dismayed by the circus-like atmosphere of the area.

It was obvious to some that sooner or later, there would be conflict. Writes Polise, "In September of 1997, Pine Bush was facing a major change — housing development! Within a month the sky watchers and local groups began noticing a property developer had purchased most of the prime viewing area on West Searsville Road."

The developers made it clear that they did not like the constant crowds of UFO nuts parading in front of their lots. According to Polise, in late 1997, a sky-watcher and a property developer got into a confrontation resulting in the police being called. Then came the announcement: West Searsville Road was now "off-limits to sky-watching."

Polise was himself approached by the police who told him that "there will be no more sky watching in Montgomery County." He and others still tried to visit Pine Bush, but the police continued to enforce the law, which was taken from a code forbidding loitering along highways.

Writes Researcher C. Burns, "Towards the end of 1996, the UFO activity in and around the Pine Bush area decreased significantly and the crowds faded to leave only the faithful local community to sky watch each night... Eventually the Montgomery police enforced the law that required all tires to be off the road in order to park roadside. This was nearly impossible now that the area was under development."

Despite the law and the constant police patrols, the lure and popularity of Pine Bush was too powerful to completely stem the flood of incoming UFO hunters.

Writes Scott Carr, "Conflict was inevitable...As of January of this year [1998], sky watching has been banned in Orange County. Though the legalities of this are uncertain at the time of this writing, apparently anyone found guilty of trespassing or parking with the intention of 'sky-watching' will be subject to incarceration and/or fine."

Carr writes that many of the sky-watchers have been forced to focus their efforts on other areas, such as nearby Wanaque, New Jersey, which has also had its share of ongoing UFO activity. Polise continued to visit Pine Bush, but only on a much more limited basis. He still had several dramatic encounters, and later had a face-to-face encounter with a gray-type ET near Wanaque, and experienced an apparent abduction from his New Jersey home.

Despite the ordinance forbidding UFO watching, Pine Bush continued to attract UFO watchers. As of spring 2003, there were local UFO meetings open to everyone held in the Walker Valley schoolhouse. At the meetings, locals and visitors shared encounters and searched for ways to support local research and find safe locations for UFO watching. Those interested in visiting Pine Bush are recommended to read Vincent Polise's book, *The Pine Bush Phenomenon.*[126]

Giant Craft emits "Rainbow"

On September 28, 1998, Mr. Bowden was driving a family member back to their home along the Saw Mill River Parkway in Ossining when he noticed a light flashing in the northern portion of the sky. Says the witness, "The object was changing colors at a very fast pace. It changed from red, to blue, to purple, to green, to yellow and to a very intense white."

Reaching the family member's home, Bowden got a closer look at the craft. "This delta shape hung low in the north western portion of the sky directly over the Hudson River...I would estimate that the object was about three to four football fields wide at the bottom points. This was a very large object."

Bowden tried to keep the object in view, but it moved away. However, he did notice that three miles from his home, his portable radar detector indicated that it needed a new battery, even though he had just replaced it two weeks earlier.[127]

UFO Changes Shape

As investigated by Sal Giamusso of Long Island MUFON, just before sunset at 5 p.m. October 30, 1998, John P. Cox and two other witnesses noticed an object moving north to south over Long Beach at an altitude of about 500-1,000 feet. Six planes passed the object while landing at LaGuardia or Kennedy airports, but paid no notice. The object first appeared red, shaped like a long, rectangular box. Then the object appeared to "bend down" at both ends, taking on the appearance of a hand-glider. The two ends then bent together to form a tall box shape. Moments later it transformed back into its original shape. Then tiny wings seem to sprout out of the sides and it assumed a compact tall box shape. By now the object had scooted out over the ocean, where it disappeared off into the distance. The witness feels certain that other people must have seen the craft.[128]

A Fiery Donut

As investigated by Jim Bouck, co-founder of LIUFON, MUFON field investigator, and then Assistant State Director of New York MUFON, a 28-year old woman from Pawling woke up at 4:45 on the morning of April 26, 1999 after a "weird dream." Looking outside she saw a giant donut-shaped object spinning and moving about a half mile away from her in a westerly direction. The entire object was so bright that it looked like it was on fire. The object hovered in place and began to pulsate in brightness, becoming brilliant then very dim repeatedly for about thirty minutes. The witness woke her brother who also witnessed the spectacle. Afterwards, the object flew up into the clouds and went away.[129]

A High-Flying Disco-Ball

As investigated by New York field investigator Bob Long, on June 18, 1999, at 6 p.m., a mother and daughter were playing softball in Montour Falls when they noticed a high-flying silver sphere glinting in the setting sun. It appeared to have a textured, faceted surface "just like a disco-ball." After five minutes of spinning and hovering, the object made a ninety-degree turn and accelerated across the sky and out of sight in one second.

Around the same time on the same day, six witnesses from the Watkins Glen State swimming pool observed what was apparently the same object, which they described as a BB held at arm's length. As they watched, the object gained altitude, heading east. After about three minutes, the object turned ninety degrees to the north and accelerated away at tremendous speed.[130]

While more UFO sightings continued into the next millennia, it is now time to take a look at the New York chronology of a different type of encounter: UFO landings and encounters with their occupants.

Chapter Seven:
Landings & Humanoids

While UFO sightings are interesting, far more compelling are cases in which UFOs land and humanoids exit the craft. In fact, we can no longer call these objects UFOs as they are neither flying nor unidentified. They are clearly a craft of some kind. There is a surprisingly wide variety of extraterrestrials (assuming that this is what they are) reported, including gray-type, short humanoids, human-looking ETs, and praying mantis type.

The New York record of UFO landings and humanoid encounters is astonishingly extensive. What follows are more than thirty New York cases, starting in the early 1940s and continuing to the present day. Some of the cases rose to prominence and are now well-known "classic" cases. Others are virtually unknown. As is the case with sightings, the following encounters should only be considered a representative sampling of the true number of cases.

Elf or Alien?

One of the earliest and strangest New York humanoid encounters on record occurred in August 1942 in Mongaup Valley, east of Monticello in upstate New York, to a young man named Ron Quinn. Then ten years old, Ron and his family were on vacation in the country. They had spent most of the day outside, however, Ron got in trouble and was told to spend an hour inside the cottage while the others remained outside to play.

Suddenly, he heard a soft tapping noise on the window. Says Quinn, "I looked in the direction of the sound and froze in fear. Standing on the outside of window ledge was a small, oddly dressed man about twelve inches high… The little fellow did not entirely resemble the traditional elf, gnome, or leprechaun we have all seen depicted in various books and movies…After all these years I can still describe that little man, down to the last detail, as his image is branded deep in my memory. He had an odd-looking hat, dark green in color. A short, dark gray beard covered his lower face. From beneath his hat, silky curly hair cascaded down and covered his ears, which I never saw. His light gray shirt fit somewhat tightly around his upper body, but the sleeves were quite baggy. The little guy's trousers were the same color and ended below the knee. Something resembling a black belt encircled his wide waist, but it had no buckle. He wore dark brown, soft-looking boots that ended just below the trousers…His extremely large eyes were his most striking feature, and the expression on his little face was that of pure friendship and love."

Despite the tiny man's friendly appearance, Quinn was terrified. Even at age ten, he knew that such things were not supposed to exist. He looked away hoping the illusion would disappear. The knocking sound came again. Quinn looked back and the man smiled and waved his hand. Quinn noticed that he held a small walking stick, which he was using to tap the window.

Quinn could hardly believe his eyes, but the figure was no illusion. As he says, "What I was looking upon was real in every sense of the word, including the movement of his body and the shadow he cast on the ledge below. Everything was there."

At this point, the figure motioned for Quinn to come closer. After a moment, he knelt forward and slowly opened the window. The little man eyed Quinn closely. Says Quinn, "He kept smiling and looking me over as if he had never been this close to a human before...As I reached out to touch this strange individual that had invaded my life, he stepped back and his head tilted from left to right as he inspected me from every angle. After smiling once more, the little guy leaped from the ledge, landing gracefully on the grass below. He ran with long leaps across the lawn, stopping momentarily to look back, then disappeared among the shadows of the trees."

Quinn jumped up and told his family. To his disappointment nobody believed him, even after he showed them a clear footprint on the grass made by the little man. His peers teased him mercilessly.

Today, however, Quinn is still sticking to his story. "In all this time, that one experience remains high on my list of pleasant memories. I've told this story numerous times at parties and so on and have received various explanations. To this day, I'm certain that the little character was real and not something conceived in the mind of a young man with a 'very active imagination,' as Mom had put it."

Could this have been the last of the elves...or perhaps an alien? One perhaps telling detail was mentioned by Quinn, who said "The most striking feature was his extremely large eyes" — a comment often made by people who encounter ETs.[131]

The Luminous Lady

In February 1954, Mr. and Mrs. Forster reported their sighting of a craft landing on the ground outside of Peekskill. They also observed a strange female figure standing next to the craft. She wore luminous clothes with a strange hood and thick goggles. She held a strange tube in one hand and a box in the other. The witnesses left the scene when they realized that they were seeing something that they couldn't explain. Mrs. Forster was so emotionally affected by the experience that she went into shock and had to be rushed to the hospital.[132]

UFO Lands at Schenectady

On the evening of October 10, 1957, Mrs. Edward Yeager was outside her trailer on Duanesburg-Church Road when she observed a large circular object zoom down out of the sky and land behind a hill near her home. She kept her eye on the area, and two minutes later, the craft reappeared, glowing very brightly, and then sped away.

The next day she was outside feeding the animals when they suddenly panicked and ran away. Looking up, she saw that the strange disk was back. This time, the craft hovered about six feet off the ground and quickly deposited two "dark little men" onto the ground. The strange figures moved quickly into the woods. The disk stayed in place for about two minutes, then suddenly took off.

A later investigation turned up no trace of the visitors, however a bus driver in the area reported his observation of two crafts that had landed in a nearby field around the same hour.[133]

An ET Walked In

Only five days following the previous encounter, on the evening of October 15, 1957, a young mother was woken up by the sound of somebody entering her home. She heard the sound of blowing wind, followed by footsteps moving up to their second floor apartment in Queens. Moments later, she was shocked to see a figure enter her room. At that point, it shined a single solid beam of light that split into two separate paths — one striking her and the other striking her newborn infant, who was sleeping in the same room. The *Being* appeared to be about six and a half feet tall, was wearing a tight gray-colored suit, and was surrounded by haze. After an undetermined period of time (two or three hours?) the *Being* left. The next day, the mother was dismayed to discover that her child's body was almost completely covered with a strange rash. She told her family about the incident many times and never changed her story. Later in 1978, she and her teenage son experienced a similar incident at their new home in Pine Bush.[134]

UFO Piloted by Huge Insects

One evening in January 1958, a woman who wished to remain anonymous was driving on the New York State Thruway near Depew. It was snowing heavily when she saw a strange object resting on top of a tall, luminous beam along the roadside. At the same moment, her car mysteriously stalled and the headlights went out. It was then that the witness noticed two figures that looked like "huge insects" standing next to the object. Moments later, the figures entered the object and the UFO took off spinning. The witness exited her vehicle and inspected the area with a flashlight. She noticed that the snow underneath where the object had landed was now melted. The ground in the area was also warm. She then returned to her car, which started up normally, and continued her interrupted journey.[135]

Human-looking ET from Saturn

New York resident Barbara Hudson is only one of many New Yorkers who claim to have had contact with extraterrestrials. Barbara's story, however, is a little different from most. Barbara doesn't claim to have been abducted and examined by gray-type ETs. Instead, she says, her contact involved an alleged friendly, human-looking extraterrestrial who knocked on her front door and said he was from Saturn!

It was a February afternoon in 1960 when Hudson's front doorbell rang. She opened the door. Says Hudson, "Standing in the hallway was a man about six feet in height, quite slender, and as I recall now, dressed in a navy blue suit, dark tie and a white shirt. Even in the darkness of the half-lit hall, he seemed to be quite fair-skinned, had dark wavy hair and deeply set eyes."

The man told Hudson he was an exterminator sent by the apartment manager. She let him in, though she wondered if he was truly an exterminator. As if reading her mind, the gentleman turned towards her and told her "not to be afraid" and that he "would do me no harm."

He walked across the room and picked up a UFO book that Hudson had been reading. He asked her if she believed in the subject, and she replied, "I do."

She asked him why he wanted to know, and he replied by asking her, "What planet do you think these flying saucers come from?"

Hudson told him maybe Mars or Venus. He asked her what she thought ETs looked like. She told him that they probably looked just like human beings — even just like him.

The man smiled, kissed her on the cheek, and then turned to leave. He told her, "I'll be seeing you again."

Right before he left, he asked her, "What planet do you think I'm from?"

"Probably Mars!" she laughed.

"Would you believe Saturn?" the man replied with a serious expression on his face. Then he quickly walked away. Hudson ran to her window to see which direction the man would go, but strangely, he never came out of the apartment building. Says Hudson, "It was almost as if he had disappeared."

Hudson is convinced that the man was an ET. She claims to have seen UFOs on several other occasions, including a close-up landing in Pennsylvania. She also claims to have witnessed an apparent UFO crash in Central Park (see chapter on UFO crashes).[136]

UFO Pumps Water from River

It was a spring night in 1960 when an unnamed electronics engineer decided to go fishing outside of Syracuse, New York. He was alongside a river-bank when he heard a loud whirring noise. Looking up, he saw a large round object with a rotating light on top swoop out of the sky and land on the shore. As the whirring sound died down, two "dwarfs with oversized heads" wearing glowing colorful clothes stepped out of the craft, carrying a large hose. They then placed the hose in the river and appeared to be pumping water out of the river and into their craft. Afterwards, they began to "play like children." Finally, they went back into the craft, which promptly took off.[137]

ETs Request Fertilizer

At 10 a.m. April 24, 1964, Tioga City dairy farmer Gary T. Wilcox was spreading fertilizer in his fields. As he approached one of his fields that was surrounded on three sides by trees, he was startled to see a large metallic object sitting in the center of the field. For a second, he thought it was an old refrigerator. But as he approached, he saw that the shape was wrong. He then speculated that it was a fuel tank that had fallen from an airplane. But as he got closer, he could see it was a large egg-shaped object, twenty feet long and sixteen feet wide. It was made of shiny metal and had no apparent windows or doors. Suddenly, however, two small male humanoids appeared standing next to the craft. They were dressed in seamless uniforms with hoods covering their faces. Each carried a tray that appeared to be heaped full of earth that had been removed from his field.

As Wilcox approached, one of the figures looked up and spoke in flawless English, informing him to have no fear, that they were from Mars, and had already contacted several other people. Wilcox thought somebody was playing a joke on him, but the "Martian" proceeded to ask him a series of questions. They gave him a prediction that a United States astronaut would die. They were also interested in the fertilizer that Wilcox was spreading throughout the field, and how it affected the growth of plants. They told him that they grew plants in the atmosphere. They then asked if Wilcox would give them a bag of the fertilizer. The farmer agreed and turned to go retrieve the fertilizer. As he left, the craft suddenly took off. Wilcox returned with a bag of fertilizer anyway, which he left in the field. When he checked the next day, the fertilizer was gone.

Knowing that his experience was unusual, Wilcox felt it was his duty to notify the police, which he did. Seeing that he was sincere, the police referred him to UFO researchers, and before long the case generated considerable interest. When Betty and Barney Hill were discovered to have a bag of fertil-izer in their car during their abduction, speculation grew that perhaps the

ETs were interested in fertilizer. Wilcox was extensively interviewed, and no inconsistencies could be found in his case. Says Wilcox, "I don't care whether anyone believes me or not. It doesn't mean anything to me one way or the other. I told them [the police] what I saw and heard. I thought I should."

In another interview, after being asked what he thought of people who didn't believe his story, Wilcox replied, "I know what I saw. We talked for two hours and we were even joking at times. I just don't worry about it. I've got nothing to hide and if I saw another one today I would report it."

Wilcox's brother, Floyd, was also interviewed as a character witness and said of his brother, "If Gary says this thing happened, it really happened. He has nothing to gain and a lot to lose by telling a story like this. I know it is true."

Today, the case, despite its bizarre elements, is considered a "classic."[138]

Children See Little Spaceman

On the afternoon of July 16, 1964, less than three months after Wilcox donated a bag of fertilizer for extraterrestrial examination, another bizarre landing case occurred. Mrs. Travis was in her home in Conklin while her two children, Edmund (age nine) and Randy (age seven), and their three friends Floyd Moore, Billy Dunlap, and Garry Dunlap played outside in a nearby field surrounded by huckleberry bushes. Suddenly three of the boys rushed into the Conklin house and requested a large jar of water. Mrs. Travis asked why, and they replied, "We are taking water over to the spaceman." Seeing that the children were excited and serious, an adult was sent after the two other children. They were found walking home from the field. When asked, they denied seeing any "spaceman." It was clear to the adults, however, that they were concealing the truth.

The adults then separated the five children and questioned them about what they had seen. One by one, they revealed an incredible story. When they were cross-examined and threatened with punishment for lying, they broke into tears, but refused to retract their claims.

The boys said they were playing in the field when they suddenly noticed a small human-looking man, wearing a black suit and a black helmet. The helmet had a transparent visor over the eyes, "antenna-like wires" on top, and was decorated with unidentified symbols or letters.

The little man kept making strange hollow noises, similar to a kazoo. At this point, the boys noticed a large object parked in the field. They described it as shiny "like a car bumper." The spaceman walked up to the silvery object and hopped up on top of it. At this point, one of the children asked the little man if he needed help or would like some water. The figure responded by falling "backwards" from the top of the vehicle. The children ran to go get some water.

When they returned to the spot, the craft and the spaceman were gone. However, in the field there was an area of crushed grass and three large depressions in the soil where the craft had landed. Like the Tioga City encounter, the case is today a well-known classic.[139]

UFO Lands for Repairs

One of the rarest types of UFO activity is known as a "UFO repair case." As Dwight Connelly, the former editor of the *MUFON UFO Journal,* points out, "there are more cases of UFO crashes than UFO repairs."

One incredible case of a UFO landing for repairs occurred during the early morning hours of November 25, 1964. The main witness, Marianne Hatzenbuhler, observed the event, which occurred on a hillside about 1,300 yards northwest of her family's home, just north of New Berlin along old Route 80.

It was a clear night at 12:30 a.m. when Hatzenbuhler stepped out on her porch. Looking up, she saw what appeared to be a shooting star zoom down out of the sky. Seconds later, another apparent shooting star appeared, however instead of fading away, it came straight down, then began traveling horizontally along and above the creek-bed parallel to Route 80, heading directly towards her. As it approached, the object became intensely bright, and emitted a low humming noise.

Hatzenbuhler called out to her mother-in-law in the house to come look, and she stepped out on the driveway to observe more closely. At that moment, two cars drove by. The second car pulled over to look at the object. The UFO started to approach the vehicle, which quickly pulled back on the highway and raced off. At this point, the UFO continued its approach directly towards Hatzenbuhler.

Hatzenbuhler turned to run towards the house. At the same moment, her mother-in-law stepped onto the porch, took one look at the object, and dashed back inside. She pleaded with Marianne to come back inside, but Marianne refused. Even the family dog refused to come out and remained cowering by the door.

A third car came along and slowed down to look at the object. The UFO immediately began to pace the car, apparently frightening the people in the car, who raced away at high speed. The object then moved north and landed on a hill about 3,800 feet away.

The two witnesses returned inside their home and watched the landed UFO through a window using a pair of binoculars. Hatzenbuhler could clearly discern a round structure that sat on landing struts. Underneath the object emitted a bright light. To her shock, she could also see five or six figures carrying boxes filled with various tools. They were carrying the boxes and working with the tools underneath the UFO.

Says Haztenbuhler, "They seemed to be dressed in something like a skin diver's wetsuit. It was a dark color, and their hands were visible apart or out from the wrist of the suit. Their skin was lighter than the suit they were wearing. They were built like men...the only difference is they were slightly taller... between six-and-a-half to eight feet tall...They seemed to have hair, like we do, although their hair wasn't long, as is the custom today for men to wear their long as they do. It seemed well-barbered, fairly close to their heads."

As she watched, the men used strange hand-held tools to extract a large contraption out of the bottom of the UFO. At that point, Hatzenbuhler's mother-in-law pointed out that another "falling star" was coming in for a landing. Moments later, the second UFO approached from the west and landed just beyond the first object. Five more figures exited the newly landed craft and joined the others who were now working hard to cut long sections of what appeared to be heavy, dark cable.

While Hatzenbuhler felt no fear, her mother-in-law was still frightened and asked if they should call the authorities. They both feared, however, that authorities might harass the UFO people, so they decided not to make the call. At the same time, both of them felt that the saucer occupants were watching them closely too.

After almost three hours of repairs, the figures surrounded the contraption and attempted to fit it back into the bottom of the craft. The first attempt was unsuccessful. Two additional attempts also failed. Another hour passed when a final attempt to replace the contraption was successful.

Says Hatzenbuhler, "I could see them quickly pick up everything they could pick up, and the men from the vehicle above them on the hill ran with their material up there. These men were running like a man running with something extremely heavy, two men with a toolbox — one that required two men to carry. There were at least two more toolboxes, because there were two other men who were laboriously running...It looked like they were picking up cable pieces these other men had left. They ran up the hill with them, and I didn't seem them anymore...At five minutes of five, the vehicle on the top left. It went straight up...almost like an instantaneous disappearance, in the direction it had come from, south southwest. A minute later the other vehicle rose straight up, went to the crest of the hill, rose a little further again, and shot off in the same direction the other one had left in, at the same speed. And that was it."

The next day she hiked up to the area where the crafts had landed. She found two sets of triangularly-spaced impressions in the ground fourteen inches wide and up to eighteen inches deep. To her surprise, she also found an apparent piece of the cable. Says Haztenbuhler, "The outer part of it looked like the wrapping, something like a brown paper towel, only it wasn't like our paper towel. It felt rather like that, and was dark brown in color. It seemed to be a wrapping for a cable, tubular. And in the center of it — it had been cut laterally — you could see the strip, maybe an inch wide, more or less, something that looked like finely shredded aluminum strips laid in there, and it was as long as the piece of paper, and that the color and feel of aluminum, although it wasn't aluminum. It didn't behave like aluminum. Aluminum will crumple and this didn't crumple. You couldn't crease it. It was inside, strips of this, laying inside this paper. You could remove the inside, for the outside paper had been cut along the length of the piece, but it was all together." Unfortunately, this crucial piece of evidence has become lost.[140]

Landing in Cherry Creek

William Butcher Sr. never claimed to see a flying saucer land on the property of the Cherry Creek farm where he resided, but his children did. Because they are often outside, children comprise a large portion of witnesses to UFO encounters. On August 19, 1965, William Butcher Jr. (age seventeen), and his brothers, Harold (sixteen) and Robert (fourteen), all observed the object, though it was Harold who saw it first.

It all began when Harold, who was in the family barn, heard their bull moaning strangely. At the same time, his radio began to static. Looking outside, he saw a metallic "chromelike" football-shaped object about fifty feet in diameter come down out of the clouds and land in their field. As he watched, the object rose up and down to ground level, emitting a strange red vapor and a loud beeping noise.

As the object landed, the electric milking machine suddenly stopped functioning. Harold grabbed the phone in the barn and called his family in the house.

Meanwhile, back in the main house, the radio stopped functioning and became filled with static. Then the phone rang and Harold's mother answered. Harold shouted out that a UFO had landed outside the barn and to come outside and look. Suddenly the phone went dead.

Back in the barn, Harold dropped the phone and ran to the window just in time to watch the object take off. It made a whooshing sound, and the weird beeping noise increased in pitch. The object ascended into the sky, emitting a bright green-yellow flame that illuminated the low cloud cover. There was a loud boom and it disappeared. Harold ran back inside the house. Only his brother Robert, however, had come outside in time to see the weird glow from the craft's departure. A few minutes later, Harold and Robert saw the craft again. They rushed inside and told their mother, who phoned the police.

Moments later, their neighbor, Kathleen Brougham, rushed inside, knocked down one of the Butcher children, and screamed, "It's here again!" Brougham and the Butcher children ran outside again and watched the object, which was now seven hundred feet away, floating slowly at a low altitude. After about a minute, the object rose up and disappeared over a hill heading towards Jamestown, leaving a red-yellow exhaust. It reappeared a few times, before finally leaving for good.

Shortly later, police troopers E. J. Haas and P. M. Neilson arrived, but by then the saucer had departed. They briefly inspected the area with flashlights, but didn't find anything unusual. All that was left was a strange pungent odor. The next day, however, the Butchers' cows produced less than half their normal amount of milk. The bull had been so terrified that it allegedly bent the iron bar to which it was tethered, though this detail has been disputed by some researchers.

The troopers were impressed by the case and called the United States Air Force in Niagara Falls, who agreed to come and investigate.

The next day, Harold was investigating the area when he found a strange deposit of purple liquid that he said smelled like "3-in-1 oil." He saved a sample that he put in a shoebox.

Later that day, five officers from Niagara Falls Air Force Base arrived to investigate. They were unable to find any further physical evidence left by the object, but they concluded that the witnesses were telling the truth, and that they definitely "did see something." Captain James M. Dorsey, operations officer of the 4621 Air Force Group, supervised the investigating team at the landing site. He also believed the case was genuine. "I don't think this is a hoax," he said. "These children saw something. The neighbors feel the same way about it." The other officers agreed that they found no evidence of a hoax. The Blue Book Intelligence officers declared the case unidentified. (Case #9806)

Dr. James McDonald was shocked at Blue Book's conclusion, mainly because they normally seemed to function as debunkers rather than investigators. As McDonald later wrote of the case, "I wonder why it happened to be tagged UNIDENTIFED so quickly. Does it imply that the credibility of all the observers and especially the son, Harold, were so high? Or was it the indentations, singed brush, and 'purplish liquid.' Or did the bull sell this one by bending the stake with his nose-ring?"

J. Allen Hynek, however, thinks that the case was so good, that the officers had no choice but to accept the case as genuine. As he wrote, "There was a strong impulse to regard this case as a hoax, but the evidence pointed in the opposite direction. In addition, the witnesses concerned were from a rural family and there seemed to be nothing to be gained by fabricating such a story. As a consequence, Blue Book reluctantly carried this case as unidentified."

The third day after the landing, further landing traces were allegedly discovered in the form of depressions or burn marks. The area was also later tested with a Geiger counter, but no trace of radiation was found.

Allegedly a team from Wright Patterson arrived August 23 and was reportedly interested particularly in the landing traces. The Air Force investigation on the landing traces revealed an unusually high presence of phosphorous.

Later, researcher Robert Galganski did follow-up research on the case and discovered that the landing trace aspect of the case may have been exaggerated, however, the general sequence of events seems to be true. He also found further confirmation of the event.

Barely two days after the Cherry Creek landing, on August 21, New York State troopers Richard Ward and Mr. Purcell were in their patrol car about one mile south of the Butcher's farm when they saw a brilliant array of seven amber-orange circles of light pass overhead at an estimated elevation of only 2,000-3,000 feet. The objected made a low purring sound "like a bagful of kittens."

NICAP investigators soon uncovered further local cases. Just days before the Cherry Creek landing, another resident saw a light that "exploded like a skyrocket." She only mentioned the encounter after hearing about the UFO landing that occurred a few days later.

But it was the days after the Cherry Creek landing that seemed particularly busy. Two days after the police officers' sighting, on the evening of August 24,

Harold and John Butcher and their cousin Richard observed "a deep yellow-orange ball of fire" rise from the woods along Route 83, less than two miles from their farm. As the object took off, their car radio and headlights both failed. Only a few miles away, Harold Butcher Sr. and two of his co-workers at the nearby cannery also saw the craft as it ascended into the sky.

Meanwhile, Dick Nelson, a dairy farmer and Butcher's next door neighbor, said that in the week following the landing, he kept hearing strange beeping sounds coming from both his television and radio. Nelson also said that two days after the landing, he was working in his garage when a speeding carload of people screeched to a stop in front of his house. Said Nelson, "That car-full of people were scared. They saw something. They said a reddish-orange ball followed them down the road."

Robert Galganski was able to locate the driver of this car who said that they had gone out driving to prove to her children that "all this talk about flying saucers was nonsense." It was shortly later that they noticed their car was being followed by a "big ball of fire." Everyone in the car became extremely excited until the object finally darted away.

Galganski also located other witnesses who said that they observed unusual light activity around that time, but couldn't be sure of the exact date. In any case, the Cherry Creek saucer landings remain one of New York's most famous UFO events. (Blue Book Case #9806)[141]

The Saucer in the Woods

On September 27, 1965, about two months following the Cherry Creek landings, Addie Jones of Fredonia observed a thirty-foot wide silver-colored flying object that suddenly rose out of a hidden forest area. The object hovered silently for a few moments—long enough for Jones to notice a strange box-like device attached to the bottom of the craft. It then moved quickly away towards the west.[142]

Aliens Seen in Window

On February 12, 1966, two teenage boys were playing outside their home in Newfield when they saw a saucer-shaped object hovering at a low altitude. Suddenly the object tilted towards them. Both boys could see a large six foot-wide window on the front of the craft and two *"Beings"* standing side-by-side inside it.[143]

UFO Leaves Burned Patch

While there are more than 2,000 landing trace cases on record, compared to the actual number of UFO events, they are still rare. At 4:30 p.m. March 9, 1966, Lawrence Rall of Alden, New York was outside his home when he observed a "huge odd-shaped object" hovering silently about two hundred feet above his home. As it hung stationary in the sky, he was able to estimate its size as 150 feet long, 100 feet wide, and twenty feet thick. On the bottom was a large porthole or opening, through which he could see a glowing red light and weird instrumentation. After a few minutes, the object glided over the wooded area behind Rall's home and departed the area.

Meanwhile, later that evening, other witnesses also observed the object about two miles outside of Alden. They watched in amazement as the object swooped down and landed in a field. After it left, witnesses found a perfectly round circle of crushed and burned vegetation about seventy-five feet in diameter.[144]

A Quick Touchdown

Why do UFOs land? This question is not so easy to answer. In many cases, it appears that the ETs are interested in the geographic area, and they are sometimes observed retrieving samples of soil or plants or even animals. However, in many cases no ETs are seen and the UFO is landing for no apparent reason. For example, on September 9, 1966, an unnamed gentleman from Franklin Springs observed an unidentified flying object swoop down out of a cloudbank, decelerate, and quickly land. The object made a soft whirring noise and emitted bands of blue, red, and green lights. No other activity was noted and after a few short moments, the object took off and moved away.[145]

Alien-MIBs in Long Island

The "Men-in-Black" phenomenon is well known among UFO researchers, but it is still unknown whether these MIB are humans or aliens, or if there are two types of MIB. This next bizarre case illustrates the dilemma. According to researcher R. Perry Collins, one afternoon in July 1967, seven members of a family were driving through central Long Island when they saw a flying object land in a field not far from the road. As they watched, a black sedan in front of them suddenly darted off the road and drove across the field to the saucer. An opening appeared in the saucer. Two men emerged from the saucer and entered into the sedan, which quickly returned to the road and drove away. At this point, the saucer rose up vertically, then accelerated quickly into the distance.[146]

Security Guard Sees Landing

Some people are more likely than others to encounter UFOs. Security guards, nightwatchmen, pilots, police officers, and other people whose jobs entail staying outside late at night are all at a higher risk than most people of having a UFO encounter. A case in point is that of New York security guard, Sidney Zipkin, age 50. On the evening of July 31, 1967, Zipkin was driving through a large parking lot in Churchville when a fifty-foot wide cigar-shaped object dropped out of the sky and landed softly on the cement. Zipkin brought his truck to a stop within one hundred feet of the strange object and aimed his headlights directly at it. At that moment, two "dwarfs dressed in shiny black uniforms" rushed by his truck and ran into the UFO, which promptly took off straight up and disappeared.[147]

Aliens Peer out of Porthole

On October 24, 1967, two youngsters, Donald Chiszar, 13, and Pat Crozier, 10, were outside their homes in Newfield when they saw a bright, glowing object hovering at a very low altitude. Suddenly, the object tilted towards them. Chiszar and Crozier were then able two see two large, square portholes, separated by a single bar. Strange lettering or symbols marked the bottom of the portholes. Inside they could see two humanoid figures sitting down in small seats, operating control panels that were filled with small lights and knobs. Moments later, the object vanished. *[Note: This may be the same case that occurred on 2-12-66: see previous story.]*[148]

Encounter at Sheraton Hotel

Another fascinating example of an alien encounter in a highly public place comes from professional violinist and highly respected UFO researcher/writer Timothy Good. In 1961, Good became interested in the subject of UFOs. He began to read about and research the phenomenon. He soon learned that telepathy often plays a powerful role during human-ET encounters, and that many people claim to have made contact with human-looking ETs through this process.

One evening in 1967, Good was staying at the Park Sheraton Hotel in Manhattan. On a whim, he decided to conduct an experiment. For about an hour, he stood in the lobby sending out the mental message, "If there any space people around, let your presence be known."

Good was amazed when suddenly his request appeared to be fulfilled. Says Good, "Finally, as I was about to give up, a very healthy-looking man, about 5'10", came over, sat down beside me, and took out a copy of *The New York Times* from his attaché case."

Stunned, Good mentally requested, "If you're a spaceman, touch your finger to your nose."

The response was immediate and positive. Says Good, "Without once looking directly at me, he did exactly as I had requested in my silent message!"

Good was so amazed that he was unable to react as the man quickly stood up and walked away. To this day, he is convinced that he made contact with a human-looking ET right there in the heart of New York City.[149]

A Saucer Nest?

In 1969, a ten-year-old boy from New York State purchased Frank Edwards book, *Flying Saucers – Serious Business*. He read it in one day. So began Bill Knell's interest in UFOs and career as a UFO investigator. One year later, his family had rented a boat to go fishing off Jones Beach. That's when Knell observed what he believes may have been a UFO landing spot. Says Knell, "We were landing on one of those shorelines there, and there was this circle, and my parents even thought it was very strange. The funny part is that the next week when we went back, every single bulrush in that whole area was completely cut down. I've never seen them do that again. That was my first experience with possible UFOs and cover-ups." Later, Knell would become an influential New York UFO researcher, investigating many significant cases.[150]

"They Were Not Human"

Late on the evening of June 10, 1972, an unnamed nurse was driving with her 65-year-old mother and infant son outside of Millerton when they noticed a "multi-colored lighted object" flashing very high in the sky ahead of them. They both assumed it was a plane when without warning it dropped down out of the sky at a tremendous rate of speed. They assumed that the plane was about to crash right in front of them when suddenly it stopped and hovered only a few hundred feet away. Only then did they realize, it was not a plane.

Says the witness, "It made a very soft quiet humming sound as it hovered just above the trees...I was terrified. My hands [were] shaking as I clenched the steering wheel. I was so afraid for all of us in the car, especially my infant son asleep in his car seat in the back. This object was absolutely huge, just tremendous in size! It was saucer-shaped with some sort of dome. Around the entire dome, we could clearly see a panel of windows. What we saw through the windows gave me nightmares for many years. There were 'beings' looking out at us! They were not human in appearance. I counted five; my mother swore she counted six. I do not know what they were, but they were not human beings. From our view, we could see large oval black eyes with big bug-like heads attached to what appeared to be very thin necks with long thin arms. My mother and I both thought they appeared gray in color."

As they watched the object, a blue-white beam of light came from underneath the craft and struck their car, illuminating the interior like daylight. The light was so bright that both women were forced to cover their eyes. After a full minute or two, the beam of light retracted.

At this point, the craft started to move. Still afraid, the nurse pressed her foot to the accelerator and raced home. To her shock, however, the UFO followed them, keeping in front of them in the sky at just above treetop level. The object remained in view the entire trip home. The frightened witnesses raced inside. They heard the faint whining of the UFO as it finally moved away. Says the witness, "I don't think either one of us actually slept that night. I was still shaking the next morning, it was such a traumatic experience for us."

The nurse was so upset by what she had seen that the next morning that she phoned the civil defense authorities, who told her that they had received "thousands" of calls. Most of the callers were reporting distant objects, but a few, they said, involved close-up encounters. Says the witness, "I have told hundreds of people about that evening, and I will continue to tell everyone that asks until I am no longer able to. There is life outside our little world. I don't understand the why's and how's, but I know there is; I have seen it!"[151]

UFO Lands in Oneida

New York MUFON field investigators Pat and Larry Clark uncovered the following case, which took place in the early summer of 1972 in a rural area of Oneida surrounded by pine forest. One morning around 1 a.m., the witness woke up to find an orangey light shining into her room. Looking out her window, she saw numerous black helicopters and airplanes crisscrossing the sky, which appeared almost bright red-orange. She first assumed there was a forest fire and that the aircrafts were spraying flame-retardants.

Says the witness, "I watched for about twenty minutes, when a HUGE blimp-shaped object, bright red with orange tinge at the bottom, rose slowly and majestically above the pines. As it hovered, I saw it was several acres big, as it overlapped the east and west borders of the pine grove. I was stunned and then realized I was watching a UFO."

At this point the planes had disappeared. The witness had her face pressed up against the window, watching the craft in awe. Suddenly the craft departed.

Says the witness, "After hovering for about three minutes, it suddenly shot upwards, and within a second it was gone. The pines leaned to the west as it left, as if a huge window was blowing them at once. Seeing that thing shook the perception of reality I had up to that time. I was too afraid to talk about it and had bad dreams about it for years."[152] *[Note: No mention is made of any possible landing traces.]*

Landing on Staten Island

Thirteen miles long, seven miles wide, Staten Island seems an unlikely place for a UFO encounter. However, the area has produced many encounters, including on February 14, 1975...a UFO landing.

For the past year, the area had experienced a number of local sightings. Then, on February 14, 1975, local resident Daniel Kish was walking his dog along Barclay Avenue. Suddenly his dog totally became unaccountably terrified and demanded on returning home. It was the most peculiar behavior Kish had ever observed in his dog. He returned home, at a loss to explain his dog's actions. He later learned, however, that a UFO was landing in the woods less than a mile away.

At the same time that Kish was walking his dog, Staten Island residents Mike Kileen and Chuck Damore were also walking along Barclay Avenue, returning home after visiting a classmate. They were going to check out a local pond, to see if it was frozen enough to go ice-skating on the next day. As soon as they arrived, they both observed a large, orange, glowing, football-shaped object hovering as still as a rock over the woods and occasionally dipping below and behind the trees. It was totally silent and about twenty-five feet in diameter. They watched the object for about ten minutes. Suddenly it changed from a football shape into an egg-shape. It then shrunk down into a small ball of light and darted away. Says Kileen, "It was definitely the oddest thing I've ever seen."

Chuck Damore agrees, "It was definitely a machine of some sort."

The two teenagers returned the next day and were shocked to discover what appeared to be landing traces. Says Kileen, "We saw that the tops of several trees had been sheared off as high as ten feet above the ground. Bark on a lot of the other trees had been burned — scorched — as if by a tremendous blast of heat. The soil itself was charred. Everything — all the shrubs and thickets — in a radius of approximately 50 feet appeared to be flattened out, as if by a giant object."

The boys contacted both the police and newspapers, who were impressed by the evidence. Word of the landing grew. Researcher Timothy Green Beckley heard about the case and conducted a firsthand investigation. He interviewed the witnesses and visited the site shortly after the landing. He came away totally convinced. Says Beckley, "Indeed, this case had all the signs of being genuine."[153]

Ellen Crystall Sees an Alien

The area of Pine Bush in Upstate New York has, as we have seen, produced a large number of sightings. During the 1980 wave, researcher Ellen Crystall and others claimed to have witnessed not only flying craft, but several landings. She had chased the craft for weeks and had experienced weird "cat and mouse" games during which they seemed to toy with her. Finally, on the evening of August 7, Crystall had her first face-to-face encounter with an actual ET.

It was one of the few evenings she had gone out alone. She saw several craft throughout the evening, but was unable to get close. At around 1 a.m., she drove slowly along the road outside of Pine Bush. She was shining a flashlight into a field where she felt a UFO might be hiding when suddenly the light from the beam glinted off something dark and moving, which she thought for a second was a moth. She shined her light directly on the movement and was shocked to see a pair of thin legs, a tight-fitting beige jumpsuit, moving arms, a thin neck, and large dark eyes on a huge head. The figure was running across the field when Crystall caught it in her beam. Suddenly, it froze in shock and looked at her in surprise.

Says Crystall:

"[It] stopped, turned and stared directly at me. It was about twenty-five feet away. I was dumbfounded. It was an alien, fully visible. I could see every detail. The 'moth' my light had caught was actually the being's huge eyes that wrapped around the sides of its head to its ears. The eyes had dark pupils, like ours, but where ours are white, its were yellow and similar to a cat's eyes with their nighttime glow. Unlike a cat's eyes, however, these were diamond-shaped but more angular, like a stretched-out diamond. The being looked to be about three or four feet tall. It was slender and weighed perhaps thirty pounds."

Crystall and the alien stared at each other for about thirty seconds. The alien stayed perfectly still. Finally, Crystall tried to speak, but instead her fear became overwhelming and she drove away in a near-panic. She went directly home to tell her family and friends, who responded with astonishment and concern. Despite her fear, she continued to do field research in the Pine Bush area.[154]

Landing in New Windsor

One afternoon in 1982 (exact date not given) a group of five children ranging in age from nine to fifteen were playing the woods outside their homes in New Windsor when they saw a strange glowing object descending into the woods. One of the witnesses (a thirteen year-old boy) described the object as "triangular or diamond-shaped" with "mainly yellow and white lights around the edges." It appeared to be about forty feet long. It swayed back and forth in total silence. Curious, a few of the children crept closer to get a better look. At that moment, the object disappeared, leaving the children terrified. They came home screaming, in an "incoherent state." At the same time, the animals in the area were affected, and the family dog "went absolutely crazy."

The next day, the mother of a few of the children returned with them to the swampy area where the object had been sighted. They found an enormous football-shaped area on the ground about forty-four feet long where the vegetation was "flattened, white, and totally devoid of any moisture." They also found several large three-toed Bigfoot-like footprints. "Whatever did it was heavy," the mother said. The case was researched by Dennis Piaquadio, a field investigator for the National Investigations Committee on Aerial Phenomena, who concluded that the case was genuine.[155]

ETs in a New York Bookstore

A startling case involving extraterrestrials mingling among the native population of New York City was reluctantly reported by Bruce Lee, a former Washington journalist for *Newsweek* and an editor at Morrow Books.

In February 1987, Whitley Strieber's book, *Communion*, had just been released, and Lee decided to visit Womrath's Bookstore on Lexington Avenue to see how *Communion* and some of the other books he had worked on were being displayed.

He found the shelf containing Strieber's book and showed it to his wife. Shortly later, he noticed a strange looking couple walk into the store and head directly for the shelf where *Communion* was. Lee was shocked that they seemed to know where the book was without any direction, so he stepped back to observe.

Says Lee, "They were short…and they were all wrapped up. Long scarves, wool hats that you pull down, and they picked up a copy of the book and they started thumbing through it — the man was doing this. And it was obvious that they were speed-reading too."

Lee was surprised to hear them start editing the book themselves, approving of some sections and disapproving of others. Curious as to how they got their information, Lee stepped forward and introduced himself. That's when he got a bad shock.

Says Lee, "I think it was the woman that looked up. She was wearing those big sort of sunglasses that the girls keep up in their hair. And they really sort of hide the face. But by God behind those dark glasses was a goddamn big pair of eyes. And I mean to say it was a big pair of eyes. And they were shaped sort of like almonds."

At this point, the almond-eyed figured glared at Lee like a "mad dog." Lee felt an intense wave of loathing coming from the woman. He quickly said good-bye and left. He says, "[I] went over and got my wife and got the hell out of there. I was almost shaking. I said, 'Did you see that couple?' And my wife said, 'Sure I saw that couple.' And I said, 'Well, they don't look like goddamn people!' ...it was really a very intense shock."

Convinced that he might have encountered actual extraterrestrials, Lee shared his story with his co-worker Jim Landis. To Lee's dismay, the story leaked out of the publishing house. When Whitley Strieber called him inquiring about the event, Lee agreed to tell him the story. Otherwise, the event would probably have gone unrecorded, as do the vast majority of UFO events.

Probably the most important lesson to be learned from this encounter is that the ETs are keeping a close enough watch on human beings to the extent of monitoring publications about human-extraterrestrials encounters. Journalist Ed Conroy writes that this event "might seem to indicate that the 'visitors' – whoever or whatever they are – took a particularly strong interest in the book from its outset."[156]

Encounter at Sebago Cabins

On January 22, 1974, a young Peruvian gentleman by the name of Sixto Paz Wells sat down in meditation with the specific intention of making telepathic contact with ETs. To his surprise, he began to channel using a method known as automatic writing. He wrote down messages from an entity who said his name was "Oxalc" and that he was from Ganymede, one of the moons of Jupiter. This was the first of several similar communications. Then Wells received a message from Oxalc saying that he would make an appearance February 7 at a predetermined location. Wells gathered a small group of trusted friends and awaited the promised contact. To everyone's amazement, the UFO showed up on schedule. A large hamburger-shaped object with portholes and lights around the circumference hovered about 250 feet above the group for about fifteen minutes.

Following this, Wells received more communications promising further contacts, all of which occurred as planned. One of these contacts involved a face-to-face meeting with the ETs, during which Paz was instructed to fulfill a project called "Mission Rama" (later designated Mission Humanity), the purpose of which was to initiate contact with ETs across the world.

In July 1974, Wells called down a UFO in the presence of several major media representatives. The successful UFO stakeout caused a sensation in the local press, leading to further publicity and a book about the case. The success of Mission Rama was assured. Wells began traveling across the world, forming groups, calling down UFOs, and spreading the word of his mission. Before long, Rama groups were thriving across South America, Europe, the United States, and Canada.

Important here is a contact Wells initiated at Sebago Cabins Recreation Park, New York, in May 1988. Eight members of the group, including Sixto Paz Wells, hosted the weekend event, which attracted more than fifty attendees. Before the event, everyone was instructed to fast and abstain from drugs and alcohol. On the Friday evening, there was an introduction and a group meditation. The entire next day and part of the next evening was also spent in fasting, meditation, and various yoga-type exercises.

As evening fell, there was another ceremony during which the men and women were grouped in separate concentric circles. Everyone then performed a specific visualization exercise involving crystals. It was at this time that the UFOs appeared. One witness, "Betty," noticed several members of the group looking at the sky. Looking up, she instantly saw the UFO. Says Betty, "There it was! It was the golden 'star' moving slowly in an arc. I followed it until it disappeared. Others later reported that it reappeared and made a circle around us."

The crystal meditation ended. At this point, two children came up to Betty and told her that they had seen two stars move. One of the children whispered to the stars that if they were really spaceships, then they should make some numbers. Instantly, the stars moved, making a "4" and a "2." The children then took turns requesting the stars to make different letters, which the stars obligingly did. As the two young children described their sighting, Betty scanned the sky and was shocked to see one of the "stars." Says Betty, "I saw one of them move sharply to the left, then to the right. It then made a zigzag, a circle and went into the other star that we all surmised to be a mother ship. What a show it was!"

The evening wasn't over yet. Wells then announced that thirty-three members of the group had been selected to receive a "Xendra" from the alien ships. An Xendra, Wells explained, was a beam of light from the alien ships used to transport a person to and from the ships, and to raise a person's level of energy and other purposes. Wells then split up the group of thirty-three people into three separate groups.

Betty was one of the lucky ones to be chosen. As the groups split up, several people noticed a large "round luminescence" hovering over the group that was about to receive the Xendra. At this point, powerful beams of light coming from above successively struck each group. When the beam struck Betty's group, she reported feeling "dizzy and nauseous," as did several other people.

Afterwards, everyone was finally allowed to eat and retire to their separate cabins for the evening. The next morning, Betty discovered that several people had reported close encounters in the night. Writes Betty, "The next morning we heard of incredible things that had happened to some during the night. One of them was told by a man, a professional dancer, who had come to the outing very ill and with his legs swollen and in pain. He was inside his zippered-shut sleeping bag next to his wife, also in her sleeping bag, when about three o'clock in the morning they were awakened by a brilliant white light that illuminated their room and soon went away. The next morning the man woke up with his sleeping bag still closed, but with his pajama bottoms on the floor. He told the group that he was stunned out of his mind because he doesn't remember taking them off. His legs were also pain-free and not swollen anymore.

"Another experience," Betty continues, "was of a group of people, some from Canada, who were sleeping in their cabin and were also awakened by a light and their beds shaking. Inside the light, two women of the group saw the projection of a being. One of the women got out of the bed and standing next to the bed, welcomed the being. The light and being then disappeared. The young woman who stood up didn't remember having done so. The only thing she said she remembered was seeing the light. It was an unforgettable weekend, one that changed my life and the way that I look at the stars at night. Because, believe me, we are not alone."[157]

The Kissena Park Landing

According to Bill Knell and other members of "Island Skywatch," a Long Island-based UFO research group, in early 1989, a UFO was sighted by a busload of passengers on the Q65 route. The UFO (described as different colored lights) was sighted hovering at ground level in center of Kissena Park by the lakeside, in Flushing. The observation lasted for three to five minutes. Afterwards, Knell and others investigated the case and discovered what appeared to be unusual landing trace evidence in the area. A strange circular mark of crushed vegetation eighty feet in diameter could clearly be seen. Soil samples were taken and analyzed by geologists at Long Island University. Nothing unusual was found except for one fact: some of the gravel in the sample appeared to be a "dio-rite" type of material, used on the surface of tennis courts. This may or may not be related to the encounter. Also, according to one version, a nearby lamppost was mysteriously magnetized.[158]

Seven-Foot Tall ET

At around 11 p.m. June 20, 1992, "Jane X" of Mamaroneck was getting ready for bed as usual. Her two children were asleep and her husband was already in bed. As she got into bed, she noticed a bright star-like object hovering in the sky outside her window. She ignored it and went to sleep. At around 3:35 a.m. she was awakened by a loud buzzing sound. Moments later, a bright beam of rainbow-colored light came through the roof skylight and hit the bed. As soon as the beam hit her body, Jane felt a sensation of heat and became totally paralyzed except for her head.

Looking at her husband, he appeared to be in a trance. Moments later, another beam came through the skylight. Inside the beam, a tall figure suddenly materialized. Says Jane, "He was dressed in blue robes and was at least seven feet tall. He had long black hair and his skin looked very pale."

The being told her that they would not be harmed. He said that the human race was approaching hard times and that he wanted to give her messages that would help the human race. Jane lost consciousness.

The next morning she told her husband what happened, but he just laughed. In the weeks and months that followed, however, Jane began receiving messages that numerous types of major disasters were going to happen in the future. Unfortunately, she received no definite dates. Nor has she sought any publicity.[159]

Columbia Crop Circle

Crop circles are much more rare than UFO sightings and their link to UFO themselves is not always present. Nevertheless, the July 1993 appearance of a 25-foot wide crop circle in Helen Pyc's oat field off Route 28 in Columbia caused a stir in the local community. The only known UFO connection is a possible sighting of a "round cylindrical shape" reported to the local newspaper by a North Carolina truck driver a few days earlier.

Two days later, the crop circle was discovered. Before long, cars lined both sides of Route 28 to take a look at the twenty-acre oat field. While some observers speculated that the crop circle was the work of pranksters or violent winds, Mrs. Pyc disagrees. As she says, "I lived on a farm for 44 years. We have windstorms, but nothing to make those oats lay so perfect as that. It doesn't seem possible that a prankster could do that."

MUFON field investigators converged on the scene, including Jim Cormia of Ilion and Ron Taylor of Baldwinsville. Says Cormia, "The oats were flattened very close (matted) to the ground and there was no apparent intertwined or braiding effect, nor was there any spiraling effect noted in any of the four circles. All the oats were bent at or just above the ground and all were creased at the bending point."

There were four circles; one was eighty-eight feet across, one was forty-five feet across, one was forty-three feet across and the smallest was twenty feet.

Cormia learned that the East Herkimer police conducted a thorough investigation under the assumption that the work was done by vandals or pranksters, though they never found the culprits. He also talked to local farmers who agreed that it was not the result of wind. Samples of the crushed oat stalks were taken for analysis. Crop-circle researchers had learned that legitimate crop-circles could be detected through microscopic analysis of the plant cells. In legitimate cases, the stalks show evidence of being exposed to "flash heat," and the stalks are bent without breaking. According to agronomist and biophysicist Dr. Michael Levengood of Michigan, the Columbia crop circle samples showed the telltale signs of genuine crop circles.

Writes Cormia, "The 4th or 5th nodes of the formation stalks were actually split and in some cases holes were blown right through the tissue. Dr. Levengood has termed these holes 'expulsion cavities.' Some of these expulsion cavities were so severe that the internal cytoplasm was blown right through onto the surface of the plant."

Cormia returned to the site two months later and found that "the seeds on the stalks within the formation were already germinating while those in the standing crop were not."

Another test involving the electrical conductivity of the plant tissue also showed unusual changes. Needless to say, Cormia is convinced. As he says, "My own 'call' is that the Columbia Center, New York crop circle is genuine and not manmade."[160]

Second New York Crop Circle

One year later, on August 14, 1994, at sometime between 9:30 a.m. and 7 p.m., a nineteen-foot wide crop circle appeared in the cornfield of an unnamed farm family in Vienna, along the north shore of Oneida Lake. Baldwinsville geologist Ron Taylor investigated the formation. "It wasn't perfectly round," said Taylor. "It was sort of elliptical, and looked almost like a comma…You could see a counter-clockwise swirl of corn, with corn near the middle interbraided and wrapped around each other."

The family had picked and eaten most of the corn, however, they did allow Taylor to collect samples for analysis. As in the Columbia case, the samples were sent for analysis to Michael Levengood. There was a thunderstorm that day, which led to speculation that the crop circle was the result of weather. Says Taylor, "I would say there is the possibility this could be from some sort of whirlwind vortex. It's hard to think somebody would want to leave a message in an 11-row wide cornfield that engulfs all but two rows. If Dr. Levengood doesn't see anything there, I guess we'll dismiss it as a freak of nature."[161] *(Note: Source does not reveal results of analysis.)*

…And a Third Crop Circle

Sometime in 1997 (exact date not given), a group of UFOs was witnessed hovering at low level over some fields in Marion, New York. Shortly later, a crop circle was discovered in the area. Samples of the affected foliage were diligently gathered by Larry Thomas and given to Dr. Michel Levengood for analysis. The results proved to be very promising, if perplexing. Writes Nancy Talbot, who published a report on the case, "In the 1997 New York State crop formation…very significant linear correlations were obtained by examining the relationship between the amount of magnetite material in the soil and the distance from the epicenter of the sampled circles. The type of linear distribution obtained was shown to agree with the fundamental physics of centrifugal forces on particles suspended in a rotating plasma system.

Increased amount of magnetic particles in the soils at unusual animal death sites have also been found to decrease in a linear fashion with sampling distance away from the carcass."[162]

A Ghost or an Alien?

In December 1998, MUFON field investigators Raymond Cecot and Jim Bouck received a call from a family in Schenectady concerning strange nighttime visitations in their home. At 3 a.m. one evening, the wife had woken up to see a "short, black, silhouette" standing at her bedside. She told Cecot and Bouck that she was unable to recall any further details and feared that it might be a ghost. She decided to call investigators only after her son also reported seeing the short, dark figure walk out of his closet through the closed door. His mother hadn't mentioned her earlier encounter, and her son was visibly shaken by the confrontation. After interviewing the witnesses, Bouck believes that the details of a short, dark figure that moves through walls might be an alien and not a ghost. As he says, "That association for me calls to mind 'the greys,' or three-foot-tall dark-skinned aliens that are mentioned in abductions."[163]

An Alien at Penn Station

By now it should be clear that ETs can (and do) appear just about anywhere. Certainly there are a lot of strange characters in any city, especially New York City. However, in this next case, the witness is certain that the character she saw in the middle of the day in downtown Manhattan was "definitely not human."

It was October 1, 1999 in the afternoon. As the anonymous witness writes, "I was ascending the escalator at Penn Station, when I reached the street level, about twenty feet away [I saw] what seemed like a male figure, standing about six feet seven inches, near the mouth of entranceway to the station. Crowds of commuters flowed around him, as though he wasn't there. He stared at the variety of passersby, as though he were trying to choose one of them. I caught a glimpse of his face, maybe his eyes too. I don't remember if he looked at me or not."

The witness looked at the figure for only a few seconds, and then kept walking, too afraid to turn around. Says the witness, "The fear instilled in me was so tremendous [that] to this day I can't explain it. His face was not human. His eyes looked right through you. It was something I wanted to forget as soon as possible, but I couldn't. It was as though he had some kind of will that said, 'Keep walking, don't stop, don't look, this does not concern you.' His face was a light gray, almost white, thick brown, menacing eyes — and the thing that stays in mind the most was his stature, or the way he was standing: his back arched, broad shoulders, his elbows pointed towards his back, his head tilted down just a bit looking at the tops of people's heads, scoping them out."[164]

An Alien in the Bathroom

At 2:30 a.m. November 18, 2003, an unnamed resident of Staten Island woke up to go to the bathroom. She sat down on the toilet without turning on the light when suddenly a bottle of shampoo in the bathtub fell over. Looking at the tub, she was shocked to see "something moving." It was too dark to make out any detail, and frightened, the witness fled to her brother's room and woke him up. At first he didn't believe her, but then they both heard another bottle in the bathroom fall.

Says the witness, "We looked at the bathroom opening and we saw something run out and down the stairs. We heard the dog's door open, even though the dog is always in my parents' room at night. We looked outside and saw a bright green light, and then it was gone."[165]

Chapter Eight:

Onboard UFO Experiences

UFO abductions are the closest of all extraterrestrial encounters and have become one of the central focuses of UFO research. Not surprisingly, New York has played a powerful role in the evolution of abduction research. Much of the abduction movement originated in the state, specifically through the research and writing of New York residents Budd Hopkins and the best-selling books by Whitley Strieber. Later, researcher Philip Imbrogno also uncovered a large number of cases, as have several other high profile and lesser-known researchers.

What follows are more than fifty cases of New Yorkers who have been taken onboard UFOs. Again, this is only a tiny portion of the actual number of cases. While there are a few cases that predate the famous 1961 Hill case (the first publicized abduction in the United States), it wasn't until the 1960s that the number of New York cases rose sharply. This trend continued into the 1980s, which remains New York's biggest decade for UFO abductions to date, apparently as a result of the Hudson Valley wave. Following the 1980s, the number of cases dropped sharply, back to the levels of the 1960s and 1970s.

Probably the most amazing aspect of the New York abductions in particular are the fact that they sometimes take place in crowded locations where such things should not be able to happen. However, as we shall see, close encounters can happen in the most unlikely places. As Whitley Strieber writes, "The visitors are certainly capable of penetrating to the center of our cities. Our society has so completely dismissed them that they have free reign here. Because of all the debunking and denial they can come and go as they please and do what they want, and be confident that they will be ignored."[166]

Abducted by Aliens in 1929

UFO abductions are often thought to have begun in the early 1960s, following the Betty and Barney Hill case in 1961 in New Hampshire. However, many cases have now been uncovered that predate even the Kenneth Arnold sighting in 1947. The following case, investigated by New York artist Budd Hopkins, remains one of the earliest New York abduction cases on record.

The incident occurred in 1929 to nine-year-old Ellen Sutter (pseudonym). She was playing outside her Spring Valley home, thirty miles north of Manhattan, when she saw a glint of light in the sky. Looking up, she saw a large metallic object "shaped like a dirigible, with, many, many portholes, and you know, this peculiar light."

Sutter could barely believe what happened next. "It was like I was rooted to the spot. All of a sudden these peculiar things…came out of it, and seemed to be floating. This is why I never told anyone, because as I said, it sounds like a dream. These people – I call them people, I don't know what they were – looked like a diving suit with a head shape at the top and a very distorted, short-looking body. It was weird."

There were about three or four short figures, each floating above and in front of Sutter at about thirty feet in the air. All the animal sounds stopped and time seemed to stand still. She's not sure how long the encounter lasted. At some point, the figures floated back into the craft through an opening that appeared. When she returned home, her mother scolded her for having been away for so long.

Following the experience, Sutter developed a phobia of being alone. She also suddenly became afraid of falling ill and having to visit the doctor, while at the same time she wondered if she might have caught a disease from the strange visitors. She also began having nightmares of being chased by the figures. In the dreams, the figures were no longer floating and had approached her on the ground.

Says Hopkins, "Ellen's account strongly implies a classic abduction scenario." He offered to place Sutter under hypnosis, but somewhat afraid of hypnosis and in poor health, she quickly declined.[167]

Abducted Next to Griffis AFB

Throughout the years of 1946-1948, Jackie X. and her family, who lived near Griffis Air Force Base, experienced many sightings of UFOs. On one occasion, Jackie, her brother, and her two cousins decided to walk to the local store. It was around 1 p.m. when Jackie saw a bright reflection coming from the woods to the left. While the others stayed back, Jackie went forward to investigate. Says Jackie, "What I saw was a large silvery round-shaped vehicle on the ground. I approached this craft, and as silly as this sounds, a fence seemed to pop up in a few seconds, surrounding the vehicle. My cousins tried to pull me back. I had a being approach and without moving its lips it asked me what we were doing there. The being also said it would not hurt me."

At this point, Jackie recalls that her brother and cousins began crying. The next thing she knew, five hours had somehow passed. Their family was out looking for them and wanted to know why it had taken them so long to get to the store.

It was only years later, after speaking with Budd Hopkins, that Jackie realized that she may have been abducted. However, a few months after the missing time incident, something happened that again betrays the United States Military's interest in and cover-up of UFO events. Says Jackie, "Almost three or four months after this happened…a knock came on our door. A gentleman in military uniform was there and spoke a long time with my parents. When he left my mom was crying and my dad was angry. I was told never to mention what we had seen again or I would never see my family again."[168]

20 Miles Above New York City

In the early 1950s, UFO abductions by gray-type ETs were unheard of. Instead, UFO contact seemed to involve friendly human-looking ETs who invited people onboard, took them on tours of their ship and through outerspace, and warned of the dire consequences of pollution and nuclear proliferation. A typical example of that is Daniel Fry Ph.D., a New Mexico scientist turned UFO contactee. On July 4, 1950, Fry claimed to have encountered a flying saucer in the New Mexico desert. He proceeded to go onboard, where he held a long philosophical and scientific conversation with "Alan," an ET who spoke remotely with Fry through an alien intercom system.

At one point, Alan told Fry, "If you would like a suggestion, we can take you over New York City and return you here in about thirty minutes. The light pattern of New York City at night from about twenty miles up has always been to us one of the most impressive sights to be seen on your planet."

Fry agreed. Without any feeling of acceleration, he watched as the landscape fell beneath him and the UFO took off towards New York. Minutes later, they had arrived. Says Fry, "If I were a writer or a poet, I could perhaps explain in some magnificent way the spectacular sight which met my eyes as the greatest metropolis in the world rotated slowly before me...As we descended to twenty miles above the city of New York, the lights were much brighter and they had greater individuality. It seemed as though a vast array of millions of blue-white diamonds lay scattered before me, scintillating and coruscating against a black velvet background...The entire city was a sea of pulsing, shimmering luminescence. 'If I were an artist,' I thought, 'this would probably be the greatest moment of my life.'"

Fry later wrote two small books about his experiences and lectured across the United States. Researchers remained divided concerning the authenticity of his story.[169]

Implanted by Aliens

The year was 1955, and Richard Price (eight years old) and his friend were playing on the street on 10th Avenue in Lansingburgh when they heard a weird sound similar to an approaching train. His friend became frightened and ran away. Price, however, became curious and ran around the neighborhood searching for the source of the sound. He followed the sound to the Oakwood Cemetery. The first thing he noticed was two strange figures, both about his height. They had dark, slanted eyes and wore helmets and uniforms.

Price became terrified and tried to run. Instead, he felt himself drawn towards the beings, who escorted him to a 150-foot wide disk-shaped craft that sat in a clearing in the woods. The beings then elevated Price up into the craft. Once inside, he was undressed and placed on a table. Two other beings joined the group and began to physically examine him. They spoke verbally in a strange language that Price compared to stereo equipment being played too slowly. He watched a viewing screen on the wall as the beings placed a small object inside in penis. One of the beings spoke to him, warning him to never remove the implant or he would die.

Strangely, he was not frightened at the time. After the implantation procedure, Price was dressed. The beings then handed him a piece of parchment-like material with an alien alphabet full of strange geometric symbols.

Afterwards, Price was returned to the cemetery. He ran home and told his father what happened. His father didn't believe him, and assumed that his eight-year-old son had a vivid imagination. Price learned to keep quiet. He later told his grandmother, who believed him but also said that he should be careful about revealing his story to people.

Unfortunately, Price didn't listen and at age sixteen shared the story with a classmate. Word spread fast and Price's classmates reacted by ridiculing and isolating him. Says Price, "The experience itself wasn't bad, but the aftereffects were bad."

He kept the piece of parchment for a while, but at one point, it mysteriously disappeared and Price never saw it again.

Years later, in 1981, he went to the doctor because there was an odd lump exactly where he recalled being implanted by the ETs. The doctor examined it and was puzzled by the swelling, but recommended doing nothing as long as there was no change. Price's condition remained stable for years until 1989. Suddenly Price noticed the object was protruding more than usual, and shortly later, it popped out with a feeling like "an electrical shock." Price saved the object and gave it to David Pritchard, a teacher of physics at the Massachusetts Institute of Technology.

Pritchard conducted an analysis using a scanning electron microscope and a secondary iron mass spectrometer. He determined that it was organic material composed mostly of "carbon, oxygen, and hydrogen" plus other normal, earthly substances. What exactly the object was, however, was not determined, and Price is still certain that it was placed there by ETs. At a 1997 conference in Albany, he said that the abduction affected his entire life. He was unable to concentrate in school and experienced considerable emotional stress, contributing to his divorce. Today Price is considering writing a book about his experience.[170]

Laura's Witches

Born in the 1950s, Laura X's experiences with ETs began around age five. Around that time, she began to see weird-looking, tall, skinny figures with long faces and dark eyes that she called witches. They would enter her room from the closet area at least twice a week. Each time, Laura would call for her mother, but the figures would disappear before her mother could arrive. Other times, she would be paralyzed and fall asleep, only to wake up later with the feeling of having been taken someplace outside.

When she was nine years old, she was outside her Newburgh home playing with her friends when a disk-shaped UFO appeared and hovered above the trees. Her friends ran home, but Laura had no fear and watched the object with her mother for about a half hour, after which it darted away at high speed.

In 1982, as an adult, she had another dramatic sighting. She was driving with her husband and two children along the I-84 in Newburgh when a gigantic gray-metal craft appeared very low in the sky. They pulled over and got out to watch. Strangely, Laura's husband remained in the car. Said Laura, "It was like he was in some type of trance."

Laura described the object as "a floating city." She could see frosted windows around the craft, with shadowy figures moving around inside. The large craft shot down two beams of light on either side of them. Then two smaller craft appeared, circled around the larger craft and darted away. The larger craft followed shortly later.

Currently Laura continues to be tormented by nighttime visitations. In one experience, she learned that a baby she had lost through miscarriage had apparently been taken by the ETs and was being raised by them. Around 1996, her daughter began to report having similar UFO experiences.[171]

The Terror Above Us...
Revisited

The first UFO abduction to be reported in the United States was the Betty and Barney Hill case that occurred in New Hampshire in 1961, but was first revealed in the 1966 groundbreaking book, *The Interrupted Journey*. The case shocked the world, and at first appeared to be unique.

However, within a few years, several other cases surfaced, and by the mid-1970s, the phenomenon of UFO abduction was well known, though still considered rare.

Unknown to many, however, is that there was another missing time abduction case that followed right on the heels of the Hill case.

Among the first few missing time cases to be revealed in the United States, it is today almost unknown, even among UFO researchers. The case took place in the summer of 1958 in upstate New York, and was first revealed in 1967 in a small paperback book by Malcolm Kent, titled *The Terror Above Us*.

The case involves two brothers in their mid-thirties, Jason and Robert Steiner (pseudonyms). The brothers were very close. They worked at the same company in New York; Jason as a computer programmer and Robert as a technical writer. They often car-pooled to and from work, and they also often double-dated.

Everything changed one day in the summer of 1958. Without warning or any apparent reason, both Jason and Robert began to exhibit strange phobias. The first fear was that neither of them could stand to drive with the other at night. They not only feared it, they dreaded it. They could drive alone at night, or even with other people, but just not together.

This fear came on slowly, and both brothers avoided confronting it until one day when they were driving home together and they approached a thick fog bank. Jason, who was driving, felt a rising wave of panic. He stopped the car and began to shake uncontrollably. He thought perhaps he was having a heart attack and turned to his brother for help. Robert, however, was doubled up on the floor of the car, also pale and trembling. Meanwhile, the drivers in the cars behind them were leaning on their horns, wondering why the brothers had stopped in the middle of the road.

When they returned home, both brothers knew that something was wrong with them. They also had other strange symptoms. Jason's job entailed working with large computer tapes in the computer room. Suddenly and for no known reason, the sound of the tapes whirring caused him intense anxiety, and he had to fight the urge to smash the computers.

Jason mentioned this weird fear to Robert, who admitted that he also had the same feelings. Astounded by this coincidence, and realizing that their work performance was suffering, they decided to seek the help of a psychoanalyst.

The therapist, Dr. Emmanuel Brant (pseudonym), interviewed the brothers and began his analysis. He first assumed that there was some traumatic childhood event. However, after several weeks of going over their childhoods, he could find nothing out of the ordinary.

Dr. Brant then focused on their relationships. Both men were young, good-looking bachelors and dated many girls. However, after the summer of 1958, Robert suddenly stopped dating. He used to brag to his brother about his sexual exploits. In fact, Robert revealed to Dr. Brant that not only had he stopped dating, he had stopped all sex completely. He had not been with a woman in five years.

Finally, Dr. Brant felt like he was making some progress. Whatever happened to the brothers, it occurred in the summer of 1958...when their weird phobias began. Brant assumed it was some type of traumatic event and he was going to find out what it was.

The next few sessions, however, proved fruitless. Neither Robert nor Jason had any explanation for their sudden change of behavior, or their fears. Dr. Brant had narrowed the change to the summer of 1958, but neither brother could remember anything unusual happening at that time. Dr. Brant had them go over the entire summer, but there was nothing.

Then came the major break in the case. Both brothers enjoyed speaking about automobiles. On a whim, the doctor asked Jason to describe his Dodge car. Jason did so easily. He then asked about his brother's car, a Ford. Incredibly, the conversation made Jason extremely uncomfortable and he could not even remember the car's color. At the end of the session, Jason was noticeably upset and told the doctor that he wanted to terminate therapy. The doctor, however, recognized this as a psychological defense, which meant he was getting close to the source of the trauma.

Dr. Brant thought this was odd and vowed to ask Robert the same question at the next session. When the time came, Robert too claimed to not really remember the car. In fact, both brothers claimed that the Ford belonged to the other brother.

This was the break in the case. Dr. Brant now assessed that something had happened to the brothers while driving the Ford late at night (probably in the fog judging from their violent reaction earlier to a foggy night). Whatever had happened left both brothers phobic of driving together at night, afraid of the computer tapes at their work, and left Robert completely sexually traumatized. Dr. Brant still had no idea what the cause was and never even considered UFOs.

He decided to use hypnosis, as this had been helpful with his other patients. Under hypnosis, he guided each of the brothers to that summer in 1958, and asked them if anything had happened while driving together on a foggy night. At first, all Robert and Jason could remember was driving into a fog bank, and then arriving home about thirty-six hours later than they should have. It took several sessions for the doctor to get past the missing time barrier and uncover what really happened during the missing hours.

Both brothers remembered driving along the Henry Hudson Parkway, then turning on the street that led to their home, when they hit a thick fog bank. For nearly an hour, Jason inched through the fog. Robert was sleeping in the front seat, but woke up just as they were exiting the fog bank.

At that point, they both heard a hollow beeping sound and smelled an odd metallic odor. Robert looked up and pointed out a group of lights hovering up in the air to the right. As the fog cleared, Jason suddenly saw what it was. As he says, "The saucer. He saw the saucer...After a while we could make out its shape. We saw the lights first. It was just hovering there. Big thing."

Next, they both got out of the car to watch the object. Says Robert, "I saw it. It was a flying saucer. What else could it be, out there in there air, shaped like a saucer, hovering, lights, over the hillside?...We came to the side of the road together and stood on the rise looking at it. It was shaped like a disc, thick in the middle with lights just above the middle section, big flashing lights that seemed kind of yellow in the fog."

As they watched the object, Robert suggested signaling it with their headlights. Jason, however, was becoming a little nervous. They got back in the car, turned off the lights, and backed up the car into the fog.

Robert was still considering the idea of signaling the object when suddenly the beeping sound started to get louder and the odor more intense. They both felt an awful wave of fear. Jason quickly turned the car around and headed back, away from their home, towards the main highway.

Again, they drove through the fog, traveling at a very slow rate. After only a few moments, they came upon a row of lights that formed a blockade across the road. They stopped the car. At this point, events occurred very quickly. Several short figures with blunt features and wearing dark uniforms with belts rushed forward, ushered them out of the car and into a craft. Neither of the brothers was able to resist. Robert was too frightened to notice much detail, and apparently lost consciousness as they were led into the craft.

Jason, however, was less frightened. He thought at first that his work buddies might be playing a practical joke. But as he and his brother were being pulled out of the car, it was clear that the beings were not human. He lost consciousness briefly, but woke up to find himself on a weird stretcher, being carried into the craft. He then lost consciousness again.

When he woke up, Jason found himself lying down naked on a table, paralyzed, and unable to open his eyes. He felt what appeared to be straps holding his wrists and ankles. A bright light shined down through his eyelids. He could feel something cold press against his thighs and then his shoulder. Uncontrollable terror gripped him and he let out a bloodcurdling scream and struggled against his bonds. Within seconds he was rendered unconscious.

When he woke up again, he attempted to remain calm. He pretended to be asleep, hoping to gain some more information. Suddenly he felt somebody reach down and manipulate his genitals. At the same time, he felt strange objects touching his skin. This continued for a few moments and then he was left alone. At this point, he called out softly for his brother. Within seconds, he was again put to sleep.

Meanwhile, his younger brother Robert woke up to find himself in a small featureless room with no windows and no doors. There was a small bed, and a table on which there was a variety of fruit. The only other thing in the room was a young attractive woman sitting on a normal-looking chair.

The woman turned to Robert and told him that she too had been captured by the aliens. Until that point, Robert had completely forgotten what had happened and where he was. He felt strangely euphoric, though the strange metallic smell nauseated him.

The girl seemed to be unconcerned about the situation and was bizarrely comfortable, Robert thought, for somebody who had just been kidnapped by aliens. On the other hand, much of Robert's fear had left him. He still found it extremely difficult to concentrate and remember where he was.

The girl suggested that if they do what the aliens wanted, they would be set free. Robert realized she was suggesting that they have sex. The idea of "voyeurs from another planet" was too much for him to take, and he began to laugh hysterically.

The girl, however, remained serious. Robert's next memory is waking up in bed lying naked beside the girl. At this point, he became horrified. He suddenly instinctively felt that the girl was an alien imposter. There was a strange smell coming off her body. He was repulsed by her advances, though powerless to resist.

As this event came out under hypnosis, Dr. Brant realized that it was this incident that caused Robert's sexual trauma. Robert estimates that he was in the room for about eight hours before being put to sleep again.

Meanwhile, Jason woke up after being examined to find himself in what appears to have been the same small room that his younger brother had been put in. The description of the room was the same. There was a table with fruit, a small bed and a young woman on a chair.

Unlike Robert, Jason suspected from the very beginning that the woman was not who she appeared to be, and was probably an alien. He believed wholeheartedly that the aliens might not return them if he didn't cooperate. And so he accepted the sexual advances of the woman/alien. Afterwards, he, like his brother was put to sleep.

Both the brothers next remembered waking up sitting on a bench in a corner. Their hands were bound in front of them with a dark rope-like material. Robert began to panic, however, Jason urged him to be quiet and not attract attention. Said Robert, "The room was very dark and very large, much larger than the cell. I was glad to see Jason, but I didn't believe it was really him until I looked straight at him."

Robert yearned to speak, but Jason refused, and instead seemed more interested in observing their surroundings.

Suddenly, a weird disk-like contraption with lights descended in front of them. At the same time, a low voice began to speak to them, placing them in a deep hypnotic trance. The voice told them that they would not remember any of the events that had just occurred. The voice then proceeded to question the brothers on various aspects of daily life, much of it seemingly trivial and meaningless. The voice repeated that they would not be able to remember anything, but that in three years to the day, the brothers would return to the same location where they were picked up. They told the brothers that the reason for their delay, if anyone asked, was because they had been unexpectedly detained at work. Afterwards, they both lost consciousness.

When they next awoke, they were seated in the car next to their home. They had no memory of the encounter. They noticed that they were late, but somehow accepted the aliens' post-hypnotic suggestion that they were late because of work.

They had no memory of a UFO, aliens, or missing time. Three years later, the brothers found themselves compelled to travel to the same spot where they had originally been abducted. They still had no memory of any encounter and wondered to themselves why they were there and what they were doing. When nothing further happened, they drove away mystified and confused.

It wasn't until 1964 that the brothers finally sought the help of Dr. Brant. After they recalled their abduction, Jason became repulsed by the subject and avoided discussing it. Robert, however, had the opposite reaction. He became increasingly interested and even obsessed with the subject. He started to investigate UFOs firsthand, traveling around to various UFO hotspots, hoping to have another encounter. He joined UFO groups, began to lecture and write about the subject. He still remained anonymous about his own experience and told only a few people.

Even after recalling the experience under hypnosis, it took several years before Robert could resume normal sexual relations with other women. Both brothers are not happy to have been abducted and have a negative attitude towards the ETs. They feel that the ETs treated them like lab rats.

Malcolm Kent, who interviewed both brothers and authored a book on the case is, of course, convinced of its validity. He writes:

"Until the strange story of Jason and Robert Steiner was revealed to me, and for a long while afterward, I did not believe in what are called flying saucers...But that was all before the Steiner case became my intimate concern...I want at this time to come straight out and say I believe. I believe that Jason and Robert Steiner while driving home late one fog-infested night were kidnapped by alien creatures and taken aboard an alien ship where strange and revealing experiments were made upon their bodies...Here it is. These are the facts. I'm going to present them, stand behind them, claim in front of my peers and my God that I believe them."

Kent, like the Steiners, does not think that many answers to life's questions are to be found inside UFOs. Says Kent, "There are those, I know, and the numbers include almost everyone interested in flying saucers, that believe we can learn untold secrets, opening amazing doors of learning, not just in science, but in philosophy, psychology, medicine. For these reasons and others, people attempt to track down the saucers and the saucer people, berate the government for denying their existence, make speeches and write books.

"I would like to suggest," continues Kent, "that this course is as mad as those disputed previously. It is nearly as filled with illogical thought and superstition. It is only too clear that the aliens are not interested in telling us or teaching us anything. And what could we learn from them if they were willing to tell us their secrets?...If the aliens treat us with impunity, assuming the right to sweep down out of the skies and kidnap us, enclose us with creatures of their manufacture, stick needles into our skin and watch us reproduce, what makes us think that whatever philosophy they have will be

An Invisible Abduction

In the summer of 1958 or 1959, eight-year-old "Marianne" and her friend "Angie" were playing in the basement of their home in a densely populated suburb of Queens. It was a warm and sunny summer afternoon. The two girls were coloring pictures for what felt like a few hours when they decided to go outside. Once outside, they were surprised to see a crowd of people, including several police officers, surrounding their home. Their parents were also there and looked very worried. Marianne and Angie approached the crowd to determine the reason for all the excitement. Suddenly, everyone turned and looked at them in shock. Marianne's mother dashed up to her and demanded to know where she and Angie had been. Only then did Marianne learn that she and her friend Angie had apparently been "missing." Although neither had any memory of leaving the basement, Marianne's mother insisted that she had checked the basement (and the entire house) and neither of the girls were there. Evidently, they had been missing for more than an hour. They called the neighbors and the police and had begun a manhunt to locate the missing children. That's when Marianne and Angie came strolling out of the house.

Later, Marianne experienced further UFO encounters. She located researcher Budd Hopkins and underwent hypnotic regression. Under hypnosis, she recalled that both she and her friend Angie were abducted from the basement, floated out of the house and into a UFO that hovered over the home. Says Hopkins, "The content of her hypnotic recall of their joint abduction conforms to the familiar patterns of UFO abduction experiences worldwide."[173]

Impregnated by Aliens

New York resident Mary B. began having UFO experiences at age five, which continued to age fourteen, and then suddenly stopped. The experiences began sometime in the late 1950s, early 1960s (exact date not given), when Mary began having dreams about "UFO people." In the dreams she would see a large ship hovering over her family's home, then a beam of light would shine down. After that the aliens would come down the beam of light into her room and examine her. Mary felt no fear, but instead was fascinated. The

ETs also seemed fascinated with her. They didn't speak, and their expressions seemed to be fixed in a "half-quizzical smile."

These "dreams" continued for years, occurring at least three or four times a year. One time, at age ten, the aliens came and lifted Mary out of her body and transported her into a warm pink-colored room. She heard soft music and felt a strong presence of love. She also had the impression that it was some kind of alien nursery, though she didn't see any details.

At age thirteen, Mary had her most traumatic "dream" during which the now familiar ETs entered her bedroom. As usual, they entered on a beam of light. On this occasion, however, a more human-looking ET (a hybrid?) was with them. He approached her and proceeded to have intercourse with her. Shortly later, she became pregnant. For the first time, she realized that these experiences were more than just dreams.

Filled with fear, shame, and confusion, Mary told no one. She knew that she had not had any contact with any other men, and yet, there was no doubt she was pregnant; all the signs were there.

Then she had another dream during which the ETs came into her bedroom and performed yet another examination. This time, however, she felt some physical pain. The next morning, she felt different. Says Mary, "I wasn't pregnant anymore. It was really weird. A short time after that dream, my periods resumed; and I knew – I knew with all my being and my inner conviction – that I was not pregnant."

A few months later, Mary had one final UFO dream. Says Mary, "I was taken aboard this craft. Once again I was in that beautiful pink room, and this time I was looking at a baby — a beautiful baby boy. The entities smiled and indicated that I could pick up the baby. I did so, and I had the strongest feeling that I was holding my own child. I caressed and held him and said, 'I love you.'"

Moments later, Mary felt her surroundings becoming hazy. The room appeared to shrink in size and she woke up in bed. Their goal apparently achieved, the ETs never returned.[174]

Extraterrestrial Gardeners

Cosmetologist Mary X. of New York has experience repeated abductions throughout her life. Starting at age five, she has been abducted as many as ten times spanning twenty-five years. Many of her family and close friends are also involved. The aliens are the commonly reported short, gray-skinned type with large, bald heads and big, dark eyes.

When asked if she felt that the aliens had used her in any way, Mary said, "...for a year I was obsessed with taking some little piece of the world with me. I took my children to the park and I collected every little seed and rock and twig I could find. My whole room looked like a nature study. Then half the stuff turned up missing."

Mary feels that the aliens came and took half of her collection. Mary's case is very extensive, involving convincing landing trace and medical evidence. Despite admitting that she has been used by the aliens for apparent breeding and other purposes, Mary does not feel that the aliens are bad or evil.[175]

"They Can't Tell Us too Much"

Jackie X., a resident of Syracuse, says that her abductions began in the early 1960s, around age three. Her father, she remembered, used to announce, "They're coming tonight." One of her earliest memories of an actual encounter occurred while they were camping one summer in the Adirondacks. Says Jackie, "I remember looking through the bars of my crib, and there were all these little creatures around my mom and dad. Then all of a sudden my parents were gone, and then they surrounded me, and I was gone."

Following that incident, Jackie was repeatedly abducted until her teenage years, when the experiences suddenly stopped. For nearly twenty years, she had no further experiences until her early thirties...when they began again.

One experience occurred in 1991. Says Jackie, "I was at home watching one of my favorite movies. Suddenly I heard this voice telling me to take a walk. The voice said, 'Come on, it's time to go.' And I did."

It was pouring rain outside. Jackie, however, was unable to resist the impulse and walked out in the rain towards the local park. She reached the park and bent down to pick up a leaf. At this point her memory ends. The next thing she knew, says Jackie, "It was a couple of hours later, and I was back at my home, and my clothes were completely dry. I reached into my pocket, and the leaf I picked up was still there, so I knew I wasn't crazy."

At first, Jackie remained in denial about her experiences. However she began to hear similar accounts, a few of which occurred in the same area, at the same time and day as her own.

Following the experience in the park, she began having memory flashbacks of this and other encounters. She recalled seeing at least two types of beings. One type are short, stocky, telepathic gray-skinned creatures whom she calls the "genetic engineers." They are the ones who perform the medical examinations. "Most of the tests they perform are over instantaneously," says Jackie. "Other times take longer, and once in a while, they leave scars."

The other beings are taller, bluish-skinned, and act as Jackie's communicators. One of the bluish beings told her, "We come from another place, and another time." Says Jackie, "It's difficult to explain. It's like being shown a map and asked where you are from, and have to tell someone that you are from about four maps behind this one."

She believes that some people are having encounters because they were aliens in a past-life. Says Jackie, "It is possible that some of us are from another planet. If we have incarnated here from another planet, there is a possibility that we wouldn't remember."

Over the years, Jackie has forged a relationship with the ETs, and has been able to extract some interesting information and strike kind of a deal regarding the frequency of her abductions. Sometimes when she isn't ready for an imminent encounter, says Jackie, "I just tell them that I'm busy, or that it's an inappropriate time, and they understand. They just say they'll be back later."

Other times, when they call, Jackie obediently walks into the woods and waits for them. She is now at the point where she can carry on conversations with the ETs. Says Jackie, "They'll tell you things about your life and about the world. They can't tell us too much about the future in terms of specifics, because the future is constantly in motion. It all depends on our actions."

Despite her evolving relationship with the ETs, Jackie still says, "I haven't gotten used to being taken. It's not just something that I expect. It comes very much as a surprise."[176]

"I'm Still Being Monitored."

James X. of Cayuga had his first UFO experience (that he remembers) in 1964, at age fourteen. He was in his backyard watching a twin-engine plane fly by when he noticed "a large red blinking object" emerge from a large cumulous cloud. James watched in amazement as the plane entered into the cloud and the red light followed. The cloud filled with brilliant flashes of red light. He heard the sound of distant explosions. The red light emerged from the cloud, but, says James, "the plane never did."

Six years later, in 1970, James was visited in his bedroom. "I was awakened and attacked by a man-like creature," he said. "I went to grab a plug-in flashlight off the night stand. I was struck in the head, and the flashlight was knocked out of my hand. When I woke up my face was sore, and the flashlight was lying on the floor next to the door."

One year later in 1971, he woke up to find two of the creatures in his room. Says James, "I got up off the bed and tried to escape. I never made it to the hallway only a few feet away. I can still remember my feet on the hardwood floor as I bent over in a very doped state." James says he was injected with a hypodermic needle, picked up off the floor, and "slammed down" on the bed, where he was immobilized by "something elastic." At this point, he lost consciousness and woke up some time later.

James wondered if perhaps he was being visited by demons, and became a born-again Christian. However, the visitations continued.

Another bizarre experience occurred in 1986, while driving late at night. He saw a strange white van pass by him. "Suddenly, my car was enveloped in a white cloud," said James, "and everything went blank. The next thing I knew, I'd lost more than an hour, and I couldn't account of the seven or eight miles I had traveled."

He had vague flashbacks of being surrounded by strange creatures, though he couldn't recall their faces, only that they smelled "like rotten eggs." He also recalled an examination. Says James, "I was placed on a table under a very bright glaring light while electrodes were placed on my limbs. This might have been a brainwashing or a punishment. I don't know why they wanted me."

One evening in 1988, he woke up to smell their familiar rotten egg odor. The next thing he realized, his head was trapped in a strange device and he lost consciousness. He woke up the next morning suffering from an unexplained nosebleed.

James has no idea why he has these experiences, only that they continue to occur. As he says, "I'd almost thought that the visitors were through with me in 1981, especially since I'd become a Christian, and had been counting on God to keep them away. But the 1986 abduction and several inside visits proved to me that I'm still being monitored."[177]

"Everything Is Okay"

Martha X is a small business owner who lives along the shore of Lake Ontario. Her first UFO sighting occurred in the late 1950s, when she and several classmates observed a "huge, oval shaped thing" fly over the school-yard where they were playing.

It wasn't until she was an adult, however, that her experiences began in earnest. One evening (date not given), one of Martha's two dogs was in her bedroom with the door closed. She was downstairs trying to close the basement door, which wouldn't remain shut. As she was closing the basement door, she observed a "small figure" standing in the basement. Strangely, she reacted by getting her other dog and lying down on the living room couch. She fell asleep and woke up a few hours later to find a bright light streaming into the house. It was 2 a.m., and her dog that had been locked in the bedroom was now running freely through the house.

On another occasion, Martha had a terrible nightmare and woke up screaming. Her terrified husband struggled desperately to wake her. When she finally woke up, she was bleeding from the ears.

Her husband also recalls an incident of which Martha has no memory. Says Martha, "My husband remembers watching little people carrying me on my side, and he was completely paralyzed. Normally the dogs start moving around and barking at the slightest little noise. They didn't move either. They just made a low, growling noise."

At this point, they considered going under hypnosis. Martha's husband tried it first, but was so traumatized by his recall that he stopped immediately and has refused any further sessions. He also told his wife that he doesn't want her to suffer the same trauma, so Martha has agreed not to undergo hypnosis.

Despite the traumatic nature of some of her encounters, Martha claims not to have been negatively affected.

On one occasion, she saw a glowing object hovering low over the surface of Lake Ontario outside her home, and then disappearing. She believes that the ETs have taken up residence on the planet, specifically in bodies of water, like Lake Ontario, and also in various desert regions.

During one of her most recent experiences, she saw an ET looking in her window. It was gray-skinned, small, and slender, with a thin lipless mouth, a large head, and deep, slanted eyes. It seemed to be there to reassure her, and spoke telepathically. Says Martha, "It was just smiling at me, and I heard it tell me that everything was OK."[178]

"You've Got to Believe Me!"

In 1964, a six year-old girl from upstate New York, "Andrea X," woke up one evening not in her bedroom where she had gone to sleep, but lying on a table inside a small round room illuminated with pink light. A small, bald man stood next to her and was doing something to her chest. When she woke up the next morning, she was back in her bed, but she found a long straight scar on her chest.

Following this incident, Andrea reports that she would regularly dream about short figures with large bald, heads and dark eyes entering her bedroom. At first she assumed these were just dreams. Then in 1971, when she was thirteen-years-old, an event occurred that proved to Andrea that she was in actual physical contact with ETs.

Says Andrea, "I just dreamed this man was in my room and I was having sex with him. He was real funny looking. He didn't have any hair on his head, and he had real funny eyes, not like mine."

In the "dream" Andrea was paralyzed while the man penetrated her. In the morning when she woke up, she had a burning sensation in her vagina, and her underclothes and sheets were wet. Shortly following the incident, Andrea began to gain weight. When her stomach showed the telltale signs of pregnancy, her parents rushed her to the gynecologist. The gynecologist was puzzled. He told Andrea's parents that Andrea was still a virgin as her hymen was intact, and yet, she was also pregnant.

Andrea's parents insisted that she tell them what happened. Andrea denied having sex with anybody and told them about her "dream." They were shocked and disbelieving. In any case, they all decided that Andrea should have an abortion.

Shortly before going for the operation, Andrea had another dream that she was taken inside a strange round room and examined. Afterwards, she went to have the abortion. Following the operation, the doctors told her that they were unable to locate any fetal tissue and that she must have spontaneously aborted. In either case, she was no longer pregnant.

Andrea tried to forget about the incident and live a normal life. As the years passed, however, she continued to have weird dreams and odd incidents.

One major incident occurred in April of 1985. One evening she "dreamed" that she woke up to find a small, gray-skinned figure standing next to her bed. She tried to wake up her boyfriend, but he would not respond. Suddenly she was levitated out of her bed, across the field behind her house and into a UFO. Inside the craft, she was placed on a table, where she was unable to move. The gray figure first did something to her back, which caused pain along her spinal column. He then took a long needle and placed it inside her nose, causing pain as it pierced into her sinuses. At this point she blacked out.

When she woke in the morning, her nightgown and bed-sheets were stained with blood. She had apparently suffered a severe nosebleed in the middle of the night.

The incident was the final straw and Andrea decided to seek help. She wrote a letter to researcher Budd Hopkins, saying in part:

> "I'm forty years old, and otherwise a normally happy wife and mother. But I've had to sleep every night of my life with a hundred watt light on in my room ever since a recurring child-hood dream about some small gray-skinned figures."

When Hopkins contacted her, she told him, "Please believe me, I'm telling the truth. You've got to believe me."

Hopkins, of course, did believe her and was able to visit her and interview her extensively. During this investigation, Andrea discovered that her body now showed another scar that had appeared following her recent "dream." This scar appeared as a faint, thin, red cut that ran about three inches down the center of her back. Says Hopkins, "This cut – of which Andrea had been unaware – was, of course, a new and unexpected piece of evidence that helped support the accuracy of her other accounts."

At the time, Hopkins had uncovered several other cases involving disappearing pregnancies, and this case helped him to develop his theory that one of the alien agendas involves genetic manipulation and the apparent creation of half-alien half-human hybrid babies.[179]

Beamed By a UFO

Mrs. Bennett (pseudonym) of DeForest Lake in Nyack, was an amateur astronomer. She and her daughter Renata (pseudonym) would often sleep outside on cots during the warm summer nights to watch the stars. One summer evening in 1965, Mrs. Bennett and her daughter were lying side by side on their cots watching the stars when a weird light appeared from the northeast. Brighter than a star, it approached quickly and stopped when it was directly overhead. It was still at a high altitude when it suddenly sent down a beam of light that directly struck the frightened witnesses. Says Mrs. Bennett, "When this light came down and shone on us, I can only tell you the feeling that you get is that you really are…dead."

At this point, Mrs. Bennett remembers running back inside the house to tell the rest of the family. However, her daughter Renata remembers things differently. Renata doesn't remember being struck by the beam of light. However, she says that at some point, two smaller objects came out of the larger object and flew away in different directions. She then ran inside with her mother to tell the others.

While it isn't certain that the mother and daughter were abducted or even had missing time, Budd Hopkins, who investigated the case, believes that the abduction scenario is likely. Says Hopkins, "The fact that mother and daughter recall two dramatically different aspects of their encounter only moments after its end suggests two possibilities: first, that one or both is an unusually poor observer, or second, that each was recalling different aspects of a longer sequence of events."

Hopkins also noted that the behavior of the UFO clearly indicated that the mother and daughter had been targeted. Writes Hopkins, "They were for a moment the center of interest, and the beam of light seemed clearly aimed at them. It isn't as if Mrs. Bennett and her daughter accidentally happened to see something passing by: rather, it is almost as if they were the reason for the UFO's trip in the first place."[180]

The Alien in the Red Vest

As we have seen, many (if not most) abductees first begin having experiences as young children, typically around age four or five up to age eight or nine. In this next case, the visitations occurred to a five-year-old boy and his four-year-old sister in their home in West Corners. There was a series of about five visitations over the span of one year.

Each event followed the same basic pattern. One morning the witness was in the living room watching television or playing with his toys when he suddenly got a strange feeling of being watched. He went to the window and looked out. Moments later a "gray alien in a red vest" popped up in front of the window. The five-year-old boy stared at the figure for about five seconds, then turned and ran, screaming for his mother. At that moment, the figure darted away.

Later that evening, after they went to bed, his sister said that she saw the strange figure come out of her brother's room and come towards her. She got up to run, but instead fell paralyzed to the floor. It came and scooped her up. She noticed that it had extremely long fingers. She told her brother that the figure took her into a strange room filled with toys. They laid her out on a table and took a glowing rod and pressed it against various points of her body.

Later in life both the brother and sister continued to have further encounters. Neither has undergone any type of hypnosis, but are able to remember their experiences in full waking consciousness.[181]

UFO Hits Windshield

When a call came into the Millerton, New York Police station on the evening of July 17, 1967 regarding a stalled automobile on Route 22, patrolman Lewis Lindsay was dispatched to the scene. Officer Lindsay found the car, and inside found Mrs. Funk, stunned and confused. Funk told Officer Lindsay that she had been traveling north when, at around 11:25 p.m., her car radio became filled with static. At that moment, a shiny, black, baseball-sized object, swooped down out of the sky, collided into her windshield, then appeared to bounce away. At the same time, her car headlights mysteriously went out, the car engine stalled, and Mrs. Funk lost consciousness. When she came to, she was dazed and disoriented. Her car, she said, was now facing in the opposite direction, and was about one mile south of where the object had struck her car.

Funk's case found its way to the Aerial Investigations and Research, Inc., a civilian UFO investigative group headed by William Donovan, which recommended hypnotic regression. Under hypnosis, Funk recalled that aliens had approached her car and struck her on the chest with a strange "rod." It wasn't clear if she was actually taken onboard the UFO, however, at some point she recalled her car being turned around. The session was filmed and was later televised during a news special on UFOs.[182]

Donestra

A unique and intriguing case of UFO contact comes from Dean Fagerstrom, a nightwatchman from Putnam Lake. Fagerstrom's UFO contacts actually began in November of 1966, while he was in the army stationed in Germany. One evening he was startled to see a holographic image of a beautiful man and woman appear in his apartment. The man introduced himself as Donestra and said he was an extraterrestrial who had been studying the Earth a long time. He told Fagerstrom that he would prove his assertions and to watch the sky. A few days later, Fagerstrom had an incredible UFO sighting involving a craft of "amazing design and aerial ability."

After his service in the army, Fagerstrom moved to Brewster, New York. It wasn't long before he began having further contacts with Donestra. On January 19, 1968, he woke up to find a weird glowing object appear in his room. It came to within three inches of his forehead, then emitted a powerful vibration that shook his head and neck.

The next day, Fagerstrom became obsessed with drawing highly technical blueprints of what appears to be alien technology. For example one of the designs includes a complicated device called a "photon accelerator." Before long, he had completed dozens of designs, not to mention countless pages of an alien language. He handed the designs over to New York investigator

Philip Imbrogno, per Donestra's instruction. Imbrogno has himself shown the designs and blueprints to many highly qualified people including physicists, engineers, a master draftsman, and professional artists. Says Imbrogno, "Everyone was very impressed, and the draftsman stated that it would take someone with at least twenty years of experience to produce something of that quality."

Fagerstrom's contacts are still ongoing today.[183]

"I Was Held Captive in a Flying Saucer"

On August 11, 1966 Marlene Travers (of Melbourne, Australia) was in New York State (exact location not given) visiting friends and having a dinner party. During the party, several guests mentioned that they had seen UFOs the previous evening. Travers laughed and told them she didn't believe in such "science fiction."

After the dinner, Travers decided to walk to the local store a half-mile away to purchase cigarettes. She was half-way through her journey when she heard a strange humming sound. Looking up, she saw a "weird light" in the sky. At first she thought it was a plane, but then it suddenly dropped out of the sky and landed thirty feet away. Says Travers, "It was a silvery disc, about fifty feet across and ten feet thick."

The disk seemed to glow of its own light. Travers realized instantly that she was seeing a UFO—an actual alien spacecraft. She could hardly believe what happened next. Says Travers, "A sliding door opened and a tall, handsome man, wearing a sort of loose-fitting metallic tunic stepped out."

She wanted to run, but was unable to resist as the man escorted her aboard the craft. Onboard, she saw an instrument panel and other "wild" furnishings. The man placed her on a table, undressed her, and told her that she been specially selected to be the first woman on earth to bear a woman from his planet. He then proceeded to have sex with her.

Afterwards, she was dressed and escorted out of the craft. While leaving the ship, she somehow burned her ankles and passed out. When she woke up, the UFO was gone. She ran back to her friends' home. They were relieved to see her and had been searching for her for hours. Travers told them what happened. They returned to the site and saw a large indentation in the earth where the craft had landed.

Travers herself had burn marks on both ankles, and also later discovered that she was pregnant. She later revealed her story to a reporter for the *New York Chronicle*, telling him, "Believe it or not, I was held captive in a flying saucer, raped, and made pregnant by a man from outer space."

Marlene Travers story, while undeniably sensationalized, is far from unique as the following case shows.[184]

"You Wouldn't Care Who We Are"

The year was 1967, and Shane Kurz was in her last year at Westmoreland High School. Because she lived close to the school, she was able to walk to and from the school. One morning while walking to school an odd-looking man approached her. He was dressed in strange clothes, and talked with a weird foreign accent. But it was his bizarre slanted eyes and ears that really caught her attention. Says Kurz, "I was fascinated by his ears, because they seemed to come to a point and were very sharp compared to ours. His eyes were gray, yet when I looked at them they seemed to go, as if I could see completely through them. They were very magnetic."

Somehow the man knew her name, but was puzzled about everyday facts that everybody should know. He asked her odd questions such as, "What is volleyball and basketball?" He asked her if she would like to go for a ride during lunch in his "white vehicle" and pointed towards the field. Kurz politely said no and walked away. Realizing how strange the encounter was, she immediately turned around, but the man was gone. Says Kurz, "No more than three seconds had passed from the time I took the steps and turned around, and there was no possible way he could have gotten out of my sight that quickly."

Kurz was stunned by the incident, but didn't think much about it. Then, one month later she was in the local convenience store when she saw another very strange man looking at her. The figure had very thin blond hair, extremely white hair and penetrating eyes. The man stared at her as she went through the store. After a few moments, he was suddenly no longer there.

A few months later, in the spring of 1968, a flurry of UFO sightings struck central New York, around the town of Westmoreland. In April, Kurz and her mother, Doris Bailey, heard about the sightings and spent several hours outside on their porch with their telescope, looking for the alleged saucers.

Having never seen anything, they were skeptical. Then on April 13, they went outside one evening and were shocked to see a bright, glowing cigar-shaped object moving in strange patterns overhead. They both had the strange feeling that were being "observed" and could feel a prickly electrical feeling.

Then on April 15, the UFO returned. Shane and her mother watched it for about seven minutes. Again they both felt like they were being watched, and felt a strange prickly sensation.

That night they went to bed earlier than usual. Sometime in the middle of the night, Shane and her mother, who shared a bedroom, both awoke to find their bedroom flooded with light. Looking out at the source of the light, Shane saw a large oval object land in the meadow behind their home. It was shining a powerful beam of light directly into their bedroom window. Moments later, the object quickly ascended and disappeared.

Shane and her mother lived only a few miles from Griffis Air Force Base, so they called the base and asked if they had any information about aircraft activity on that evening. Officials at the base denied any activity.

It wasn't long, however, before the UFO returned. On the evening of May 2, Shane stayed outside looking for UFOs when she saw what appeared to be the same cigar-shaped object. It came from across the horizon, stopped overhead, then shot straight upward. Again, Shane had the feeling she was being watched.

She went to bed. Meanwhile, her mother woke up in the middle of the night and noticed that Shane was not in her bed. At first she assumed that Shane had gone to the bathroom, and went back to sleep. Doris woke up shortly later to find Shane lying on her bed, with her feet and robe covered with mud. The front door was wide open and muddy footprints led from there to the bedroom.

Shane, who had no history of sleepwalking, had no explanation for the muddy footprints, or where she had been earlier when her mother couldn't find her. Shane had no memory of anything strange occurring, however, she did notice two reddish ring-shaped marks on her abdomen. She also began to suffer migraine headaches, nausea, nightmares, worsening vision, and depression. She also noticed that her menstrual cycle stopped completely. Other strange effects followed, including an increase in psychic abilities and wristwatches that acted strangely whenever she wore them. About nine months after the incident, she experienced a sudden unexplained weight loss.

She went to the hospital, but they were unable to diagnose any specific condition. Meanwhile, Kurz dreamed over and over that she was in her backyard when a UFO appeared overhead, struck her with a beam of light, and lifted her into the craft. As the years passed, the experience faded into the background.

Kurz eventually connected her experience with UFOs, and joined a local UFO group. Then on the morning of January 23, 1975, she woke up feeling as if she had been drugged. Checking her body, she was dismayed to discover burns on her chest, neck, and face. There was also a needle mark on her arm. She decided it was time to take action, and sought out paranormal researcher Hans Holzer to help her uncover what happened on that fateful night.

Holzer placed her under hypnosis and regressed her to the incident. Under hypnosis, Kurz recalled waking up and walking into the muddy field where she was sucked up inside a UFO. She found herself unable to move, lying down on a table in what looked like a hospital room. Several identical-looking, hairless figures with white pale skin, large dark pupil-less eyes, and small mouths surrounded her. They spoke telepathically and told her that she was special, and that she was a good subject for breeding. When she tried to resist, they told her to relax and applied a strange lotion on her body. One of them was wearing a strange scarf around the neck and appeared to be the leader. He undressed her and then proceeded to have sex with her. He told her, "We've watched you. You're the one...I want to mix with you...We want you as a mate."

Kurz was unable to resist. As they had sex, the leader seemed particularly fascinated by her hair and eyebrows, which he picked at and stroked. Afterwards, they poked her naval with a needle-like device and gave her a shot in the arm with a box-like instrument.

At one point, Kurz asked them who they were, and where they were from. The leader gave her a typically evasive answer, saying only that they were "from very, very far" and that "you wouldn't care who we are."

They then dressed Kurz and told her she was ready to go. She screamed at the leader that he had just raped her. He seemed confused and said, "No, we want to let you go…You won't remember."

Kurz insisted that she would remember. He insisted that she wouldn't. They placed her on a device. A light came from the ceiling and suddenly, Kurz found herself floating down to the ground. The UFO darted away and Kurz walked into the house, tracking muddy footprints into the bedroom, where she went to sleep.

Since then Kurz has reported no further encounters. However, she is convinced the ETs either took her ovum or impregnated her. In either scenario, she believes that she has an alien child somewhere out there. She also believes that the strange man she met while walking to school and the alien who raped her onboard the UFO were actually the same person.[185]

"We're Going to Check You Out"

In the last week of March 1969, seventeen-year-old Denis McMahon and his friend Paul Federico (not their real names) had pulled over in their car at around 11:45 p.m. while driving near Pearl River.

Looking up, they saw a round, flattish object with red and white lights moving overhead. Unknown to the teenagers, more than a dozen other witnesses in the area, including a few policemen, also observed the same UFO traveling about fifty feet above the railroad tracks through downtown Pearl River.

One week later, at around 7:30 p.m. April 5, 1969, McMahon, Federico, and another friend parked their car along DeForest Lake in West Nyack to make plans for the evening. As they talked, one of them noticed a strange light reflecting brightly off the dashboard. Jumping outside the car, they were shocked to see a large oval-shaped object identical to their earlier sighting hovering about thirty-five feet overhead. It was shining down a beam of light.

At some point, they experienced a lapse of time and suddenly found themselves back in the car, trying to start the engine, which would not turn over. After several attempts, the engine finally started and the boys raced off to the police station to report their encounter. The UFO had already left, moving in a westerly direction.

The teenagers arrived at the police station at 10:23 p.m. The police filed an official report. At the time, although the boys noticed the strange time discrepancy, they didn't know what to make of it.

Federico began to dream about the incident. In his dream, they were looking at the object hovering in the air. But instead of moving away, the object suddenly landed next to the boys. Shortly later, a beam of light came out and shined on Federico. While he was nervous in the dream, as soon as the light hit him, says Federico, "I was not scared at all. I felt very relaxed, very calm, and very at ease, almost as if I was in my mother's arms as a little baby."

Ten years later McMahon heard Budd Hopkins on a local radio show. He called Hopkins, who agreed to conduct an investigation. Only then did McMahon find an explanation for the missing time sighting: he may have been abducted.

McMahon and the others considered hypnosis, but finally decided against it. However, McMahon did allow himself to be interviewed. This apparently was enough to crumble the wall of amnesia, and in the weeks that followed McMahon spontaneously and without hypnosis recalled what happened during the missing time.

Like Federico, he recalled the UFO landing and a beam of light striking them. His next memory is of being in a room inside the craft. The room was about twelve feet across, brightly illuminated, and very clean. In the center was a white Formica-like examining table. With no sign of his companions, McMahon found himself laid out on the table surrounded by three short figures with big black eyes, large bald heads, and grayish, plastic-looking skin. Otherwise, they had a powerful, muscular build and seemed very much like humans. One of the figures was dressed in a loose, medical-looking outfit with a high collar and was five feet tall. The other two wore grayish-green form-fitting coveralls and were only about four and a half feet in height.

McMahon tried to struggle, but found that he was paralyzed and partly numb. The figures also grabbed him and held him down. He says that while they had no fingernails, they had very hard fingers. He was subjected to some sort of bizarre examination or operation that eludes his memory. Says McMahon, "I don't remember the actual thing that happened. I do know something happened. It felt like I was being ripped to pieces and put back together again."

He felt no pain, though he does admit that during the episode he was alternately panicked and extremely calm. He reports that the ETs communicated telepathically, a detail that bothered him because of its strangeness.

He doesn't feel that the ETs were evil, nor however, does he feel that they are friendly space-brothers. Says McMahon, "It wasn't an antihuman attitude. It was more of a, 'We're going to check you out, pup. Get up there on the table' sort of deal. I get the same impression when I take a dog to the vet...That's sort of the impression I got from these people. 'Hi, pup, get up on the table here, sit down nice, don't wet yourself.'"

Incidentally, this incident occurred only one mile from the previous 1965 encounter reported by Mrs. Bennett and her daughter, Renata, of DeForest Lake.[186]

Alien on the 7ᵗʰ Avenue Subway

In the summer of 1969, a young lady was returning home from work on the subway when she had an incredible alien encounter in a very unlikely location. Says the understandably anonymous witness, "In the middle of the 7ᵗʰ Avenue subway rush hour crowd I saw a little man about four feet tall. He had a huge head, but it was the quality of his skin that first caught my attention. It didn't look like human skin, but more like plastic or rubber. I knew he wasn't human. I tried to follow him with my eyes, but he quickly got lost in the crowd. No one else seemed to notice. This disturbed me: I thought I was seeing things."

One year later, in the summer of 1970, another experience occurred that gave the witness reason to believe something unusual was happening in her life. She was visiting a commune near New Paltz, New York. As she and her boyfriend sat outside with a group of about twelve people, suddenly everybody stood up and, as if in a trance, walked to their cars. Says the witness, "We found ourselves sitting in our cars, revving the engines and realizing that we didn't know why we were doing this, but we were unable to stop. Then we all drove off, one car behind the other. I was then with my boyfriend in his van. One of the cars in front fell into a ditch alongside the road. The procession stopped; the guys got out, helped push the car back on the road, and we all drove off again. I remember being in a trance and watching the scenery as if it was a movie screen. The next thing I recall is the sky becoming very bright. It was already a sunny day so it had to be very intense. There was an electrical quality to it. Then I perceived what seemed like the sky opening. A force was coming towards me. The last thing I remember was finding myself outside of the car, lying alongside the road, trembling uncontrollably, in fear. My boyfriend was also lying alongside the road, but he wasn't afraid. I had always thought I'd had some sort of religious experience."

Later, the witness got married and rented a house outside of Woodstock, New York. One night in the summer of 1983, they were both simultaneously woken up by "an extremely loud whirling noise." The witness turned to her husband and joked, "I think the spaceships have landed."

At this point, a bright light filled the bedroom. The husband went downstairs to investigate, and returned saying it was just a whippoorwill. They both returned downstairs and looked outside in time to see what appeared to be a large bird swoop through the trees. The witness, however, feels that something else may have occurred. As she says, "There remained, however, a feeling of unreality about the whole incident."

It wasn't until she read Whitley Strieber's book, *Communion*, that she remembered (and had a possible explanation for) all the weird events that occurred to her, especially one from early childhood involving night terrors. "The more I read of your book," the un-named witness wrote in a letter to Strieber, "the more weird memories come to mind…It wasn't until I almost finished your book that a series of memories came to me which gave me goose bumps and chills. When I was about four years old I suffered from 'night terrors.' I would wake up in the middle of the night screaming…I would have these dreams that I was looking over our apartment window on West End Avenue and see spaceships hovering over the Hudson River and the Palisades. The dreams were always very vivid and powerful. The ships were distinct with bright lights. I had completely forgotten those dreams, even though I've had them since childhood."[187]

Pregnant Woman Abducted

The gray-type ET's interest in human reproduction is typified – and perhaps partly explained – in the following case.

Barbara Kent of Westbury, Long Island was eight and a half months pregnant with her first child. At this stage in her pregnancy she had some trouble moving around and sleeping. It was just after 11:30 p.m. on the evening of January 17, 1970, and Kent was watching the beginning of "The Tonight Show," waiting for her husband (a night-shift city police officer) to come home before going to bed. Suddenly, she heard a strange, high-pitched beeping noise coming from the television.

As she wrote in an article for *Fate Magazine*, "I watched the first minute or two of Johnny's monologue and was greatly annoyed by the beeping and the prospect of eventually having to get up and investigate. My next memory is of lying uncomfortably on my back in a very dark and cold room. I blinked my eyes because my sight was blurry, and I tried to make some kind of noise, but was unable to. I could not even move my lips."

The entire room was bathed in a red light that came from a single source above her head. She could barely make out a few shadowy figures standing around her. One said, "You'd better hurry, she's starting to come up."

Another voice replied, "I'm finishing up right now."

Kent reports that she wasn't terribly afraid and assumed at first that it was a strange kind of waking nightmare. She tried to look at one of the figures, but he placed something over her face and she lost consciousness.

Says Kent, "I woke up in my bed, in a freezing sweat. My feet were cold and dirty. I tried to jump up, but I couldn't, so I slowly rolled of the bed and waddled into the bathroom. My stomach was as hard and as cold as ice. There was a drop of blood on the front of my nightgown, over my stomach, where there also seemed to be a cold spot."

Kent lifted up her nightgown and examined her body. To her shock, there was a small puncture similar to a child's tuberculin tine test. She looked at the clock; it was 2:15 a.m. In the living room, the television and all the lights were still on. Kent reports that she never went to bed without turning off the television and lights. She was a little frightened by this fact, and when her husband came home, she revealed the whole story. He told her she must have fallen asleep and had a nightmare.

However, three days later she went to the doctor for a pregnancy checkup.

He immediately noticed the puncture spot on her stomach and, puzzled, asked her, "We didn't order an amniocentesis on you?" When Kent denied having a test, the doctor passed the wound off as a strawberry mark. However, says Kent, "This mark never went away and is still present to this day."

Her baby was born three days later, and was, says Kent, "a very, very difficult birth...a double footling breech."

Kent pushed the dream into the back of her mind and continued with her life. Five years later, she was sitting in their new home in Dix Hills, New York when she heard the same strange beeping sound coming from the television. She was instantly transported mentally to that night five years earlier. Suddenly she remembered what had occurred during the missing time.

Says Kent, "The television set was on, just like it had been that night, only now I remember the beeping getting louder and louder, and a man's face appearing on the screen and talking to me. He had said, 'Do not be afraid, we will not hurt you, do not be afraid...it was what is recognized as an alien face today, but back in those days it was grotesque, unlike anything any of us had ever seen before."

She told her husband what she remembered and that she thought it was an extraterrestrial. He was incredulous. However, Kent wasn't finished with her story yet.

She also recalled that after she was "taken," one of the examining ETs asked her if she knew how her child had gotten inside her. Says Kent, "They thought it amusing that I had a baby inside of me."

At that point, she began screaming. The ETs somehow silenced her and returned her to her room. Why were the aliens amused by her pregnancy? Kent speculates, "If the aliens are nocturnal creatures, or come from a planet with a red sun, that would account for the red light. If they are reptilian, or do not bear their young live, that would account for their being amused by the baby being inside of me."

Former MUFON president John Schuessler was impressed by the case and included it in his groundbreaking catalogue of physiological effects resulting from abduction. Writes Schuessler, "On January 17, 1970 a pregnant woman was abducted from her home in Westbury, Long Island, New York. She was returned with a mark on her abdomen like that from an amniocentesis test, marked with a spot of blood on her gown. The spot on her abdomen was very cold to the touch. She recalled the smell of ozone."[188]

Executive Loses 24 Hours

"It was as though I did not exist for a day."

In the summer of 1973, Wall Street executive Frank Hoffman (pseudonym), was returning home to New York from a business convention in Hawaii via 747. When he looked out the window, he was shocked to see a glowing red UFO pacing the jet. Nobody else saw it, and after five seconds it disappeared.

Hoffman was amazed, but remained silent about his sighting and continued to flirt with the lady who sat next to him. He returned home. The next day he had a date with the lady he'd met on the plane. She was also from New York, and they agreed to go out for dinner that night.

Hoffman arrived at her East End Avenue Apartment that evening. However, his date, it turned out, was very upset. She asked him why he had broken the date. He told her that she was wrong, he hadn't broken the date. He was exactly on time. She disagreed and showed him a newspaper, and pointed to the date. Hoffman was shocked. It was a full twenty-four hours later than it should have been. He was missing one entire day.

When Hoffman returned to work, his co-workers also demanded to know where he had been the previous day. They had made several calls to his residence, but nobody answered. Hoffman had no explanation, nor any memory of what happened during the missing twenty-four hours. His only theory is that it had something to do with the UFO he had seen the day before. Says Hoffman, "It was as though I did not exist for a day."[189]

Aliens Warn of Global Warming

According to UFO researcher Thomas Bullard's landmark study of 303 abduction cases, the most common onboard experience is a physical examination. However, the second most common is being given messages, usually warnings of pollution and nuclear proliferation and/or other spiritual type messages. A good example comes from upstate New York resident Norma Shelton (pseudonym).

As with many people who have extensive UFO experiences, they began in early childhood. On one occasion, Norma was playing with her sister behind their house when they had a missing time experience. It wasn't until years later, during the early 1970s, however, that she saw her first UFO. Says Shelton, "While out on a summer evening ride with my husband at the time, I called attention to a large metallic object, clearly hovering near the Shawangunk Mountains. It was still daylight, and we were both amazed at such a large object in plain view."

Around this time, Shelton began having vivid out-of-body experiences during which she'd visit other dimensions and/or planets where she was taught knowledge and given a boost in psychic and healing abilities. On a few occasions, she saw aliens. Says Shelton, "At one time, some beings with bald heads were staring at me and one was saying, 'She's not ready yet.'"

After a decade of alien dreams and OBEs, Shelton found herself increasingly curious about her experiences. Then one summer in the early 1980s, she was treated to another sighting. "I was living in the Hudson River area at the time. Looking up at the summer sky, I saw seven small disks flying overhead. I felt very excited, yet peaceful. The sighting seemed to have a reassuring effect on me."

Three weeks later, Shelton's sister called and said that after returning home from visiting Shelton's home, she saw "a large and well lit UFO" that slowly approached her car, hovered for a few moments, and then darted away.

In 1986, she had a vivid dream in which she was taken onboard a UFO and told by the aliens, "Come, I have something to show you." The alien then showed her an image of the planet Earth. Shelton could see that "the polar icecaps on the earth were melting, causing massive flooding and imbalance." Then the ETs told her, "This will affect the tilt of the Earth on its axis. We cannot intervene." The ETs warned her that there was a problem with the ozone layer and that the Earth was in "great danger."

Shelton's most recent experience occurred in the 1990s. She was at a party with some friends when the subject of UFOs came up. She recounted a few of her recent UFO dreams. After an hour or two, she returned home. Ten minutes later the phone rang. Says Shelton, "The remainder of the party was on the deck viewing a fascinating group of UFOs. Because of trees obscuring my property, I couldn't see them, but they did make the evening news. Someone had videotaped them."[190]

Abducted from Café

Brenda X., a successful commercial artist and a resident of Bronx, New York, is one of many New Yorkers who have gone public with her experiences. Like many abductees, she believes she has been having experiences her whole life. It started out with flashbacks and partial memories of encounters. Then in 1975, at age twenty, Brenda says she was taken by gray-type ETs from the rooftop of her Bronx home to a secret underground alien base somewhere in the southwest. There she saw several different types of ETs – Nordics, Grays, and Hybrids – all working together.

In another abduction, Brenda recalled being made to wear weird "glass or plastic" shoes on her feet. Later, when she read that Massachusetts's abductee Betty Andreasson had described the same thing, she burst into tears. The corroboration of such an unusual detail made her finally accept that she was an abductee.

Another major encounter occurred in 1995. This is one of the many New York encounters that occurred in broad daylight and in full public view. Brenda was eating at an outdoor café near Battery Park City when she saw the short, hazy silhouette of a gray being approach her table. As soon as it reached the table, the gray being became fully visible and commanded Brenda to come with him. Brenda suddenly found herself holding onto the being as they flew up over the Hudson River and into a dark UFO hovering high in the sky. Inside Brenda was subjected to the typical examination procedures before being returned.[191]

A Mass Abduction

Sometime in the late 1970s, an unnamed woman from New York City claims to have been a participant in a bizarre mass abduction event that she didn't recall until ten years after the fact. According to the woman, she woke up one night to find her self in a large silver-walled room with about thirty other women. They were all being undressed by ETs who looked like a cross between humans and cats. They had brown skin, and green-skirted uniforms.

Says the witness, "They took us all together into a medical bay of some kind...They placed our hands and feet in loops attached to ropes that came down from the ceiling. They didn't put us on tables; we just hung in the air. They stuck something up our noses that sort of looked like a plastic ball."

The ETs then told the woman that they were studying human female reproduction systems because their own females died soon after menopause. Researcher Jack Grimes who interviewed the woman, writes, "It is one of the most interesting abduction stories I have ever heard."[192]

"You Have No Right to Do This!"

It was around 6 p.m. November 15, 1978, (November 23?), and Joseph X., age 24, was driving his car through Islip on Montauk Highway in Long Island. Suddenly, his vehicle became enveloped in a blue-white light and came to a sudden stop. He first thought that he must have hit a tree.

His next memory was waking up at 1:37 a.m. He found himself lying on his back in a wooded area alongside a road in Ronkonkoma, which he would later discover was twelve miles from where he had been taken. The former contents of his pockets were in a neat pile next to him. His socks, which he was no longer wearing, were folded neatly in his back pocket. His shoes were untied and had been placed backward on his feet. His shirt was buttoned incorrectly. Worst of all, he had defecated in his pants. Vivid flashbacks of short gray-skinned figures approaching his car raced through his head. He also had vague recollection of being physically examined.

After hiking around for several minutes, he finally found his car, headlights still blazing, sitting directly on top of some crushed bushes in a field. There were no tracks to show how the truck had gotten into the field. The paint surface on the car was also strangely faded.

He returned home where he discovered a red scar under his naval. He became nauseous and vomited "a ferocious amount" of blood. Realizing something was wrong, he rushed to the doctors. After examining him, the doctors asked him if had recently been exposed to a source of radiation.

Joseph denied any such exposure. At first he didn't connect it to his experience with UFOs, but as he began having more flashbacks of being pulled from his car by the short gray figures and physically examined, he made the connection. He sought out the help of researchers Budd Hopkins and John Ford. Later, under hypnotic regression, he was able to recall most of what happened during his UFO abduction.

He remembered driving along the road when a bright light enveloped his car. Again, he first thought he hit a tree. Under hypnosis, he recalled that he re-opened his eyes and saw four, short, gray-skinned figures moving through the bright light towards him. He received an incredible shock as he realized they were not human. Says Joseph, "God, those eyes. I couldn't deal with those eyes."

He tried to hide by curling down on the floor of his car. The next thing he knew, the car itself was inside a huge room. He was pulled out of his vehicle and ushered to the next room.

He was then placed in a chair-like device, and the ETs passed a glowing wand over his head. Moments later, a transparent screen dropped down from the ceiling, showing the witness sections of his body in full color.

He was stripped of his clothes and placed on a table where he was probed "like a lab rat" with various instruments. One instrument like a fountain pen pierced his stomach and "hurt like hell." They extracted semen. Says Joseph, "I was screaming, 'You have no right to do this to me!'"

According to the witness, he next suddenly found himself marching through an "Arctic scene," where he was able to physically feel the cold wind on his skin and the heat being painfully sucked from his body. Moments later, he was back in the chair being physically examined by the ETs.

Next he suddenly found himself in a desert-type scene where he was exposed to "searing heat." Again, he was pulled from the scene and subject to another physical examination. His next memory was waking up in the field, disoriented and nauseous.

Obviously Joseph is not happy to have been abducted, but he is certain that it did happen. As he says, "There is no way anybody is going to tell me that this didn't happen to me. I'm telling you, this was real."[193]

"An Eye Implant Operation"

In 1982, Budd Hopkins investigated the case of a young New York woman who, under hypnotic regression, recalled a missing time incident and remembered observing an alien eye implant operation being performed on an unknown male before she herself underwent the same procedure. Writes Hopkins, "She stood inside a round room observing an apparatus consisting of long, telescoped sections, which descended towards the eye of a reclining male abductee. While he lay naked upon the examination table, the needle-tipped end of the apparatus touched his eye, apparently piercing it. Though his body suddenly quivered, she assumed he was paralyzed and could move very little. After this operation, the young woman was, herself, placed on a table for the same operation. She felt the pressure of the needle but recalled no pain."

After her session, Hopkins had her draw a picture of the instrument used by the ETs. The instrument looks like a large cylindrical object with a needle and syringe at the end.[194]

"I Am Not Afraid of Them"

During the Hudson Valley UFO Wave of 1982-1986, the number of UFO abductions in the area rose sharply, practically tripling in number. On February 26, 1983, Monique O'Driscoll and her daughter witnessed the Hudson Valley UFO. O'Driscoll had mentally asked the UFO, "Don't go," and it had responded by approaching her more closely.

Now, two months later in April 1983, she was walking her dog outside her home in Lake Carmel when she saw strange lights hovering nearby. She returned home thinking only that she had just seen the UFO again, but discovered that it was an hour later than it should have been. She agreed to undergo hypnosis.

Budd Hopkins hypnotized her and she recalled that she was walking her dog outside and the next moment she was lying on her back in a small round room covered with computer panels being examined by little people with big, bald heads. They placed a small silver instrument that vibrated on her chest. Despite the unusual nature of her experience, she remained calm throughout. Says O'Driscoll, "I am not afraid of them. Right now I feel restful."

During Imbrogno's investigation into the Hudson Valley UFO wave, he spoke with Hopkins and asked him what he thought was the reason for the wave. Hopkins replied, "They are looking for people."

At the time, Imbrogno says he was "not convinced about the reality of abduction claims. But I soon changed my mind when I discovered that over eighty-two percent of all the abduction cases I looked into were people who had been scanned previously by the UFO's white light."

Imbrogno suddenly found himself on the forefront of UFO abduction research as he began to deal with the incoming flood of onboard UFO reports during the Hudson Valley wave.[195]

Struck by a UFO Beam

As investigated by Philip Imbrogno, in the a.m. hours of March 19, 1983, engineer Jim Falkworth was driving past the New Croton Falls Reservoir located near Yorktown when he saw a large dark mass hovering just above the water. He pulled over and turned off his car lights. After looking more closely, he could see that the object was chevron-shaped. At one point, the object lit up with red lights and began to scoot over the surface of the reservoir. Amazed, he got out of his car and walked to the edge of the water.

He thought the object might be an experimental government craft. But then it approached within two hundred feet of him. It was totally silent and was composed of a gray metal that seemed to absorb the light.

As he watched, several cars came up and down the road. On each occasion, the lights on the object switched off and came back on when the cars left. The object then made wide sweeping movements, approaching to within one hundred feet of Falkworth.

Suddenly, a red beam of light came out from beneath the object and played across the surface of the lake. The object then moved to the center of the reservoir and emitted a white beam of light that struck Falkworth, knocking him back, and rendering him unconscious.

His next memory was getting up off the ground. It was daylight and the UFO was gone. When he got home at 8 a.m., his wife was very upset and worried about his absence. Falkworth reports that he cannot account for several hours. His wife says that in the days following the incident, Falkworth was disoriented and distant.[196]

Abducted During the Hudson Valley Wave

On March 24, 1983, one of the biggest nights of the Hudson Valley UFO wave, John Wright was driving with two teenage friends when they saw a huge boomerang-shaped craft hovering over a utility pole in Stormville. Meanwhile, another separate group of people watched the same object from a further distance. Wright pulled over and walked until he was directly below the craft. They watched it for the next twenty minutes. He finally had to leave because his friends had become frightened. They drove away, but the craft began to move with them. They followed it for the next hour, passing many other people who were also watching the object. At some point, some of the lights separated themselves from the craft, flew around and then rejoined the craft which then flew away.

At first, the encounter seemed to be nothing more than a simple sighting. However, in the days following the sighting, Wright had a dream in which he and his two friends were abducted inside the UFO where they were examined by short creatures with large heads. He later underwent hypnosis and recalled further details. The ETs were just over five feet tall. They wore black uniforms that buttoned up the front. The interior of the craft was filled with numerous computer-like panels with bright colored flashing lights. Wright and the two teenagers were placed in large chairs and examined with strange instruments. One of the ETs told Wright that their mission was scientific and peaceful, that they were there to study the people in the area. They told him, "Don't worry, we won't hurt you." This was repeated several times throughout the experience until suddenly, Wright and the others found themselves back in the car. Later, investigators contacted the other two witnesses and discovered that both had been having dreams that they had been taken onboard the craft, placed in chairs, and examined by large-headed ETs.[197]

Probed by ETs

One evening in April 1983, Jane X. of Westchester County was awoken from a sound sleep by an unusually bright beam of light coming through the window. The beam engulfed her entire body and felt like it was actually penetrating her. Says Jane, "I felt it and was shocked, as my entire body from head to toe was paralyzed. I lay there about ten minutes, and all the time I felt as if my insides were being probed, like a doctor was probing my insides. I was terrified, but there was nothing I could do."

Strange images suddenly filled her mind, starting with flashing colors and then turning into an image with a large hairless head, big eyes, and claylike skin. Says Jane, "He assured me that I would come to no harm and said that I was being tested. He told me, in my mind, that he was part of a team of explorers studying the people."

At this point, she lost consciousness. She was so upset the next morning, she told nobody what happened. She later contacted investigators who offered to put her in touch with a hypnotist, but she declined.[198]

"Do Not Be Afraid"

Also in April 1983, one morning at around 2 a.m. Ellen X. also of Westchester County was awakened by a voice that said, "Do not be afraid. We will not harm you." She tried to awaken her husband, but he wouldn't wake up. Through the skylight, she could see a large object with multicolored lights hovering above the house. A low hum reverberated through the bedroom. She tried to get up, but found herself paralyzed. At that point, a beam of light came from the object, through the skylight, and engulfed the bed.

They woke up the next morning, exhausted. Ellen told her husband what happened, and he told her that he had dreamed that a UFO had hovered over the house and taken them onboard. Ellen later contacted investigators, but her husband refused to discuss the incident.[199]

"They Come from a Place Which is Very Ugly"

"Bill X." is a computer programmer for a major engineering company that helped design components of the Hubble space telescope. At about 10:30 p.m. July 19, 1984, during the peak of the Hudson Valley UFO wave, Bill was driving home from work along Highway I-84 in Dutchess County. As he neared the Taconic Parkway ramp, he was shocked to see a bright disk-shaped object hovering in the north sky. He soon lost sight of it, and thought to himself that it was probably a one of the ultra-light planes that were making headlines across New York for allegedly provoking UFO reports.

He kept driving, turning onto Route 52. Shortly later he noticed a large, dark, barn-like structure sitting in a nearby field. He was sure there was no structure there as he had driven the route many times. As he watched, the structure rose quietly into the air and started to approach his car. Bill's was the only car on the road. When his radio started to sound tinny and full of static, he became frightened and accelerated out of the area at top speed.

After a few minutes, the object was out of sight and Bill slowed down. However, looking ahead of him, he saw a bright glow at the crest of the next hill. It was the UFO, lit up with a row of bright lights, waiting for him. Bill slammed on the brakes, shut off his lights, and turned off his car, hoping that the UFO hadn't seen him.

At that moment, however, the object also turned off its lights and glided quickly towards him until it was directly over his car. The next thing he knew, the UFO was gone and his car was six hundred feet away from its original location. He was emotionally upset and his neck was very sore.

When he arrived home, his wife was worried because he was an hour late. That night, he woke up from a nightmare, screaming, "Get away from me!"

The nightmares continued, and Bill soon became afraid to drive alone at night. Realizing that his fear was a result of the missing time/UFO incident, he sought out information on the subject. He learned that hypnosis was a tool often used to recover memories. He contacted Phil Imbrogno, who put him in touch with a qualified psychologist.

Under hypnosis, an incredible abduction scenario emerged. After the object hovered over his car, Bill recalled seeing a figure standing in the road, telling him, "Don't be fearful. We need you. You have been selected."

Bill screamed at them to "Get away!" Nevertheless, he found himself inexplicably floating in the air. Next, he found himself lying on a table, paralyzed, and surrounded by short beings. As he said under hypnosis, "These guys are small. They have large heads with round eyes. The eyes are all black. I can see no pupils in them, they remind me of shark eyes. They are dressed in some type of black and white skin-tight suits."

Although he couldn't move, he could still see. The ETs proceeded to place a loud device at the side of his head, which vibrated his entire head like a drill. One of the ETs told him that they were looking for something, and had found it.

Afterwards, he was allowed to sit up. He asked the ETs where they were from and they replied, "We are from here."

He asked if they planned to let him go, and they said, "Yes, but we will see you again."

However, it was what the ET said next that was most revealing. Says Bill, "He told me that they need us because they have trouble living in our world. He said they come from a place that is very ugly when compared to our world, and they would rather live here, but can't."

Bill told them he was going to tell everybody about them. They told him that he wouldn't remember at first, but would later. He was then returned to his car with almost total amnesia of the onboard segment.[200]

"I Felt Like a Specimen"

At around 2 a.m. August 15, 1984, construction worker Shawn X. and his girlfriend Sally were driving home to Mahopac along Route 6 when they noticed a weird glow off Drewville Road. Sally wanted to call the police, but Shawn drove toward the glow. Looking ahead, they saw what they assumed was an emergency vehicle with flashing lights blocking the road. Two figures began to approach the car. Shawn exited and began to walk towards them when he realized that they were too short to be adults. For a few seconds he wondered if they might be kids playing a prank. Then he got a good look at them. He saw that they had large, hairless, pear-shaped heads and huge insect-like eyes that curved around the sides of their heads. He jumped back into the car, locked all the doors, and yelled at Sally to hide in the backseat.

Seconds later, the figures surrounded the car and attempted unsuccessfully to open the doors. At this point, strange images filled Shawn's mind. He felt the ETs trying to convince him that the car was unlocked and to open the door. When this didn't work, they showed him images of the car on fire, blowing up. Shawn knew that they were after his girlfriend. He yelled at them to leave her alone.

Says Shawn, "I then felt very light-headed and the next thing I knew I was outside the car and Sally was nowhere in sight. I don't know how I got out of the car, but now there were six of those alien guys all around me."

Shawn screamed in fear, and yelled at the beings to let him go. One of them told him that they would let him go when they were finished. Says Shawn, "This guy was very cold. It was like it was his job and no matter what I did, he was going to do what he had to do. I felt like some type of specimen."

The next thing Shawn knew, it was early morning. He and Sally sat side by side in the car alongside the road. They didn't discuss the incident and just drove home. One week later, their relationship ended. Shawn refused to investigate with hypnosis. Sally moved away to an unknown location.[201]

Chapter Nine:

More Onboard UFO Experiences

Whitley Strieber, *Communion*, & Beyond

In July 1984, novelist Whitley Strieber was reading in his bedroom at around 11:30 p.m. when he heard the sound of footsteps outside his front door. When his motion sensor light went off seconds later, he dashed to the door to see what was there. To his shock, nobody was in view. Whoever it was should have been visible as only a few seconds had passed.

Just over one year later, on October 4, 1985, Strieber and his wife invited two friends over to spend the night at their cabin. In the middle of the night, Strieber woke up to find a powerful blue light streaming into the cabin. Thinking that perhaps the cabin was on fire, he tried to get up to investigate. Instead, he unaccountably fell back asleep. Sometime later, he woke up to hear an explosion. His wife woke up and cried out, and his son downstairs began crying. Strieber jumped up to find a weird glow surrounding the house. Seconds later the glow was gone.

He went downstairs to comfort his son. Meanwhile, Strieber's friends had been in the downstairs bedroom when they woke up to find their room flooded with light. They both assumed it was morning and began to get up. However, seconds later the light winked out, and when Strieber told them everything was okay, they went back to sleep. Strieber's son, however, later told his father that on that night a group of "people" came into their home, and told him everything would be "okay."

The next morning, Strieber had all but forgotten the incident and his friends didn't speak of it. Within days, however, he began having flashbacks of having heard an explosion and seen a strange light. Next came a flashback of seeing a large crystal-like object hovering above the home.

Not believing in UFOs or aliens, Strieber went on with his life. Then two months later, on December 26, 1985, a wave of sightings struck the area. On that night, he woke up to hear what sounded like a group of people scurrying around in his living room. Moments later, he saw his bedroom door begin to move. He sat up in bed and saw a short robotic-looking figure about three and a half feet tall, wearing a large rounded helmet, a square chest-plate etched with concentric circles and two dark holes for eyes. The figure rushed towards him, and he fell unconscious. Moments later he woke up to find himself paralyzed and being carried out of his home by short broad-faced, bluish-skinned figures and deposited in a hollow in the woods behind his home. A thin gray-type ET with large almond eyes, a very large head, and a tan jumpsuit sat next to him. Seconds later, he was sucked up into an object in the sky. Inside he remained conscious, but in total terror.

He found himself inside a small, stuffy, tan and gray room. Several short gray-type ETs darted quickly around. He was placed on a table and undressed. One of the ETs showed him a long thin needle and told him that they were going to operate on his brain. Strieber began screaming in terror. One of the ETs asked, "What can we do to help you stop screaming?"

Trying to ground himself in reality, Strieber replied, "You could let me smell you."

The ETs obliged, then shortly later, placed the needle in his head. He heard a bang and saw a flash. He was then passed into the next room. Says Strieber:

> "My memories of movement from place to place are the hardest to recall because it was then that I felt the most helpless. My fear would rise when they touched me. Their hands were soft, even soothing, but there were so many of them that it felt a little as if I were being passed along by rows of insects. It was very distressing."

Strieber was then given an anal probe. Following this, one of the figures grabbed his right hand and cut Strieber's forefinger. His memory of the experience ends there.

The next morning, he had forgotten virtually everything, except for a memory of an impossibly large owl outside his window. That day he felt terrible and had "strange recollections of people running, of being pulled and shoved."

He also had a strange memory of being woken up by a light in the woods. Nor could he explain the cut on his finger, which quickly became infected.

The next week he suffered from anxiety, insomnia, fatigue, and flu-like symptoms. Then, on January 3, 1986, after a day of skiing, Strieber discovered what looked like a needle mark behind his right ear. This was the final straw that caused the wall of amnesia to crumble, and before long, Strieber had recalled much of the December 26th incident.

Thinking he was losing his mind, Strieber sought outside help. He went to a psychiatrist to see if he was suffering from any mental disorders. He wasn't. He went to medical doctors to check for temporal lobe epilepsy or anything else that might cause these types of "hallucinations." He was diagnosed with excellent health.

Later, he sought help through hypnotherapy in order to recover any further memories that may have been blocked. Under hypnosis, he recalled that on October 4, after waking up to find the house glowing, he recalled seeing a short bug-like figure with enormous dark eyes standing in the corner of the room. The figure rushed forward and struck him in the head with a wand-like instrument. He recalled that he was shown images of the Earth blowing up, and of the death of his son and father. The ET then caused the explosion type noise and departed.

After being regressed to the December 26, 1985 incident, Strieber recalled numerous other details, such as the cot that was used to transport him out of the house and into the craft. He recalled that after being taken into the craft, the ETs told him, "You are our chosen one."

Strieber told them, "I don't believe that for a minute."

The ETs asked Strieber how he knew that, and he replied, "Because it is ridiculous."

The ET simply repeated, "You are our chosen one."

Strieber also recalled being sent back into his home where the ETs remained until he was back in bed.

Strieber's wife Ann consciously remembered strange activity such as the sounds of people moving around in their house on both the nights in question.

Strieber decided at this point to investigate his childhood to search for further encounters. Like many abductees, he discovered several events that pointed towards ET contact. At age twelve he and his sister saw what they thought was a fireball. Under hypnosis, Strieber recalled having an encounter with a praying mantis-type ET. In another childhood memory, Strieber recalled being abducted with his father from a moving train into a UFO where he saw dozens of soldiers laid out on tables, being examined by an old-looking gray-type ET.

In 1967, he was reading in his grandmother's house in New York, when suddenly there was a short figure with "a very fierce strange face like a giant fly" standing next to him. Before he could react, the figure struck Strieber on the head with an instrument like "a bright silver nail," causing a strange out-of-body type experience.

Some of his New York City contacts show how far the ETs have gone to interact with Strieber and other abductees. Strieber and his wife lived for seven years in a two-room flat on the top floor of a building on West 55th Street in Manhattan. In April 1977, the Striebers had an experience there that they would only later connect to the UFO phenomenon.

Writes Strieber, "With both of us sitting together in our living room, somebody suddenly started speaking through the stereo, which had just finished playing a record. We were astonished, naturally, when the voice held a brief conversation with us. The voice was entirely clear…Never before had it happened, and it didn't happen again. I do not remember the conversation, except the last words: 'I know something else about you.'"

A few weeks later Strieber had "an overwhelming desire to move." One month later, they moved to a brownstone on West 76th Street. They lived there for one year until June 1978. Writes Strieber, "In June of 1978 something terrible happened in the middle of the night. I have variously thought of it as a phone call followed by a menacing visit, and as a series of menacing phone calls…I remember only looking out our bedroom window onto the roof garden and seeing somebody standing there. Just a prowler, perhaps, but it has always seemed to me that there was more to it than that."

Strieber called the police, but they found no evidence of any prowler. Shortly later, they moved to Connecticut. One year later, they were again drawn back to New York City. In January 1980, they rented an apartment on the top floor of a thirty-three-story building on East 75th Street. Despite the crowded urban environment, it wasn't long before the ETs made an appearance. One evening in September of 1980, Strieber glanced outside to see a "strange streak of light streak down the night sky." He had the feeling that the ETs were coming. That night, he awoke to his son screaming in terror. He rushed into his bedroom. Says Strieber, "I recall the impression of a small dark figure dashing toward the sliding doors that led to our thirty-third floor balcony." At the same moment, a piece of glassware in their pantry suddenly exploded.

Within a few months, the Striebers moved again, this time to the Village. About one year later, Anne Strieber woke up screaming. A strange "white thing," she said, had poked her in the stomach. The next night, Strieber had just gone to bed when he too felt something poke his arm. Turning, he saw "a small, pale shape withdrawing into the hall." Strieber jumped up to chase the figure, but it had disappeared.

Then a few nights later, Strieber's son reported the same experience. A few weeks later, a baby-sitter also saw the same short white, glowing figure. The Striebers decided to move again.

They found an apartment on the Upper West Side. Not surprisingly, the move had no effect on the frequency of Strieber's encounters. Despite living in the heart of one of the biggest population centers on the planet, Strieber was regularly "taken" by the ETs. One afternoon in March of 1983, he stepped out of his apartment and lost three hours of time.

A year and a half later, in October 1984, he was driving home from the grocery store when he encountered a thick fogbank. Says Strieber, "The next thing I recall, I was in the fog in my car and two people in dark blue uniforms were leaning in the windows. Then I was back on the highway, returning home."

Like many other incidents, Strieber dismissed it and didn't think about it. Later, under hypnosis, he recalled being taken into a craft where he was examined both physically and mentally.

Up to this time, Strieber was still unaware that he was having encounters with extraterrestrials. It wasn't until after the visitations on October 4 and December 25, 1985 that he became aware of the underlying strangeness in his life.

Meanwhile, his encounters continued at a prodigious rate. On March 15, 1986, the Striebers were at their cabin with some friends. Before dinner, he saw "a hair-thin streak of light come straight down out of the sky." Again, the thought that the visitors were coming came into his head.

As they ate dinner, their son's friend ran inside and said, "A little airplane with lights just flew through the front yard!" Both Strieber and his wife looked at each other in shock. The UFOs had arrived. That night, Strieber awoke to see three dwarf-like beings with gray human-looking faces, dark glittering eyes, and wearing blue coveralls. He tried to move, but found himself almost fully paralyzed, though still totally conscious. On the other side of his bed, he saw a taller, thinner gray type being with a large hairless head and dark almond-shaped eyes. Says Strieber, "It appeared to be wearing an inept cardboard imitation of a blue double-breasted suit, complete with a white triangle of handkerchief sticking out of the pocket."

Strieber was consumed with terror. He had earlier meditated on initiating contact, and now, here they were. He made a valiant attempt to smile at them. The action caused them to dash out of the room, and he fell asleep.

Strieber's encounters, while numerous, were not unique. By this time he had discovered that, despite the lack of media coverage, many other people were also experiencing close encounters with what appeared to be extraterrestrials. What made Strieber's case different, however, was not the fact that he was a successful and famous author. Likely there are many other famous people in the world who are also having encounters. Unlike these people, however, Strieber decided to come out of the closet. Shortly after recalling his encounters, he wrote the book, *Communion: A True Story*, vividly reconstructing his experiences in narrative form. The book was rejected by nearly all the major publishers before finally being published by Morrow Books in 1987 with a million dollar advance.

The media reaction was nothing less than the explosion of an atomic bomb. Never before had such a high-profile public personality claimed something so outrageous as alien abduction, and then backed it up with such convincing testimony. The book quickly rose to the coveted number one spot on the *New York Times* best-seller list and remained in the top ten for more than a year, making it the most successful UFO book in publishing history. As millions of copies flew off the shelves, Strieber began to receive upwards of twenty letters per day from readers sharing their own encounters.

Meanwhile, talk show hosts, journalists, newspaper columnists, and other media representatives lined up to get a piece of the action. Appearances on the "Tonight Show," "Larry King Live," and other major outlets fanned the media flames.

The UFO community rejoiced that the subject was finally getting some attention. Of course there were detractors; some pointing out the million-dollar advance for the book, others saying that as a horror novelist, Strieber may have concocted the entire story.

Despite these minor controversies, Strieber's obviously sincere and honest book was not only accepted by the public, it became one of the seminal books on UFO abductions, and was responsible for introducing millions of people to the idea that aliens are visiting our planet. It was a watershed event for UFO research.

Communion was followed by three other books that told the continuing saga of Strieber's encounters.

One of the most striking aspects of the Strieber story is the huge number of supporting witnesses. It is well known to UFO researchers that friends and family of UFO abductees have a much higher likelihood of also experiencing encounters than does the average person. This "contagion factor" was particularly prominent in Strieber's case.

Almost from the beginning, Strieber found that he was the "Typhoid Mary" of UFO encounters. Although he was the apparent focus of most of the activity, many people closely associated with him would sooner or later experience contact.

In August 1986, Dr. John Gliedman visited the cabin and witnessed a star-like object perform "odd maneuvers" and then disappear. Gliedman, who is an amateur astronomer, is convinced the sighting was "inexplicable."

In September 1986, Strieber invited his brother and a friend to visit the cabin. Later, Strieber, his wife, son, brother and friend were walking behind the house when a star-like object began moving in strange patterns overhead. Says Strieber, "All five of us observed this phenomenon clearly...Richard and Denise were changed by what they saw. No rational person could attribute the sighting to a known source. Now my brother listened to me with new interest. Denise went from believing the standard debunking scenario to realizing that there was actually something quite astonishing taking place...they both commented on their change of perspective."

On December 29, 1986, yet another neighbor became infected. The neighbor, Barry, reported a vivid bedroom visitation by a short entity with large dark eyes. Strieber says, "Barry's case was special to me because he seemed to have experienced some sort of face-to-face interaction that could be connected to my situation."

In January 1987, another neighbor reported a "huge lighted object hanging a few hundred feet above a road."

In 1987, more of his neighbors soon joined the growing ranks of Strieber's UFO witnesses. At least two neighbors both observed a bright, glowing light above the house.

The epidemic continued to spread. Says Strieber, "In the summer of 1987 a number of people who came to our cabin had visitor experiences."

Among these was film director Philippe Mora. While staying at the cabin, Mora was woken by a bright light shining through the window. This was followed by a dream-like visitation with an apparent gray-type ET.

As time went on, Strieber could no longer deny that he was a lightning rod for UFO contact. As he says, "In 1988 we were making the *Communion* movie and I was worried that it might cause the spreading incidence of contact to become an avalanche."

Not surprisingly, the epidemic continued to spread. In the fall of 1988, Strieber had invited several people to stay at his cabin. Among them were two friends, Lori Barnes and Raven Dana. One of the people there, Cummings, had arrived in the hopes of filming an encounter. On the second night, Strieber and his son simultaneously saw a small silver figure outside their home. When they returned inside, several of the guests reported unusual knocking sounds on the wall. Incredibly, Cummings reported seeing a small figure that he at first thought was a child, until he saw that it had big black eyes and a strange narrow face. Before his eyes, the figure transformed into a bird and disappeared.

Moments later, Raven Dana came out of her room and described an intensely vivid and fully conscious face-to-face encounter with a small gray-type extraterrestrial that had come into her bedroom and stood on her bed. "It communicated the sense of curiosity and wonder to me that you get from a small child that still hasn't made judgments about the world, and sees everything as fresh and new. I had the feeling that it was looking at the world that way. There was a certain sense of innocence that you don't find in adults, yet at the same time the wisdom and serenity you see in somebody very old, who has reconciled to life."

Raven Dana and the extraterrestrial stared at each other for a few moments, then reached out, and touched hands in a peaceful way. "Although I was frightened, I was very drawn to the creature. I was very emotionally moved by it, and I just reached forward and touched its hand with mine."

Afterwards, the figure left down the hallway and entered the room of Lorie Barnes. Lorie woke up when she heard someone outside her door. The door opened and she saw a small figure with dark eyes glide across the floor. "It stood slightly below me and stared. It was a being with a long face and huge eyes. It reminded me of a small deer."

In the summer of 1989, Strieber's brother Richard had another UFO experience, only this time it was a face-to-face encounter with a gray-type ET who appeared in his bedroom. The encounter had understandably frightened him, and he told Whitley, "Look Whitley, this has something to do with you, and I'm telling you right now I don't want to be a part of it...tell them they got the wrong Strieber. That thing scared the hell out of me and I want no part of it."

In 1992, another of Strieber's friends, Michael Talbot, had an encounter at the cabin in upstate New York. Years earlier, Strieber had joked with Talbot, as he writes, "We laughed, and I promised to introduce him to the visitors. At the time, of course, I hardly thought that such a thing was possible. Little did I know."

Talbot came to visit Strieber for many reasons, one of which was his illness. Talbot was suffering from Hodgkin's disease that, unfortunately in his case, proved fatal. He asked Strieber for a healing from the aliens, but as Strieber sadly pointed out, although healings do occur, they are on the aliens' terms and not ours.

Nevertheless, hopes were high for an encounter. As it turns out, Talbot did have an apparent encounter. He had a lucid dream experience in which he woke up, went to the front door, and conversed with a gray-type alien disguised as a bag-lady. Because he didn't remember going back to sleep, Talbot assumed the experience was some type of dream.

What's interesting is that Strieber had the same experience, only Strieber insists he was awake. He woke up because he heard noises downstairs. He went down and observed Michael at the front door. As he says, "I was actually there...it was no dream."

Following the publication of *Communion*, newspaper journalist Ed Conroy became interested in the case and conducted a thorough investigation into Strieber's encounters. He quickly verified what Strieber already knew—that the encounters were, in fact, spreading.

Says Conroy, "Strieber has on occasion said to me that he seems to have something of a 'Typhoid Mary' effect on others, passing on the 'visitor experience' as though it were some kind of contagion. Mora wouldn't go any further in speculating about his experience, but it is a rather curious one in the context of the experiences of other people who have visited his cabin. I have spoken to two other women who remember sleeping on cots in the living room of Strieber's house only to be awakened, they said, by brilliant light streaming into the house from all the windows."

By the time Strieber sold his cabin, dozens of people had reported encounters there including the lead investigator of the case, Ed Conroy.

The huge number of corroborating witnesses has been a mixed blessing for Strieber. On one hand, he is not alone with his experiences. On the other hand, as he says, "my experience has come to include too many witnesses for me to consider that it is internal to my mind."

Evidently, the old adage of six degrees of separation holds true, even for UFO encounters. While those around Strieber experienced the "fall-out," it was Strieber himself who remained the focus of the encounters.

On April 1, 1986, he woke up to find himself already in a craft, being escorted by blue beings. He was taken into a chamber filled with beings with milky white skin and wearing uniforms. Strieber was then asked to lecture about why the British Empire had collapsed.

The next night, on April 2, 1986, he woke up in his upstate New York cabin to find that his son was missing from his bed. He ran outside in time to see a large craft lift up into the sky and dart away. At the same time, Strieber was escorted back inside by the ETs who made sure that he stayed in bed during the abduction. Strieber fell asleep. In the morning, his son had been returned.

On May 30, 1986, the ETs visited Strieber in his cabin. On this occasion, the purpose of the visit was a warning and a prophecy. The ET told Strieber, "Your metabolism has been altered. If you continue to eat sweets you cannot hope to live long, and if you eat chocolate you will die."

Then came the prophecy. "In three months' time you will take one of two journeys on behalf of your mother. If you take one journey, you will die. If you take the other, you will live."

Meanwhile Strieber experienced a wide variety of paranormal-type events including strange knocking noises, levitation, out-of-body experiences, and more voices giving strange messages. At the same time, he continued to experience visitations and onboard experiences.

Then, in 1992 and 1993, his experiences seemed to come to a climax. In the summer of 1992, he had been meditating on the purpose of the alien agenda. Writes Strieber, "One thing had become clear was that they didn't want slaves or genes or souls or anything remotely like that, or they would have taken them. You don't get wooed by somebody who is attacking you and we were being carefully wooed. The visitors were here to become a couple with us, and they were acting much more like an impatient, imperfect, and over eager lover would act than like a predator. Virtually the day I realized this, everything changed."

At the time, the Striebers had just moved into a brownstone apartment in Brooklyn Heights. One evening Strieber heard the familiar sound of soft, precise footsteps moving downstairs. He quickly jumped up and searched the house. Finding no intruder, he climbed the stairs to his bedroom. At that moment, something pounced on his back. Writes Strieber, "I was jumped from behind. I staggered, I shouted — and then I realized that I had one of the visitors on my back."

Strieber became overcome with emotion, but still had the presence of mind to observe what was happening. "Two thin arms were protruding in front of me, pinning my own arms to my sides. They were more than strong, they felt like steel. Struggle got no results at all. The one thing I could do was to bend my forearms so I could touch the wrists. They were hard inside, soft on the surface, as if made of bone covered by deerskin. There was no feeling of muscle or fat...The person was heavy, too, weighing easily forty or fifty pounds."

After a few moments, the figure jumped off Strieber's back and disappeared. Strieber rushed into his bedroom and told his wife what happened. He searched the house, but the visitor was gone.

One afternoon a few weeks later in July 1992, he was walking in the woods behind his home when he saw what he assumed was a twelve-year-old boy with a cigarette in his hands. As he approached, however, the image changed. Writes Strieber, "Then I realized that he was wearing a tan jumpsuit. I saw that his eyes were deep set, and his skin was...old. And it wasn't a cigarette, it was a little silver wand, and here came my old friend fear."

When the strange figure began to growl at Strieber, he took off running and never looked back.

Meanwhile, back in his apartment, the activity became more pronounced. Both Strieber and his wife continually heard noises in and around the house at night. On several occasions, they heard the sound of small bodies landing on their roof. Each time they checked, however, there was nothing to be found.

One evening Strieber heard the familiar thuds on the roof. On this occasion, however, the ETs came through the roof and into the house, surrounding him. Writes Strieber, "They came roaring down around me right through the beams, a crowd of racing shadows, shabby and stinking of sweat. I could see that they looked human, but they were crouching, they backed into the corners, they acted like I was the wild wolf."

Strieber panicked and ran out of the room. The ETs followed. Writes Strieber, "Then the visitors all trooped down the stars, some of them jumping up and down on the runners, other leaping off the landing and dropping with soft thuds. They moved fast and I didn't see much."

He continued to meditate to try and improve his communication with the ETs and eventually was able to reach a point of "communion" with them.

One year later, in the summer of 1993, Strieber got his wish. He woke up one evening to find an ET standing next to his bed. On this occasion, Strieber reacted not with fear, but by reaching out. Writes Strieber, "I crawled toward him until I was sitting on my knees right beside him. He was just a little slip of a thing. I don't think he was even three feet tall."

Strieber said, "Hi." The ET held up his hand and Strieber took it. Writes

Strieber, "I took it – cool and quite oily – and inhaled the scent of the skin... His hand lay in mine like a cool little bird, absolutely still."

They stared into each other's eyes for a few more moments, and then the figure darted away.

The very next night, however, Strieber walked into the room where the encounter had occurred and there was the ET again. He sat down next to the figure and prepared to ask questions. Instead, he was instructed by the figure to calm down and meditate. After an hour, the ET left.

Over the next week, the ET came every night at midnight. Each night Strieber sat down next to the figure and meditated. During the meetings, the figure communicated to Strieber various messages about his own psychological and emotional states.

The Striebers found that although the visitations occurred at night, the visitor was also there during the day. Writes Strieber, "Incredibly, he appeared to be living with us."

They continually found that the bed in the spare bedroom was mysteriously disturbed. The figure also left bits of candy in front of books that it apparently wanted Strieber to read. The ET then began waking up Strieber at various times in the night to meditate.

He had finally reached the kind of ET contact he had been searching for. Writes Strieber:

"I kept working and meditating with him. It was a wonderful, incredible period in my life, and I wish dearly that I could share him with every single soul in the world. My hope is that contact will lead to friendships like this for everybody who seeks them...I sought to free myself as he was free. I was fascinated with his physical abilities. I'd seen him disappear. He levitated at will. When he left, he'd shoot through a wall...How I loved him. I had never loved anybody else like this. I didn't know his name. I rarely saw him, I'd never heard him speak. But he knew me vastly better than anybody else ever had...He was a teacher, a real one, not the sort of egocentric fake that usually treads the path of enlightenment. By any human standard, he was totally enlightened."

Following this intense period of communion, Strieber's contacts suddenly diminished in number. While he continues to have encounters he has to this point stopped writing about them. His case, however, remains one of the most famous, influential, and extensively researched cases in UFO history.[202]

A Family Affair

In late June of 1987, an anonymous seventeen-year-old girl was driving with her father along Route 116 near Croton Falls when they saw "a large dark craft, triangular in shape" that paced their car just above treetop level for an apparent duration of five minutes.

The next day, the daughter returned to her mother's home in New Jersey. Her mom revealed that the previous evening, at the exact time that her daughter had seen the UFO, she experienced a terrifying bedroom visitation by gray-type ETs, who placed an apparent implant in her nose. The fact that both the father and daughter and the mother had UFO encounters at the same time seemed beyond coincidence. Researcher Philip Imbrogno heard about the case and began an investigation. He soon learned that the sighting by the father and daughter might have been more than just a sighting. Writes Imbrogno, "There is more to this case than meets the eye. The daughter and father according to my finds may have had as much as thirty minutes missing time. If this is so, and if both were abducted, then the experience happened to father, mother and daughter all at the same time!"[203]

"I Think They're from Outer Space!"

One evening in July 1987, two couples were driving home from New York City when they felt themselves compelled to turn onto a dirt road called Reservoir Road in the Croton Falls area. Half way down the deserted road, the car engine suddenly died. They debated what to do next when suddenly they heard the sound of something approaching. One of them went outside with a flashlight to investigate. Seconds later he came running back into the car screaming, "Let's get out of here! I think they're from outer space!"

The others thought it was a joke until they saw a row of figures with large bald heads and claylike skin dressed in tight fitting jumpsuits approach the car. One of them shined a flashlight at the beings, which caused them to scamper away into what looked like a cave. Seconds later, however, they saw a giant triangular-shaped object with rows of colored lights appear right over the spot where the beings were. The object hovered over the car, sending down a bright beam of light. Moments later, it suddenly disappeared. After it was gone, the car engine worked fine, and the two couples left the area quickly.

Following the experience, all four experienced dreams about having been taken onboard the craft and examined. In the days and weeks that followed, some of them experienced subsequent sightings and bedroom visitations by the same type of entities.[204]

"Tell Us About This Music"

While ETs show an undeniable interest in the human body, they also appear to be equally interested in human emotions and other uniquely human traits. For whatever reason, they are apparently gathering as much information about human beings as they can. The following case, investigated by Philip Imbrogno, is a good example of the aliens' intense interest in all things human.

On May 13, 1988, "Ray X," a computer programmer from New Castle, was driving home from a friend's house along Route 116 in Croton Falls at around 10 p.m. when he saw a group of lights just above the reservoir to his left.

The lights appeared to be moving too slowly to be a plane. As he drove closer, he realized the lights were attached to an object that was coming towards him. He stopped his car, climbed up, and sat on the window-ledge and stared at the object, which passed over his car at a height of twenty feet. All he could see was a dark triangular mass about one hundred feet across. Only the front was lit, and the bottom appeared to have inset sections of different levels that would flash strobe-like lights.

Suddenly, without warning, he was back in his car, driving down the road, and the object was gone. He kept driving and went to bed, though he was unable to sleep. For the next few weeks, he suffered from nightmares.

He contacted Imbrogno who arranged for Dr. Jean Mundy to place him under hypnotic regression. Only then did the full story come out.

Ray recalled being drawn out of his car and into the UFO. He was placed on a table in a dark room. Several beings surrounded him and began to examine him with strange instruments. He was unable to move, but could see the figures, which he described as typical grays, excepting having very round eyes.

Next, he felt something being inserted inside his nostril, causing considerable pain. Afterwards he was escorted to "a control panel" with many projections and knobs. Ray was apparently supposed to learn how to manipulate the controls.

He then found himself back in his car. After recovering his memory, Ray fears that the ETs are definitely coming back for him and that the next time he won't be returned. He says that the incident has changed his entire life. He feels like he is in constant mental contact with the beings, and that they are using him to gather information.

Writes Imbrogno, "For example, Ray may be listening to music, and a voice inside his head will say, 'Tell us about this music? How does it make you feel?' Ray is not able to control these requests. They can come at any time while he is experiencing something in his every day life. Ray's case is unusual, but not unique when compared to others I have investigated in the Hudson Valley."[205]

"This Was No Frisbee!"

Many UFO witnesses learn the hard way not to talk about their experience, and that many people will react with disbelief and even ridicule. A UFO sighting can be a very difficult thing to accept, both for the witness and those who surround the witness. This is, of course, especially true for skeptics. And when a case moves beyond a simple sighting and into a close encounter of the fourth kind, this difficulty of dealing with an encounter can divide friends, family, and co-workers.

At 1 p.m. on the afternoon of July 15, 1989, Nathan J. of Rochester was out hiking with his two young sons. Looking up, they saw a metallic silver disk-shaped object approaching from the southwest at just above treetop level. The craft began to maneuver in a slow circle around them. Nathan whipped out his camera and quickly snapped several photographs. At this point, the craft "shot away" in the direction where it had come from.

Immediately afterwards, Nathan and his two sons discussed the incident. Only then did Nathan realize that they were missing time. As Nathan wrote in a letter to Florida-based abductee/researcher Ed Walters, "One of the strangest things is that my youngest boy [age eleven] said he did not see what my older boy and I saw. I did not understand how this could be because we were all together and looking up at it. So at first I thought that he was only scared, but as we talked about what had just happened, I stopped and saw it was almost dark. I don't know how, but it was suddenly 1700 [5 p.m.]."

Shocked by the encounter, Nathan returned alone to the same location the next day to investigate and survey the location. As if lying in wait, the UFO appeared again. Says Nathan, "I was standing at about where the boys and I were standing when, bingo, there it was again, a little more distant but the same disk."

Nathan quickly snapped one additional photograph. Later he told friends and coworkers about the sighting and showed them photographs. To his disappointment, their reaction was not positive. Says Nathan, "A week later I was told that it was a trick done with a Frisbee, and told to drop it...THIS WAS NO FRISBEE!"

Nathan next found that even his family was not comfortable discussing the subject. Says Nathan, "My eleven year old son (who saw nothing) does not answer when I ask him about that day. It all sounds crazy and even my wife now does not want to talk about it, but I feel something else happened. I don't bring it up anymore."

Later, Nathan's neighbor approached him and referred him to researcher Ed Walters, who published one of Nathan's photographs in his book, *UFO Abductions in Gulf Breeze*. Writes Walters, "Nathan's photographs are astounding and I believe them to be valid...Of great significance with Nathan's sighting is the loss of time from 1300 to 1700. He indicates that he has no recall of those four hours from 1 p.m. to 5 p.m. As I learned from my own missing-time incident, the possibility of an alien encounter is almost a certainty."[206]

Friends abducted from Trailer

On Labor Day weekend in September 1989, Farmingdale resident Curtis Walton, a store manager, and his friend James LeFante, a messenger from Merrick, were spending the weekend with friends in a trailer in upstate Saugerties. What was supposed to be a fun holiday, however, turned out to be one of the strangest weekends of their lives. Walton and LeFante claim that both they and their friends were all taken onboard a craft and subject to medical examinations at the hands of gray-type ETs. (No other details were provided.)[207]

Family is Abducted

On July 24, 1984, during a peak sighting of the Hudson Valley UFO wave, Brewster resident "Jake X" was driving home from work along Highway 84 when he saw a weird string of light approaching from the east. He stopped his car and got out to observe. Suddenly the UFO appeared to single him out, coming straight for him. Jake jumped back into his car and tried to accelerate away. At that moment, a beam of light came from the object and shut off his engine. He felt the car begin to lift up into the air while his entire body began to buzz and vibrate. Suddenly he heard a voice in his head say, "We have seen your light and we need you to return." The beam then retracted and Jake raced home.

At his home, he discovered that his wife and two children had just watched the UFO come directly over their home and then circle the neighborhood for about five minutes.

Five years later, on October 27, 1989, the UFOs returned. There had been a rash of sightings in the area, though Jake hadn't seen anything. Then, on October 27, Jake, his wife, and both their children went to bed as normal. Sometime in the middle of the night, they all woke up to find themselves standing in the living room with no memory of how they got there. Jake's son screamed that a UFO was hovering over the house. They all ran into the basement as the entire house became bathed in a brilliant red light emitted from the object. After five minutes, the beam turned off. Jake ran outside to see a "dark triangle about 100 feet long with a big red light in the center and several white lights on the front" move slowly away. He called the police who told them that they had been receiving calls all night long.

The next day, the son revealed that just before the UFO appeared, he saw two "little men" in the house, and then a third who came through the wall. Jake and his wife revealed that they both had dreams of "little bald men with big round eyes leading us down a dark corridor."

Imbrogno, who investigated the incident writes, "This case could represent an abduction of an entire family…It seems that once again the witness was scanned and then later the intelligence behind the UFO came back for him, and his entire family."[208]

The Brooklyn Bridge Abductions

One of the most bizarre and controversial New York abduction cases took place in the heart of Manhattan November 30, 1989 and is known as the "Brooklyn Bridge Abductions." What makes this case unique is that – unlike the vast majority of cases – it was apparently observed by several outside witnesses, including allegedly, a highly placed world leader.

The main witness, "Linda Cortile," had a history of encounters before the November 30 abduction. She had written to researcher Budd Hopkins earlier in the year when she discovered that she had an apparent implant in her nose. She had recently found a strange lump on the right side of her nose and went to the doctor. The doctor X-rayed Cortile's head and discovered a strange "foreign body" in her sinus area. It was this discovery, in addition with memories of numerous other strange events, that prompted Cortile to write to Hopkins. However, when Cortile experienced another abduction on November 30, 1989, she called Hopkins the next day to tell him what happened.

On that night, she was awakened in her high-rise apartment, which is adjacent to the Brooklyn Bridge, to find three small gray-skinned figures with large bald heads and dark wrap-around eyes in her bedroom. At this point, her memory becomes fragmented. She recalled being pulled out of her apartment by a blue-white light and levitated into a UFO. She had some flashbacks of being undressed and examined, and was then returned to her apartment. At this point, she tried desperately to wake up other members of her family, but they could not be awakened. She then went back to sleep.

Hopkins agreed to hypnotize Cortile. Under hypnosis, Cortile recalled a typical onboard abduction. The ETs undressed her and placed her on a table. They examined her body, paying particular attention to her nasal area. They examined her with several instruments. At some point, they spoke to her in what sounded like gibberish, though Cortile had the impression that they were trying to teach her their language. There were other incidents that she was unable to recall.

At the time, Hopkins assumed that the case was no different from the hundreds of others he had already investigated. However, Hopkins was soon to learn that he was wrong. Just more than one year later, he received a letter from two gentlemen claiming to be police officers. "Dan" and "Richard" wrote that they were beneath the Brooklyn Bridge on November 30, 1989 and actually witnessed Cortile's abduction in its entirety. They wrote that they were guarding a highly placed world leader, who sat in the back seat, when suddenly they noticed a reddish glow coming from above. Looking up, they saw a large fiery-red object hovering next to Cortile's building. Seconds later, they watched as several small gray-type ETs floated out of the building with Cortile in a beam of light and into the UFO. At this point, the object plunged into the East River. The gentlemen waited for about an hour for the object to surface, but it never did.

Hopkins quickly realized that the gentlemen had actually witnessed

Cortile's abduction. Over the next several months, he would receive several more letters, not only from Richard and Dan, but from nearly a dozen other independent witnesses to the same event.

What at first appeared to be a routine abduction event now presented itself as unique, groundbreaking, and of tremendous importance. Writes Hopkins, "Over the past five years I have interviewed and communicated with nearly a score of individuals involved in this New York City UFO abduction case. After conducting many hypnotic regressions and studying the various types of physical evidence, I have come to a firm conclusion: This abduction event so drastically alters our knowledge of the alien incursion in our world that it is easily the most important in recorded history. No previous case has had such a profound effect on so many lives, and none has ever been observed by so many independent witnesses...Among the many stunned observers was a political figure of international significance, whose presence was the likely reason for this demonstration of alien capability."

One letter came from "Janet Kimball" who was driving across Brooklyn Bridge at the time of the incident. Suddenly, says Kimball, her car and several other cars on the bridge suddenly stalled and rolled to a stop. At the same time, all the headlights on the cars were mysteriously extinguished, as were the streetlights on the bridge itself. Looking up, Kimball saw a large aircraft hovering next to Cortile's building. Moments later, she observed Cortile and the ETs exit the building and ascend up a beam of light into the craft. At the time, she wasn't sure what she was seeing, and thought that perhaps Kimball was a manikin and that the ETs were deformed children. She also considered that it might be a movie production. It wasn't until she watched a program about UFOs that she connected the experience to the UFO phenomenon and wrote to Hopkins. Kimball reports that several other people on the bridge also observed the event. As she says, "Some of them were running all around their cars with their hands on their heads, screaming from horror and disbelief."

Another witness to the incident is bookkeeper and Brooklyn resident, Cathy Turner. She was driving near the bridge at the time of the incident, when she saw what appears to be the same UFO, which she described as a fiery red "like the sun," a description repeated by most of the witnesses.

Another possible witness was Cortile's neighbor, "Francesca," who lived in the same building. Francesca reports that on what was apparently the evening of Cortile's abduction, she was woken up in the middle of the night to find "everything lit up outside like daylight." The event so upset her that she made her husband move their bed away from the window.

With so many outside witnesses, the Brooklyn Bridge case is clearly unique and significant. Hopkins theorizes that the event was a staged demonstration. At first he believed that the case involved only the abduction of Linda Cortile and an unknown number of people who observed the event from the outside. However, he later learned that Cortile may not have been the only person who was abducted into the UFO that night.

In the months following the incident, Dan and Richard became obsessed by the incident, and intent on locating Linda Cortile. After writing Hopkins a letter about their sighting, they sought out Cortile and confronted her. They questioned her about the incident and then left. Unfortunately, their obsession with Cortile and her case grew, and they ended up actually kidnapping her on more than one occasion.

Dan and Richard, it turned out, were not policemen as they claimed, but covert members of an undetermined governmental security agency (possibly the CIA, FBI, or the NSA), who were put in charge of guarding the world leader. While at first they believed they had only sighted the UFO, they revealed in their continuing letters to Hopkins that after the sighting, they began to have recall of having been abducted. All three eventually recalled being taken onboard the craft and examined. They were then set down on a beach area. Cortile came out of the craft and, speaking for the aliens, lectured them and the world leader about world peace, the importance of environmentalism, and the dangers of pollution.

Following this revelation, Hopkins again hypnotized Cortile. She was also able to recall being taken onboard and then set down on a beach area where she saw Richard, Dan and the third man. She was then taken back into the UFO and returned to her apartment, and the three men were returned to their location under the bridge, where they witnessed the UFO diving back into the river.

If this isn't complicated enough, both Richard and Cortile both began having memories of having met each other several times in the past—onboard a UFO! They remembered meeting each other as children, as teenagers, and as young adults. The meetings were always at night and took place in a dreamlike state. It was only after Richard had been manipulated to be at the location of the abduction that he witnessed Cortile and recognized her as the girl from his "dreams."

Both Cortile and Richard have independently recalled numerous corroborating details of their encounters that seem to prove that they did, in fact, take place and are not imaginary.

Today several other cases of relationship manipulations have surfaced, however, this was the first time that Hopkins had encountered this new twist to the ET encounter phenomenon.

A final complication to the Brooklyn Bridge abductions comes from yet another witness identified by Hopkins as "Erica," a resident of the east side of Manhattan (about three miles from Cortile's apartment). On the same date and time as the Brooklyn Bridge case, Erica woke up to find her bedroom flashing with strange light. Moments later, three typical gray-type ETs appeared in her bedroom. The strange figures told her that she should go with them while her husband remained asleep.

Erica consciously recalled being floated out of her apartment to the edge of the East River near 38th Street. Looking towards Brooklyn Bridge, she saw a fast-moving bright red craft. Unable to resist, she found herself floating a few feet above the pavement. To her shock, she saw that many other people beside herself were also being abducted and brought to the same predetermined location: a large, empty parking lot. Hopkins was shocked to discover that the Brooklyn Bridge case may actually be "a mass abduction" and that Erica "saw about twenty other people being similarly taken."

Erica saw several other UFOs, besides the fiery red one that she observed hovering near the Brooklyn Bridge area. How many people were abducted that night and were these abductions connected?

Hopkins theorizes that there are likely hundreds of other witnesses (or participants) to this event who have never come forth. His four hundred-page book, *Witnessed: The True Story of the Brooklyn Bridge UFO Abductions*, presents the case in detail and the investigation that followed. The book contains several of Cortile's abduction experiences and also includes the X-ray of her nasal implant.

Since the case was first revealed, speculation has run through the UFO community and beyond as to the identity of the mysterious world leader, who told Hopkins himself that he would always remain anonymous. However, in 2006, researcher Steven Greer, MD wrote in his book, *Hidden Truth – Forbidden Knowledge*, that the mysterious leader was allegedly none other than the Secretary General of the United Nations, Perez de Cuellar.

Greer's understanding of the event, which he learned from various inside sources, is that Perez de Cuellar was part of a group of highly placed world leaders who were planning to make an official announcement of the extraterrestrial presence. According to Greer, the world leaders were convinced that Perez de Cuellar was abducted by the ETs who allegedly told him that if his group didn't stop their plans for disclosure, the ETs would abduct all the other leaders involved, including the United States President. Greer, however, believes that the entire event was, in fact, a "staged abduction" done by humans using psychotronic weapons. Writes Greer, "The goal of the operation was to stop this entire attempt by the world's power elites, including Gorbachev, to disclose the truth to the world...these abduction events are paramilitary operations run by humans, using things that look like UFOs and even having creatures on board that look like extraterrestrials but are disguised humans or manmade creatures."

Greer asserts that many missing time abductions blamed on gray-type ETs are actually hoaxed abductions done by humans from the "secret government" in order to put a disinformation spin on the phenomenon. And so the plot thickens...[209]

A Lifetime of Contact

Kenneth Anderson (not his real name) began having contact with ETs as a young child in his home in upstate New York. From age six to nine, he suffered from a series of severe unexplained nosebleeds. At the same time, he often woke up to see shadows of strange figures shuffling through his room, making weird "clicking" sounds when they spoke.

Then in August 1991, Kenneth had an experience involving missing time. It was late at night and he was driving home with a co-worker from the local hospital where they worked as nurses. While driving along the rural mountain roads, they saw a "white orb" pacing their car.

The radio then started to exhibit a strange sort of static. They were listening to a local station that usually had great reception. After several minutes of being followed by the light, Kenneth stopped the car and got out. The orb hung above the field ahead of him. He marched out into the field, but the orb quickly retreated. He returned to the car and tried to start the engine. However, when he turned the key, nothing happened. After a few more tries, the engine suddenly turned over. As they drove home, the white orb followed them into town and then darted away.

Once he got home, Kenneth discovered that it was nearly 3 a.m. He and his co-worker had somehow lost about two hours of time. The next day, he learned that there had been a wave of sightings in the area, and that both of his older brothers had also witnessed the strange orbs.

Over the next weeks and months, Kenneth found himself experiencing strange psychic visions. At the same time, he began experiencing strange phone problems. He also began dreaming about the UFO sighting, however, in the dreams, he saw two weird-looking figures coming towards the car.

For the next few years, nothing else unusual occurred. His life returned back to normal. The UFOs, it seemed, were gone from his life.

Then, in 1998, seven years following the missing-time incident, he had another major encounter.

It was near the end of 1998. It was around 12:30 a.m. and he was driving alone, again on his way back home from work. As he crested over a small hill, he was shocked to see a huge white sphere of light blocking the entire width of the road. Says Kenneth, "I had to slam on my brakes. I was afraid if it was a solid object, it would damage my car. So my car is skidding on dry pavement until this thing is just a few feet in front of my windshield. It was practically hovering over the front hood of my car, it was that close. The light was blinding."

The face-off lasted only a few seconds before the craft lifted up and darted away. Kenneth raced home, and had no further sightings during the trip. He checked all his clocks and watches and confirmed that he didn't have any missing time. He arrived home at the correct time and there were no discrepancies between any of the clocks. He made a sandwich, watched a little television, and went to bed.

When he woke up the next morning, he received a minor shock. Says Kenneth, "I had a very curious triangular burn on my left shin. It didn't hurt. I remember pressing on it, and it felt a little warm, but it didn't hurt. It wasn't a bruise; it definitely looked like a burn. And I thought, what the hell happened? Where did this come from?"

About one year later he had another bizarre missing-time encounter. It was sometime in the summer of 2000. He and his friends decided to go out for the evening. They planned to meet early at a local bar and spend the evening there together.

Shortly after night fell, Kenneth got ready, then hopped in the car, and drove to the bar. The journey passed without incident, however, when he arrived at the bar, his friends were already getting ready to go. He had lost three hours of time.

A few weeks later, he dreamed that he was back at that night, driving on his way to meet his friends at the bar. In the dream, he saw another one of the white spheres race up from behind his car and then flood his vehicle with blinding bluish-white light. At that point, the dream ended.

Kenneth decided to move to Florida, but he continued to have encounters with the orb there. He experienced a missing-time incident with the orb in 2003 and another in 2004.

Following a car accident, Kenneth found himself suddenly out of work and with no income. The bills piled up quickly, and by January 2005, Kenneth decided he would return to New York. He was sure he could get a job there, and start over.

His encounters had been occurring steadily at about the rate of one every year or so. So by the time 2006 rolled around, Kenneth knew that he was overdue for another encounter.

Right on schedule, on January 16, 2006, Kenneth had his next white sphere encounter. He had just dropped his friends off and was driving home alone. It was a cold evening, so Kenneth turned up the car heater and continued his drive. Way off in the distance, he suddenly saw a tiny ball of light. In a matter of seconds, the white sphere swooped forward until it was thirty yards from the side of the road.

The object darted off into the woods. Kenneth continued to drive, nervously glancing to either side, looking for the object. He came around a corner and there was the sphere, hovering at ground level, covering both lanes of the road.

He slammed on his brakes. "There it was in the middle of the road. And I thought to myself, My god, here we go again! Do what you have to do. Take me, whatever you going to do — just do it! This time I do remember being surrounded by a column of bluish-white light. And it only surrounded me, not the car, not the road. It was just me, the driver's seat and the steering wheel. It was really strange."

Kenneth's next memory is waking up and finding himself sitting in the front seat of his car. His car was parked alongside of the road. The engine was running and the heater was blasting, making the interior of the car extremely warm. The gas-tank dial registered half-empty, which was impossible considering it had just been near full.

When he arrived home, it was 4:30 a.m.—a full two hours later than it should have been. Kenneth lay down in bed and just prayed that this whole problem would just go away.

When he woke the next morning, he was dismayed to see two perfect triangular-shaped bruises on the same exact location on the top of each forearm.

Feeling overwhelmed, Kenneth sought a therapist, who worked with him for several months and then finally recommended that he see a UFO specialist.

In July 2006 Kenneth had gone down to the basement to shut off the electrical circuit box so he could do some wiring work on the house. Says Kenneth, "When I turned towards the stairs, there were two figures standing there. Each one at approximately four and a half feet in height, no clothes, large heads, black eyes that wrapped around towards the temples. They just stood there. They had two little slits for nostrils. There was no nose visible at all. I didn't know what to make of it. I let out a scream. I remember I shut my eyes, I shook my head, and I looked back at the stairs, opened my eyes and there was nothing there."

Kenneth began having nightmares and flashbacks. Then in July 2006, Kenneth was disturbed to receive a telepathic message from the ETs. It came loud and clear in his mind, saying, "We are coming for you soon. Be prepared. It will make sense to you when we come."

One month later, in August 2006, Kenneth was driving home from work at about 3 a.m. He had his cell phone with him, just in case the car broke down. Suddenly, the phone started beeping a series of random tones. The ringer was actually set on a particular song, and had actually never made these kinds of tones before. Kenneth picked up the phone and answered it. The line was totally dead. He shut off the receiver, shut the phone, and put it back on the front seat.

Moments later, it started beeping weirdly again. Kenneth picked it up and looked at the digital screen to see who was calling. It read: NO NUMBER. He answered the call. Says Kenneth, "I heard funny clicking noises, not like a mechanical click, more like a person with their tongue at the roof of their mouth and then snapping it down — that kind of click. But it was very rapid. I thought, 'Wow, this is nuts!' I began to get a little freaked. And I heard a voice say, 'The time has grown closer.' I got so scared, I didn't even realize I was going 90 miles an hour."

Kenneth hung up the phone and threw it on the seat. He raced back home at top speed and tried to ignore the creepy feeling that he was being watched and hunted. He saw a small white sphere darting around, but decided to just ignore it.

Over the next few weeks, the telepathic alien message came a few more times. "We are come for you soon. The time is coming soon. It's only a matter of time. Soon you will know."

One month later, events finally came to a dramatic climax. A few days earlier, the aliens had repeated their same message, this time saying, "We're here. Be prepared, and all that you want to know will be revealed."

At around 11 o'clock p.m. on September 29, 2006, Kenneth sat us pin his bed, watching television. Then came the voices. Speaking in their character*isting simultaneous chorus, they said, "It's time. And it's also time for you to know why."

Kenneth kept the television on and went to bed. As he lay there trying to fall asleep, he suddenly felt like somebody was in his bedroom. Opening his eyes, he was shocked to see that his bed was surrounded by four gray-type ETs, two on each side and one at the foot of his bed. They told him, "Don't worry. We haven't come to harm you. But you need to know why."

Says Kenneth, "All of a sudden, things just seemed so screwy. I wasn't even in my bed anymore. The next thing I knew I was in a room with gray metal walls. The floor was made of the same material. And there was a much taller being, I would say about six feet, although he looked the same. And it motioned for me to come closer. I could feel one of their hands on my back pushing me forward gently, not too rough. And the next thing I see is a child being. It came out behind the tall one."

Kenneth's reaction surprised him. As he says, "I was so overcome with grief and sorrow, because this being was mine. Its head was a little smaller in shape. Its eyes were still black, almond-shaped and wrapped towards the temples. But it had signs of a nose and lips, and I could see it smile. I knew immediately that this was a child, and it was mine. No one told me it was. I had paternal instincts; I knew. And yet it looked repulsive. It looked nothing like a human being. And yet it had a few characteristics that made it seem like it was more human than its alien counterparts that were standing in that room with the rest of us. There was an attraction I think only a parent can know, and never having had these feelings before, that's the best I can describe it. There was a paternal attraction. It was like giving up a child for adoption and meeting years later, and not knowing what he or she is going to look like. But the moment they walk into the room, you know it's your child."

Kenneth's mind was reeling. He was fully conscious and found himself in a constant state of reality-checking. This can't be happening, Kenneth thought to himself. Incredibly, the ETs responded, saying, "Yes, this child is yours."

Kenneth had a further conversation with the ETs and then was returned to his bedroom. As of 2007, he has experienced no further encounters.

Today Kenneth has become increasingly concerned with the idea of upcoming Earth changes. He feels certain that there will soon be climatic changes on such a massive scale, that it may cause widespread death and destruction. Most recently, he has been having a bizarre series of vivid dreams on this theme.

Says Kenneth, "This is a recurring dream. I have it several times a month and this has been going on for a few years. I have dreams where I'm seeing people crawling in the streets, and I'm trying to warn them, 'Don't drink the water! Don't go near the water!' I can see the sun. I can even feel in these dreams. I can feel the heat. I can see people dying or near-death in the streets. I can see people who are alive and I can see them crawling towards a stream or even towards a ditch that might be filled with water."

In the dreams, the Earth's atmosphere has taken on a hazy golden hue, as if the air has been somehow changed or polluted. The food is gone, the water supply is poisonous, and people are dying by the hundreds of thousands in every town and city across the world. The dreams are frightening, and have reinforced his fears that humanity is on the brink of major disaster.[210]

"They Looked Like Insects"

Madison Sorenson believed in UFOs from an early age. One summer evening in 1984, when she was ten years old, she and her family had a dramatic sighting while driving from Peekskill to Ossining. Four years later, in 1988, the entire family observed an enormous egg-shaped object that hovered at treetop level right in their own backyard. After a few moments, the object floated lazily away.

Following this sighting, Madison had no further encounters for at least a decade. Then in 1994, she gave birth to her first child, a son. He was only three months old, so she kept his crib next to her bed in her own bedroom. On the evening of May 15, 1995, Madison woke up to the single most terrifying experience of her entire life. She had gone to bed early and woke up to find eight strange beings surrounding her bed.

Says Madison, "They were ugly. They had big heads, and I know they had suits on. I don't know if they were gray or white, but they were ugly. They had big heads and black eyeballs. They looked like insects."

Madison's first reaction was to kick and scream. The ETs, however, just continued to stare coldly at her, pressing her down into the bed. Says Madison, "I remember cursing at them. I told them, 'Get the f— off me! Leave me alone!' and 'Where's my baby?!' They were surrounding me. It was dark. I remember looking up and they were pressing against my chest and my forehead. It was a weird feeling. I don't know if they were physically touching me. It was like a weird force, I don't know. It was very, very weird. I can remember kicking my feet. They just stood there. It was scary. They just stood there looking at me like I was some kind of animal or something — like we do with animals, like experimenting on them."

Madison was too shocked and frightened to carefully observe what was going on. She fought, cursed, and screamed for just a few moments. The last thing she remembered was screaming for her baby when she suddenly lost consciousness.

When she woke up, she immediately looked at her clock. It was 11 p.m. She couldn't believe that she had actually fallen asleep so early. She jumped up and checked her son. He was sleeping peacefully. She checked over her own body, but noticed nothing unusual. The room itself, however, seemed to be crackling with a weird energy.

At this point, there was a knock on the front door. Madison suddenly remembered that her friend was coming over at 11 o'clock. She rushed to the door and told him what happened.

He looked at her in shock. It was obvious she wasn't lying. "Maybe you just had a dream?" he offered.

"No," she said. "I don't think so."

Madison reports no other encounters, except perhaps as a young child when, one evening, she remembered being dropped back into her bed from above. The next morning, she found dirt in her bed and soiled footprints leading out to the closed window.

There were other profound after-effects from Madison's 1995 encounter. Probably the biggest was a feeling of anxiety. Says Madison, "I feel ridiculous but sometimes I feel like they're there watching me or something. I'm always dreaming of them...sometimes they're just there, like they're in my room. I sometimes sleep with the light on because I'm thinking of that experience."

Ten years later, in 2007, Madison is still unnerved by the encounter. As she says, "I just hope that they don't come around again. It was scary. Put it this way: I cannot be by myself in a house sometimes, and I live in a building. I cannot be alone because I'm afraid that they-- ...I can't leave the door open in my room at night. I have to close it and turn my light on, or at least leave the TV on...When I think about it, I get scared."

A final strange effect that she feels might be connected to her UFO encounters are a series of recent dreams, which she is wondering might be prophetic. As she says, "My dreams are mostly about water...major floods. What could this mean? I don't know."[211]

Scarred by Aliens

Erica X. is a designer for a popular New York clothing store. She has had UFO experiences her whole life. Although she lives in a large apartment building in Manhattan, her abduction experiences continue. One particularly dramatic encounter occurred in 1995. She was taken from her apartment and into a UFO, where she was examined and operated upon. After cutting open her leg, one of the aliens placed his hand over her wound and healed up the cut. Says Erica, "I was looking at this as if in shock, and then the wound in my leg kind of sealed up."

The next morning, Erica checked her leg and found a faint hairline scar, already completely healed. Unfortunately, Erica has a medical condition which normally causes very slow healing. She has to be very careful because cuts usually take weeks or months to heal and always leave noticeable rough scars. This scar, however, was not only healed, it was practically invisible. For Erica, this was proof that her encounters were real, and even her doctor, she says, was impressed by the scar.[212]

Giant Peanut over Ticonderoga

Ticonderoga is a small New York town with a population of only about 4,000. On July 2, 1998, at about 8 p.m., Fred & Mary X. were working in their yard. Looking up, Fred saw a giant, glowing, beige-colored, peanut-shaped object cruising overhead. He immediately noticed that there were no wings and no sound. It was a UFO, he realized. He ran inside and got his video camera. Fred obtained about twelve seconds of video before the object disappeared above a cloud. The footage taken of the object was later analyzed by physicist and expert photo analyst Dr. Bruce Maccabee Ph.D.

After analyzing the footage Maccabee concluded, "The MUFON investigation indicates that this was not a hoax, since the witnesses are upstanding citizens of the community, are both employed in law enforcement, and have requested anonymity. Since the aircraft and hoax explanation are ruled out, the image can be considered to be that of a single unidentified flying object with two major whitish sections connected by a narrow structure not seen on the video, or of two whitish elliptical objects traveling in close formation."

A photograph taken from the videotape was later published in the *MUFON Journal*. Budd Hopkins heard about the case and learned some starting details.

Fred, who is a retired corrections officer, says that after taking the video of the object, he actually forgot about it, and didn't even remember seeing the UFO for about two weeks. Also, after he took the video, he remembered going into the kitchen, and from that point, he doesn't remember the next four hours. Hopkins recognized the missing time as a red flag pointing towards the probability a UFO abduction.

Hypnosis was arranged. Under hypnosis, Fred X. recalled taking a videotape of the object. He then stepped into the kitchen when suddenly a beam of light came through the ceiling and levitated him into the craft. Inside, he was laid out on a table, undressed and examined by gray-type ETs. While the account of the sighting has been published, the extended "abduction version" was revealed only in a lecture by Budd Hopkins March 7, 2004 at a monthly meeting for Northern California MUFON.[213]

"We Want You!"

Pauline Darcy Roger of Bronx, has always considered herself psychic. Throughout her life she has experienced several episodes of telepathy, however, they were usually brief and only with other people. Then, in 2001, while living in her 236th Street apartment, she had a week-long series of telepathic communications with the occupants of a UFO, which culminated with her being abducted inside that same UFO.

It all began one evening when Roger glanced out her window to see three objects hovering near the chimney of the building across the street. Says Roger, "Though I'd never before seen any UFOs, I knew what they looked like from pictures. The three objects I saw were definitely UFOs. I wondered what they were doing in the Bronx."

As she watched, one of the disks disappeared, and the other two began a pendulous, seesaw movement, edging closer towards her window. Becoming frightened, Roger left the window and went to bed.

The next night, before bedtime, she recalled the experience from the night before, and looked out the window again to see if the UFOs were there. To her shock, they were. As soon as she saw them, they began to move in a weird pattern, playing follow-the-leader. At the same time, she suddenly felt and heard a loud buzzing noise in her head. Again frightened, she fled the window and mentally commanded the weird sound in her head to stop. To her great relief it did. Again, she went to sleep without returning to the window.

On the third night, Roger wasn't as shocked to find that the UFOs were back. However, on this occasion, as soon as she saw the UFO, she received a strong telepathic message from a male entity: "You speak English, don't you?"

Shocked, Roger didn't respond. "Answer me!" the voice insisted. When she refused, the voice repeated, "Talk to me."

Roger screamed mentally at the UFO to go away, and stay away. The voice said, "All right, we'll go away."

However, the UFO didn't go away. Instead, the occupant tried other methods to get her attention. In the middle of the night, she heard the entity's voice again, screaming, "Help me! Help me!"

When morning came, she heard a female voice ask her name. She rushed to the window, but the UFOs were gone. When the voice insisted she say her name, Pauline lied and mentally projected the name, Alice.

The next night, the UFOs were back again. The man's voice asked if she was Alice or Pauline. Confused and scared by their meaningless questioning, she turned up her stereo to blast out the voices. However, after five minutes, the tape began to weirdly malfunction and the voice said, "The tape won't play anymore."

That was enough for Roger. She looked up a hotel in a phone book and prepared to call them. However, when she heard the UFO occupant repeat the address, she realized the futility of trying to run. The voice told her, "We'll contact you tomorrow."

By now Roger was nearing the end of her rope. "Why?" she asked. "Why are you doing this? What do you want with me?"

"We want you," the voice responded.

At this point, Roger felt something like a physical electric shock run through her body. She thought to herself that she must escape, but the voice said, "We'll find you wherever you go."

She dashed to her phone to call a cab, but now the phone wasn't working and only making weird mechanical noises. She hung up and tried the phone again, but again, says Roger, "I heard an ugly medley of mechanical noises.

They gimmicked my phone just as they had gimmicked my tape player! I cursed them with every obscene word in my vocabulary."

Feeling on the verge of a nervous breakdown, she ran out of her apartment, hailed a cab, and rushed to the hospital. At the hospital, she was given a tranquilizer and told to go home and rest.

Reluctantly, she agreed. Seeing a church on the way home, she decided to stop and pray. The voices screamed out, "Don't go in there!" She ignored them and entered the church to pray. While inside, the voices were silent.

She returned home, and at around 10 p.m., the UFOs arrived right on schedule. As she observed them from the window, she suddenly realized that she heard no voices in her head asking her strange questions. Suddenly one of the UFOs began to approach her window. Says Roger, "The next thing I knew I was seated on my couch, my clothes in disarray. I couldn't remember how I had gotten there, and when I looked at the clock it was midnight. Where had the two hours gone?"

The UFOs were gone, and Roger felt strange and disoriented. She instantly wondered if she had just been abducted by the UFO. She had no memory of anything happening, just the missing time.

The next night, she anticipated that the UFOs would return, but thankfully, they did not. As the days and weeks passed, it became clear that they were gone for good. As far as Pauline Darcy Roger is concerned, things can stay that way. As she says, "Now, three years later, they still have not returned... Three years ago I communicated telepathically with aliens from a UFO. And I've never stopped wishing someone else had that 'privilege' instead of me...I fully believe that the aliens and I will never meet again."[214]

Demonic ETs?

Most abductees believe that they are dealing with biological extraterrestrials. However, some abductees feel that interpretations such as angels or demons may also have some validity.

In 2003 (exact date not given), Paul Davis and his cousin were in Russell Park where they saw "several UFOs" resulting in twenty minutes of missing time. In the weeks following the incident, he began having "awful demonic alien nightmares." He suffered from acute anxiety and had to take medication.

After several nightmares, he recalled the entire incident. He saw a large craft land in the park. A ramp opened up and he walked inside. Says Davis, "Before me were huge, octagonal, metallic walls or doors, about nine feet high. The inside of the craft appeared to be larger than the outside of the craft. Each wall had a large symbol that looked like a different complex pattern burned into it. I began to receive messages in my head and turned to see three gray aliens with large heads and child-like bodies sitting around some sort of biological high-tech computer device, wearing tight diver-like suits."

Davis says that the ETs did not look at him, but answered whatever question he posed to them. He asked them who they were and where they were from. The ETs told him that they were advanced bipedal animals with a scientific knowledge way beyond human understanding. They told him that they had "the soul or spirits of demons," and that each of the symbols on the door was an advanced demonic language.

He asked them how they navigated through space, and they replied that they used their minds to interface with a "biological to digital control." They showed him various star-charts, symbols and control panels. Of the control panel, Davis said, "It was clearly an advanced computer keyboard."

Former MUFON director John Schuessler investigated this case, which is apparently ongoing.[215]

Chapter Ten:

Celebrity Encounters

A surprising number of famous New York celebrities have come forth revealing their own incredible encounters. The first, of course, being actor Robert Whitman, who had an extensive encounter during the famous New York blackout.

Celebrities, because of their ability to communicate to large numbers of people, can have considerable influence over public opinion in regards to UFOs. The explosive reaction to Whitley Strieber's book *Communion* shows how powerful this influence can be.

What follows are some high-profile New York celebrities who have experienced the UFO phenomenon firsthand. Credit should be given to researcher Timothy Green Beckley, author of *UFOs Among the Stars*, for convincing these celebrities to come out of the UFO closet.

Neal Sedaka's Sighting

World famous singer-songwriter Neil Sedaka owns a home in the Catskill Mountains in upstate New York. As this is one of the most active UFO hotspots in the state, it was only a matter of time before Sedaka joined the ranks of New Yorker who have seen UFOs. Early one Sunday evening (date not given), he and his son were playing outdoors when they saw something weird very high up in the sky. Says Sedaka, "There, moving slowly but steadily across the sky, was what appeared to me at first to be nothing more than a shooting star. However, its subsequent action convinced me this object was no ordinary aircraft...because the behavior – movement – of the UFO was erratic."

The star-like object accelerated, decelerated, and maneuvered at strange angles. Sedaka and his son watched it for long enough to conclude that it was not a satellite, plane, or any conventional object. After several minutes of observation, they finally began to lose interest. The strange object was still cavorting around when they returned inside. Sedaka granted an interview to researcher Timothy Green Beckley, but otherwise has remained silent about his encounter. As he says, "Some people are still prone to laugh, though the number of skeptics are getting to be fewer and fewer in number."[216]

Muhammad Ali

Probably the world's most famous prizefighter, Muhammad Ali also claims to have had multiple UFO sightings.

His first sighting occurred over a period of two nights on August 9th and 10th, 1974 when he saw a strange light over his gym in Pennsylvania.

His New York sighting, however, occurred a few years later. At the time, Ali was training to fight Oscar Bonavena. Ali used to train before his fights by jogging in the early morning hours through Manhattan's Central Park. One morning around 5 a.m., (date not given), Ali was jogging near 80th Street in Manhattan. Says Ali, "I happened to look up just before dawn as I often do while running, and there hovering above us was this brilliant light hanging as if by an invisible thread."

Seconds later, another identical object showed up. Both appeared to be "round and big." Ali pointed out the objects to his trainer. Together they watched the UFOs maneuver across the sky for more than fifteen minutes. As soon as the sun rose, the objects darted away.

Ali had seen UFOs before and he takes the subject very seriously. He immediately notified reporters of his encounter, telling them, "This is no joke. All my friends here saw it." Ali later learned there were other reports on the same night.

He also admitted that he's seen them several times while out jogging in the hours before sunrise. Says Ali, "I've seen them on many a morning. I'd look up, and there among the stars would be these objects playing tag. They definitely weren't satellites. They'd scoot back and forth, move this way and that, traveling a thousand miles per a second."

Ali revealed his encounter to researcher Timothy Beckley, and is willing to tell anyone who will listen that UFOs are real. He even mentioned his sightings to Johnny Carson while being interviewed on "The Tonight Show." Says Ali, "I'm convinced UFOs are of tremendous importance to the whole world."[217]

Mel Torme

One early morning, around 2 a.m., in 1953, world-famous singer Mel Torme stepped out onto the courtyard of his downtown Manhattan apartment building located at 61st Street and York Avenue to walk his dog Spooky. Looking up, he was startled to see a small red light flying in strange patterns. At first he thought it might be some type of illuminated balloon. But then it did something no balloon or plane could do. Says Torme, "It moved horizontal, faster than my eyes could follow it, before stopping dead in its path as though it had hit a barrier. Then it did lazy loops almost like a figure eight. Next it made a few more circles and then noiselessly it went zap again to another part of the sky."

Torme estimated that the object was about 5,000 feet up. He could just make out "a strange saucer-shaped craft of unknown dimensions" behind the powerful red glow. He looked down at his dog Spooky who was staring at the object "totally transfixed and...shaking."

After several more minutes of silent maneuvering, the UFO zipped off into the sky faster than the eye could follow. Torme is convinced he saw a genuine UFO. As a pilot, he is familiar with aircraft. While he admits that it could have been a secret government craft, as he says, "Nothing I know of that we have could move about so quickly and yet make absolutely no sound whatsoever."[218]

Punk Rocker Helen Wheels

Born in 1949, Helen Wheels was one of the pioneers of the New York Punk Rock scene. She composed songs for the musical group, Blue Oyster Cult, and has gold and platinum records testifying to her achievements.

What few people know, however, is that Wheels is also a UFO abductee. It was only two weeks after her twelfth birthday when her life changed forever. One Saturday around noon in June of 1961, she and her younger brother, Peter Robbins (now a well-known UFO researcher), saw five distant objects in the sky above their Rockville Centre, Long Island home. At that instant, the objects zoomed down and hovered just above the children. Both Helen and Peter could see that the objects were metallic craft. The UFOs formed a V-formation directly over the house across the street. Says Peter, "I could certainly see what they looked like — five, silvery-white disk-shaped objects. Each was about the size of a commercial airplane at several thousand feet, or a smaller, private plane at several hundred. Around the edge of each were regularly spaced, pale-yellow lights that appeared to be windows. The two of us just stood there, about six feet apart, and looked at them."

Peter was fourteen years old, and concluded very quickly that the objects were not normal. Frightened, he turned to run into the house. At that moment, he suddenly and inexplicably forgot about the UFO. Time seemed to move in slow motion as a blue beam of light came out of the UFO and struck him. Says Peter, "Everything went blue for a second, then everything went black. I think I was unconscious before I hit the ground."

Meanwhile, as Helen stared at the objects, she experienced a period of missing time. Her next memory involved watching a large UFO scoop up the five smaller crafts and then move away. At the time, neither Peter nor Helen understood what had happened, nor did they discuss it. It wasn't until years later that they realized that there was missing time to the incident.

As an adult, Peter went under hypnosis, but didn't recall any significant new details. Helen, however, also went under hypnosis and recalled being hit by a beam of light and sucked up into one of the UFOs. Says Helen, "I was in a small, round, dark area and a tall being came and got me. For some reason, I wasn't really afraid of him, as he kept reassuring me through messages in my mind...Taking my hand, he led me into a control room in which there were all sorts of dials, meters and lights — kind of like a cockpit."

Once there, Helen was place in a chair before a wide television-like screen that showed the blackness of outer space filled with millions of bright stars. The ET was about six feet tall, with a large bald head, large dark eyes and gray skin. He wore a one-piece metallic jumpsuit. He stood beside her, mentally reassuring her.

She was then taken to another room where she was put on an examining table and surrounded by shorter identical-looking grays. Says Helen, "Something very painful was shoved up my nostril to the extent that it put a hole in my nose and blood poured out."

Afterwards she was placed back on the front steps of her home via a beam of light with no conscious memory of the onboard experience. Later she would have other bedroom visitations with the same gray-type figures. Numerous other strange poltergeist-like effects occurred, and continue to occur on random occasions. Even today, however, Helen is still dealing with the trauma of her abduction at age twelve. Says Helen, "I felt totally violated, as if they had proceeded against my will, and for this reason I do not know if I can ever completely trust them."[219]

Jimi Hendrix

One winter evening in 1965, Jimi Hendrix, Curtis Knight and other band members were driving through upstate New York. It was 4 a.m. in the morning and snowing heavily. They had been driving for more than one hundred miles when it suddenly became clear that they had missed their turn-off. At that moment, their car became entrenched in a snowdrift that reached up to the hood of the vehicle. Unable to go forward or backwards, the group turned the heater up, rolled up the windows and waited for morning.

As time passed, the temperature dropped. Knight and the others realized that they were in actual danger of freezing to death. Then at some point, something incredible happened. The road in front of the car suddenly lit up brightly. Looking upwards, they watched as a glowing object that was "cone-shaped, like a space capsule" land in the snow in front of the car.

Knight, who was driving, says "At first we thought it was an apparition caused by the cold and our confused state of mind. I mean, we just couldn't believe our eyes."

Knowing that Hendrix had seen UFOs on several prior occasions, Knight looked at him to see his reaction. Says Knight, "Jimi didn't answer, but sort of smiled. He seemed to be staring out into the night, his eyes riveted on this thing resting within a stone's throw."

Knight turned to alert the other members, but strangely they were all asleep and could not be awakened. Knight looked back at the craft. Suddenly a door opened, a figure appeared and began to glide towards their van. Says Knight, "He stood eight feet tall, his skin was yellowish, and instead of eyes, the creature had slits. This forehead came to a point, and his head ran straight into his chest, leaving the impression that he had no neck."

The figure floated towards the van. Knight and Hendrix watched in amazement as the snow melted and disappeared around the creature in all directions. The figure then approached the right-hand side of the van where Hendrix was seated and looked straight at him. Says Knight, "Jimi seemed to be communicating telepathically with it."

At this point, the interior of the van began to heat up. Says Knight, "Suddenly I was roasting!" The figure then circled their van, melting the snow all around it. Says Knight, "As it glided behind our truck, I saw that the drift had completely vanished. Turning on the ignition key I gunned the motor and got the hell out of there...The object – the strange craft – was at the same instant lifting off like a rocket from a launching pad."

Knight knew that Hendrix believed in UFOs as he had seen one during an earlier concert in Maui. Says Knight, "Jimi never did talk much about what happened. He sort of let me know that the cool thing to do was not bring up the subject. It was to be our little secret. However, from what he did say, I sort of suspect that the object arrived to save our necks chiefly because Jimi had been practicing trying to communicate by ESP with the beings on board. I know this may be hard to believe, but I'm putting it straight, just like it happened, you hear!"

A few of Hendrix's songs reveal how he may have felt about UFOs and aliens. For example, his song "Up from the Skies" is actually written from the point of view of an ET who has come back to visit earth after a long absence. The song begins: "I just want to talk to you/I won't do you no harm/I just want to know about your different lives/on this here people farm." Interestingly, ETs often introduce themselves saying some variation of: we mean you no harm.

The ET goes on to say that he has come back "to find the stars misplaced and the smell of a world that has been burned...Well, maybe it's just a change of climate." Again, nuclear proliferation and climate change is a common theme of extraterrestrial contact.

Another song, Castles Made of Sand, describes the story of a young girl who – being confined to a wheelchair – became suicidal. She was about to end her life, then, as the song says, "But then a sight she'd never seen/made her jump and say/'Look, a golden winged ship/is passing my way.'/And it didn't really have to stop/It just kept going/And so castles made of sand/slips into the sea, eventually." After the UFO left, the girl was healed, another common theme of UFO contact.[220]

John Lennon

As a member of the hugely influential musical group, the Beatles, John Lennon's report of a UFO sighting is of particular interest. At the time, August 23, 1974, Lennon had separated from Yoko Ono and was in a relationship with his assistant, May Pang. Lennon stepped out onto the balcony of his 53rd Street Penthouse apartment in Manhattan. Suddenly, a classically-shaped metallic flying saucer appeared over the East River. Lennon began screaming at Pang to come immediately out on the balcony and look. At first she ignored him but finally relented and went outside. Says Pang, "As I walked out onto the terrace, my eye caught this large, circular object coming towards us. It was shaped like a flattened cone, and on top was a large, brilliant red light, not pulsating as on any of the aircraft we'd see heading for a landing at Newark Airport."

To their amazement, the strange craft approached to within a few hundred feet. It was easily the size of a jet, but was totally silent. Says Pang, "When it came a little closer, we could make out a row or circle of white lights that ran around the entire rim of the craft — these were also flashing on and off. There were so many of these lights that it was dazzling to the mind."

Incredibly, the object scooted directly overhead. Says Pang, "John estimated its size at 'about as large as a two-man Lear jet...There was no noise — not a sound coming from it."

The saucer then scooted away and disappeared from view. A few minutes later, however, the UFO was back. Lennon and Pang grabbed their telescope and observed the object. They grabbed their camera and snapped a couple of photographs, but they came out overexposed.

Afterwards, they called the newspaper and the police. Both the newspaper and the police said that numerous other people had called in to report the object.

According to Pang, Lennon was deeply affected by the sighting. He kept saying, "I can't believe it...I can't believe it...I've seen a flying saucer."

Says Pang, "John always had an interest in UFOs. He even used to subscribe to a British UFO magazine, *The Flying Saucer Review*. But after seeing what we saw that night, he became even more fanatical, bringing up the subject all the time." He told her that he would like to be taken up inside of one.

While Lennon was never interviewed about his sighting, he did write about it in his song, "Strange Days Indeed." Writes Lennon, "There's UFOs Over New York, and I ain't too surprised...Nobody told me there'd be days like these. Strange days indeed...Most peculiar Mama."

Twelve years later, on a summer evening in 1986, Pang had another sighting while driving with a friend on 8th Avenue in downtown Manhattan. Says Pang, "I saw something in the distance. As we got closer, I saw this thing hovering."

They pulled off the road near the Tavern on the Green restaurant. At the same time, another car stopped. Pang asked them what they thought the object was. They said, "A blimp." They all got out of their cars and looked at it. Pang asked them if they still thought it was a blimp. According to Pang, they looked confused, hopped back in their car, and sped away. Pang and her friend continued to watch the object that appeared to be "in the shape of a flat iron, with many white lights outlines the shape." There was no sound. After a few minutes, the object quickly rose straight upwards very fast and disappeared into the distance.[221]

Chapter Eleven:

UFO Crash Retrievals

Perhaps the most rare and controversial types of UFO encounters are UFO crashes. The alleged UFO crash at Roswell in 1947 is undoubtedly the most famous. However, unknown to many people, there are literally hundreds of cases that have occurred across the United States and the world.

The State of New York is surprisingly rich with accounts of UFOs crashing to the Earth. In each case, they were recovered by apparent secret military forces and a cover-up was quickly enacted.

The Central Park UFO Crash

New York's Central Park may seem an unlikely place for a UFO crash. But in July of 1952 – during the now famous Washington National sightings – this exact event apparently happened.

According to New York resident Barbara Hudson, she was driving with her mother and brother on 110th Street at around dusk when they noticed a large group of people gathered and pointing at something in the sky. They pulled over and joined the growing crowd. Looking up, they observed a "strange craft" surrounded by a blue halo of light. It was barrel-shaped and had a large porthole in the front.

Hudson says that hundreds of people stopped to observe the UFO as it glided at a low altitude over Eighth Avenue, lighting up the street like day. It then passed over Wadleigh High school.

Suddenly, Hudson heard a few loud explosions, like the sound of "large guns being fired." At the same time, several storefront windows shattered. She stood among a crowd of people at the 110th Street entrance to Central Park and watched as scores of military personnel swarmed onto the scene.

However, before the military were able to cordon off the area, Hudson saw that a huge metallic section of the UFO had been apparently shot off the UFO and was lying in the park. Says Hudson, "One side was a dull metallic color, similar to aluminum, and the other side was a pale lavender color. The outside rim of the jagged chuck of metal seemed to be glowing a blue shade, exactly as it had done in the sky."

Barbara and the other witnesses attempted to get closer, but the military police were roughly escorting everybody away. Says Hudson, "People were shouting. Some women screamed. Everyone was getting excited."

Hudson was forced away from the scene, so she retreated to her apartment, which actually overlooked this area of the park. Looking out her window, she observed large floodlights being set up. She saw other large scraps of metal being retrieved. One large chunk had fallen in the street. The military personnel carted it away, and then re-tarred the street where the object had made a hole.

Then, says Hudson, the military police conducted a door-to-door search. They knocked on her door and told them to remain inside and keep all windows and doors locked. Hudson's mother asked them why, and the MPs replied enigmatically that if they knew what they were looking for, they would be glad to tell them.

Hudson says that the entire area was swarmed with military personnel for the rest of the evening as they searched the entire area, including every square foot of their back yard.

The next morning, it was as if nothing had happened. New York-based researcher Timothy Green Beckley investigated the incident and found Hudson to be a reliable witness (who incidentally, also claims to be a UFO contactee). He spoke with her father who also witnessed the UFO and confirmed that all the streets had been cordoned off. He received signed statements from them, but was unable to locate any other witnesses.

Says Beckley:

"If this case really took place, undoubtedly hundreds, perhaps thousands, of New Yorkers must know of this incident, but because of a tight wall of security and seventeen years of absolute press silence, this important and dramatic UFO event has never been publicized."

Another bizarre encounter that occurred around the same time comes from respected UFO researcher Morris K. Jessup. During the summer of 1952, the Cathedral of St. John the Divine was being rebuilt. One Monday morning, the construction workers arrived at the worksite and were shocked to see the body of "a little man with one eye in the middle of his forehead." He had apparently fallen from above and died when he hit the scaffolding.

The body was removed and the authorities were called. A reporter from the *New York Times* arrived and investigated the account. He wrote a story on the incident, but the editors killed the story for fear of sensationalism. Army officials retrieved the body of the alleged alien "cyclope," and at this point the story ends. Dr. Jessup was apparently convinced of the genuineness of the incident, but was unable to explain it. He says, "Perhaps little men occasionally fall from the sky — as well as frogs, snakes, periwinkles, and fish."[222]

The Mattydale Incident

An intriguing case of a possible UFO crash took place in late 1953 or early 1954 in Mattydale, a rural suburb of Syracuse, New York. The main witnesses are a couple, Bill Marsden, Information Manager of a large electronics firm, and his wife, a prominent lawyer employed by the German military.

One morning at 3 a.m., they were driving through Mattydale when they noticed flashing red lights and five police cars at an upcoming intersection. Marsden slowed down the car in case there was an accident. Instead, he saw something much stranger. "I looked over my right shoulder," said Marsden, "and saw an object which appeared to be twenty feet in diameter and possibly fifteen feet high at the center, and having phosphorescent lights of several colors spaced over the surface."

The object was a typical flying saucer shape and was covered with blinking multicolored lights. It was glowing brightly enough to illuminate the surrounding area. The Marsdens also observed several men – some uniformed and some in civilian clothes – surround the object, examine it, and take photographs. Mrs. Marsden turned to her husband and remarked that perhaps it was the Canadian AVRO flying disk she had recently read about.

The next day, Marsden called the newspaper about the incident who referred him to the local sheriff's office. Marsden then called the police and described the incident. The officer who answered the call replied, "Yes, we know about that, but it is a military secret and we cannot discuss it."

Marsden called the newspaper again who agreed to conduct an investigation. However, the reporters later contacted Marsden and told him that the police had denied any knowledge of the case whatsoever. Raymond Fowler interviewed the witnesses. He later attempted to locate other witnesses, but was unsuccessful.[223]

The Moriches Bay Retrieval

Many people assume that UFOs are crashing to Earth accidentally. However, in some cases there is persuasive evidence that some of these crafts have been intentionally shot down by our own people. According to the Long Island UFO Network, one such incident occurred on the evening of September 28, 1989 in Moriches Bay, on the south shore of Long Island, one of the most active areas of Suffolk County, New York.

About a month before, the area experienced a wave of sightings involving a large, triangular-shaped object. One such sighting occurred on the afternoon of September 4, 1989. John Fitzgerald and his three sons were hiking along Gardner's State Beach when they observed a large dark-colored boomerang-shaped object approach them. The object passed directly overhead without making a sound.

After Labor Day weekend, the popular Smith's Point Beach campground was closed down for the first time in eighteen years. The official reason was lack of funds, however, LIUFON investigators later learned that the real reason was the alleged planned downing of an extraterrestrial craft that was known to be scouting the area.

On September 24, LIUFON investigators Bruce and Martha Richardson were on their boat in the bay when they observed a large amount of unusual military helicopter activity over Moriches Bay.

At around 5:30 p.m. September 28, 1989 – the night of the incident – Mary McLaughlin and her two sons were in their home in Kings Park along the north shore of Long Island when they observed two large triangular-shaped objects hovering in the sky. The objects were separated by about a mile. Then, in the space of one second, one of the objects darted over to join the other, and then both moved away.

At 6 p.m., residents living near the East Moriches Coast Guard Base observed an unusually heavy amount of military and civilian traffic entering the station. There were so many vehicles that the base parking lot became filled and numerous cars were forced to park along the shoulder of the entrance road. Other witnesses reported that a roadblock was set up to turn away unwanted civilian traffic.

At 8 p.m., Setauket resident Mona Rowe was heading west along Route 25 when she observed a formation of amber lights in the sky. She assumed that the lights were conventional aircraft or flares, and has not deviated from this assertion. Rowe also happens to be a public relations official employed by Brookhaven Labs, which has been implicated in the Moriches Harbor retrieval and other New York UFO incidents.

Also at 8 p.m., Mrs. P. G. and her teenage son were heading east on the Long Island Expressway towards their home in Riverhead when they noticed six large amber lights hovering over a nearby field. As they approached, they realized that the lights were attached to one dark-textured triangular-shaped object at least twice the size of a football field.

At around 8 p.m., Larry S. and his son were fishing at the mouth of Moriches Bay when they immediately noticed heavy helicopter activity. They stayed fishing until 11 p.m. During this time, they saw numerous other helicopters, and also observed what they assumed were amber-colored flares being dropped all night long. They observed the activity from the far end of the bay and were more interested in fishing than the weird activity taking place at a distance.

Just after 8 p.m., Susan G. was heading west along North Highway near Southhampton College when she saw a semi-circle of eight amber lights hovering in total silence at about five hundred feet over the highway. The lights were as bright as stadium lights and appeared to be attached to a large object that she estimated to be about 1,000 feet across. Susan made a U-turn and pursued the object in her car. She followed it as it moved over Tuccohoe Lane and turned south along the shoreline. At this point, the object extinguished it lights and moved away.

At 8:15, dentist Dr. John Sykes was traveling south along Sunrise Avenue towards his home in Quogue when he saw a large, bright amber-colored light hovering in the sky. He assumed at first that it was a flare. However, it was a windy night and, when the object remained in the same position for more than two minutes, Sykes discarded the flare theory and realized he was seeing a UFO. He reported his encounter to LIUFON almost two years later, in April 1991.

At 8:45 p.m., Paul Peterson was in his home in Center Moriches when he saw a series of six extremely bright amber lights flashing on and off in sequence over the bay to the south. Moments later several dark green military helicopters moved at treetop level over his home, heading towards the lights. Peterson was going to videotape the amber lights, but first grabbed his son Robert and drove down to the Union Dock to get a closer look. At the shoreline, Peterson and his son observed the lights hovering about fifty feet above the water. Peterson had brought his Kodak instamatic camera and quickly snapped two rolls of film.

They remained watching the lights for nearly two hours. During the entire time, numerous military helicopters performed wide sweeping maneuvers around the amber lights. The witnesses were unsure if the lights were separate or connected to one large object. They were very emotional during the incident, and were terrified at the thought of being discovered.

At around 11 p.m., the amber lights moved away towards the east, still being circled by the military helicopters. The Petersons returned to their home. However, at around 11:25 p.m., Paul Peterson was drawn outside by the sound of helicopters and saw that the strange activity had again resumed over the bay. He remained on his deck, observing the lights from a distance. Around midnight, the activity came to an abrupt end and all was quiet. The photos were later analyzed in depth. Engineer Ron Sierra examined the negatives and noted the lack of any parachute harnesses or smoke trails normally apparent in photographs of flares. A comparison of actual flare photographs also proved the lights not to be flares. Scientists and MUFON researcher Bob Oeschler also analyzed the photos with expensive computer equipment and concluded that the lights were not flares. However, neither were they incandescent or fluorescent. The computer analysis showed them, in fact, to be sources of "cold light" emissions, meaning that whatever they were, they gave off no heat signature.

At around 9 p.m., when Peterson and his son were arriving at Union Dock, Carol Olivieri was in her Center Moriches home. Looking out the window over the bay, she saw first one, two, and then three amber lights appear over the bay. At the same time, a group of helicopters flew overhead towards the lights.

Olivieri called her husband Frank, and for the next hour, the couple observed a formation of three to five lights that would appear high in the sky and then descend slowly to ground level near the shoreline. They estimated that each of the lights was the size of a large house. The lights were so bright that the witnesses were able to read the Air Force markings on the nearby helicopters. The activity lasted until around 11 p.m., and then appeared to end.

Two other witnesses interviewed by LIUFON are Kathy and Kevin O'Donnelly. At around 9:30 p.m., Kathy was traveling along Sunrise Avenue when she saw six amber lights pacing her car, filling the interior with bright illumination. She became frightened and raced to her home, still followed by the object. When she arrived, she honked her horn to alert her husband, who ran outside. Together they observed the formation of lights hover at treetop level above the potato farm across the street, turning the sky to daylight. The lights were totally silent and appeared to be connected to one large object. The field is ten acres in size and both Kathy and Kevin agree that the object encompassed the field from end to end.

Seconds later, the object lifted up and scooted away over the trees.

Yet another interesting piece of testimony comes from New York State Court Officer and Quogue resident Frank D. Having observed what he assumed were an unusually large number of flares being dropped into the bay, Frank drove down to the shore to get a closer look. It was around midnight when he saw what appeared to be an Air Force C-130 fly over the bay and drop a string of parachutists into the water.

Two and a half hours later, at 2:30 a.m., John D., a commodities broker who was staying with his sister in Quogue, was woken up by the sound of helicopters. He looked out to the main runway of the West Hampton Air Guard Facility located a quarter mile to the south. John was shocked to see two large helicopters with large steel cables hanging from them, each carrying some very large object. The helicopters hovered for forty-five minutes, lowering the strange objects to the ground. Unfortunately, John was too far away to discern what the objects were. LIUFON investigators speculate that John observed the actual transport of the objects, which had been shot down by the military.

Meanwhile, numerous witnesses reported their observation of a large convoy of military flatbed trucks escorted by jeeps and police vehicles. The convoy was seen traveling from Smith's Point Beach up to William Floyd Parkway, towards Brookhaven Labs.

At around 5 a.m., a resident who lives adjacent to the main gate of Brookhaven Labs reported that the entire street was cordoned off to traffic to allow for the quick entrance of the convoy into the facility.

These testimonies, while compelling, only suggest a possible UFO retrieval. However, shortly after the incident, several inside witnesses stepped forward and revealed further information about the case.

A few days after the incident, independent UFO investigator George Dickson was contacted by a friend who is a colonel attached to Air Force Intelligence at the Pentagon. The unnamed colonel told Dickson that on the evening of September 28, 1989, the United States military shot down a UFO using a "Star Wars Weapon." After being struck by the weapon, the craft crashed into the dunes, where it was quickly recovered. However, the incident was not without problems. According to the colonel, the ETs retaliated, striking a group of military personnel on the scene with a weapon that emits a focused beam of low frequency sound waves, destroying the cohesiveness of human cells. Reportedly there were more than eighteen fatalities, including several psychics who had been brought to the scene to communicate with the aliens.

Dickson has refused to reveal the name of his source, but insists that it is genuine. He contacted LIUFON investigators on October 4 and told them his information. At this point, the incident was known only to LIUFON investigators and the several witnesses who had contacted them immediately following the event.

About one month later, LIFUON had amassed enough information to make a public announcement. On October 21, LIUFON held an official press conference revealing their assessment that a UFO had been shot down by the military and transported to Brookhaven Labs.

The next day, Copley News Services told John Ford that they were going to run the story nationally. They had received confirmation from both the police and the Coast Guard that there was helicopter activity over Moriches Bay. Furthermore, when they contacted the Suffolk County Police Headquarters, the public relations officer confirmed that that there had been some type of UFO incident over the bay.

Unfortunately, follow-up calls asking for further confirmation resulted only in blanket denials. The cover-up and disinformation was about to begin.

Following the publicity of the incident, LIUFON was contacted by several people claiming to have first-hand knowledge of the incident. One man, Joseph Z., an electronics engineer, claimed to have access to classified government records that said that there was a recovery that evening, but that it was of a nuclear-powered Russian satellite that had crashed in the area.

A few other witnesses called to say that they observed the activity, which they believed was part of a large drug bust operation. According to LIUFON, however, the D.E.A. received a call about strange activity over the area and actually dispatched an aircraft. However, the D.E.A. officials were ordered to turn back and told by Air Force officials that the area over Moriches was currently closed to all air traffic.

LIUFON was also contacted by two New York State Air National Guardsman who said that the incident was really just an Air Sea Rescue training operation and that LIUFON was mistaken about the nature of the incident.

Probably the most controversial of the witnesses is an unnamed scientist who claims to have been involved in the incident. Referred to LIUFON investigators by George Dickson, the scientist, "Dr. Nick," claimed that he had been involved with UFO crash/retrieval incidents since the 1970s.

Dr. Nick claims that he and his team developed a "Star Wars" weapon using a focused radar beam that could turn at right angles and thereby pierce the plasma shields that surround and protect the alien craft. Dr. Nick was told that the targeted object had been tracked by satellite for several months, and that the military knew it would pass over Moriches Harbor on September 28. According to Dr. Nick, the incident was actually part of a larger series of confrontations with one particular race or group of ETs. He said that the wreckage and alien bodies were recovered and sent to Brookhaven labs for study.

Dr. Nick says that he was only on the scene long enough to set up the weapon and shoot the alien craft down. Afterwards, he was immediately escorted from the scene. He refused to reveal any further information to investigators and then terminated contact after claiming to have been threatened by his employers to stop discussing the incident.[224]

The Southaven Retrieval

Probably the biggest and most controversial case revealed by John Ford and the Long Island UFO Network is the alleged downing of a UFO on November 24, 1992.

The first news of the crash came a few weeks after the incident when Walter Knowles of Mastic Beach called the LIUFON hotline to report his sighting of an apparent alien craft impacting in the woods on the western edge of the park near Gerard Road.

Knowles told LIUFON that he had been driving east on Sunrise Highway at about 7 p.m. when he saw an unusual cylindrical-shaped object with blue and white lights hovering low in the sky. Suddenly the object executed a ninety-degree turn and tumbled end over end into the woods. Upon impact, the object emitted a huge flash of light, making the sky bright as daylight. Knowles reports that several other motorists also stopped when they saw the light, which now began to fade to an amber glow.

The area of impact appeared to be on fire. Knowles got in his car and proceeded down the road. Moments later he saw four unmarked, black helicopters heading straight towards the site. He rushed home and turned on the television. There was no news of the incident, so he and his brother-in-law got in the car and returned to the site.

Unfortunately, by this time, the main streets and most of the side streets to the location were cordoned off by military personnel. Knowles knew the area well, however, and was able to take Victory Boulevard west towards the area, which gave him a view of the park. From that location he could see that there was, in fact, a large fire in the park. He also detected the smell of burnt insulation. Unable to see anything else, he returned home.

At around 7:15, Brookhaven Hamlet resident Bob Harrison was traveling east on Sunrise Highway when he saw an oval-shaped object pass over the Brookhaven town dump, leaving a trail of green exhaust. The object appeared to be on a descending course.

Another well-known witness is Reverend Stanley. On the night of the crash, he was shocked to hear his car engine suddenly start by itself. At the same time, his wall clock suddenly stopped and his phone began ringing. He picked up the phone, but nobody was there. Looking outside, he noticed his car had burst into flames. He called the fire department who quickly sent a truck and doused the flames. Stanley's story was leaked to the media and he was later hounded by the press.

According to researcher J. B. Michaels, three teenagers – Jennifer Biels, Richard Grayson, and Todd Phillips – were driving through the area on the night of the UFO crash. Looking up, they saw a large glowing sphere eighty feet in diameter, surrounded by three smaller triangular-shaped objects. As they watched, their car headlights flickered in rhythm to the humming of the craft. Next, the entire area was hit by a power failure. Moments later, a beam of light rose from the ground and struck the spherical object, which promptly exploded and plummeted into Southaven Park. The smaller craft darted away. One however, didn't move away fast enough and was struck by another beam of light coming from the ground and crashed to the earth. Shortly later, numerous helicopters and police cars showed up and the witnesses were ushered from the area.

J. B. Michaels says he interviewed more than a dozen firemen who were called to the scene to put out the fires in the park. The firemen said that they observed a crashed UFO and three aliens; two dead, one alive. They were not able to approach too closely because the guards warned them away.

Around this time, an eleven-year-old boy was riding his bicycle near the park when he saw several fires burning and being doused by fire-trucks.

LIUFON's investigation and the investigation of J.B. Michaels turned up many other confirmed details. According to John Ford, they discovered evidence of "extensive vehicular traffic" in the area of the crash. The park was closed down for a few days after the crash. This was at first denied by county officials, though later they said that the park was closed for duck hunting season. LIUFON found that roads had been widened, trees were chopped down and reduced to woodchips, and the entire area was flattened with tire tracks.

They later brought radiation detectors, which registered mildly elevated levels of radiation in the area. Magnetic detectors showed that the fencing along River and Gerard Roads exhibited signs of "reversed magnetic polarity."

LIUFON researchers contacted numerous federal, state, and local agencies, including local fire departments — they all denied any knowledge or involvement in the alleged incident.

However, this is contradicted by the many reports received by LIUFON of fire trucks entering the park that night. In addition, investigators also found fire department equipment in the park at the area of the crash. After more questioning, an inside source from the Brookhaven Hamlet Fire Department revealed to Ford that "their department was indeed there that night to put out fires that were caused by something which fell out of the sky." The source told Ford that "they are prohibited from speaking about it due to Federal Government orders."

Other details pointed towards a large-scale operation in the area.

LIUFON later learned from confidential sources and from the editor of the *South Shore Press* that as many as seven fire departments responded to the incident, including Medford, Coram, Yaphank, Middle Island, Brookhaven Hamlet, Mt. Sinai, and Ridge, though some had to be turned away as they did not have experience with "radiological fires."

LIUFON discovered that there was a county-wide alert issued by the Suffolk County Police, ordering all units to use landlines to receive instructions for emergency mobilizations, though again, official spokespersons have denied this.

Also, numerous other witnesses contacted LIUFON and said that on the night of the crash, there were helicopters hovering over the park for several hours. Other people called to report odd electrical disturbances and failures that seemed to be related to the incident. Still numerous other witnesses from as far north as Ridge and as far west as Coram all reported seeing the huge flash of bright light reported by Knowles and others.

According to Ford, some witnesses have been harassed by the military and coerced into keeping silent about what they witnessed.

Two years after the incident, new witnesses were still coming forward. In 1994, Ford received an anonymous package sent to his home. The package contained a videotape and a note from a man claiming to be an analyst for the Department of Defense. The video, he said, showed the retrieval of the wreckage of the UFO, including the recovery of several gray-type extraterrestrials. The tape was allegedly confiscated from one of the fire departments on the scene.

LIUFON learned that the wreckage was allegedly taken directly to nearby Brookhaven National Laboratories for study.

The LIUFON investigation was not without its problems. Relationships between LIUFON members and local police became heated when police detained LIUFON members to dissuade them from distributing UFO literature about the incident to residents along Gerard Road. At the same time, there were rumblings within the LIUFON membership itself, with some members claiming that Ford was too controlling and threatening when dealing with fellow researchers.

The situation came to a bizarre head June 14, 1996 when Ford was arrested for alleged attempted murder!

In the November 1996 issue of the *MUFON UFO Journal*, researcher Elaine Douglas called John Ford's arrest a "sting operation" and wrote that Ford was being "seriously persecuted by authorities."

LIUFON member Harry Hepcat disagreed, and in a follow-up article in the January 1997 issue of the *MUFON UFO Journal*, gave his version of events. Hepcat was a founding member of LIUFON and in his article, described Ford as a paranoid, unreliable, and dangerous researcher.

Like many extensive UFO cases of this kind, events have evolved into a murky fog of truths, half-truths, un-truths, misinformation, disinformation, allegations, accusations, character assassinations, denials…and so on. In any result, the Long Island UFO Network was unable to survive the scandal and was dissolved.

Meanwhile, in 1995, researcher J. B. Michaels published a book detailing his investigation into the alleged Brookhaven UFO crash. Writes Michaels, "I personally interviewed over one hundred individuals who had either seen or had evidence concerning the crash in Southaven Park…Many of the people I spoke to were not just scared, they were terrified."

Michaels also interviewed an insider who works at Brookhaven Labs. According to this witness, the craft had been tracked on radar prior to the incident and was shot down over Southaven Park using a "quark-gluon plasma beam" that had been specifically developed for that purpose. He also claims to have interviewed another employee, a specialist in nonverbal communication, who says she was hired to communicate with a gray-type ET who had been taken from the downed craft and was being held at Southaven Laboratories.

Today the Southaven Park UFO crash has gone down in the annals of UFO history as yet another crash/retrieval incident that remains clouded in controversy and apparently covered up by the United States Government.[225]

"Something Crashed"

While UFO crashes are considered very rare events, they are probably more common than people realize, simply because the events are usually effectively covered up. Take, for example, the experiences of Sheryl Wade of Long Island. On Easter morning in 1999 at 12:15 a.m., Wade observed a large, silent UFO flying just overhead at treetop level. Says Wade, "The amazing part is that if I wasn't looking up I would never have seen it. It was big, fast and quietly moving southwest towards Amityville."

The object moved off into the distance and that was where the story seemed to end. However, Wade learned later that the object may have actually crashed. As she says, "That same morning something crashed right of the Southern State Parkway at Exit 32 that took down trees in a field and accomplished a lot of damage to the land. They quickly tried to plant new vegetation and blocked off the view from the public what happened. It was chalked off in the news as a meteor."

Not sure who to report her story to, Wade finally contacted MUFON, who recorded her account.[226]

Chapter Twelve:

Conspiracies & Cover-ups

In 1981, New York psychic healer Jane Allyson told listeners at a conference in New York City that she received her healing power as the result of a close encounter with a UFO on the roof of her Manhattan apartment building.[227]

This is just one of the many ways that UFOs are having a profound influence on people and human society. Probably the most profound effect, however, is the UFO cover-up.

Is Griffis AFB Hiding Information?

Griffis Air Force Base has already been implicated in several New York UFO sightings, with at least three abduction cases occurring adjacent to the base, and several sightings occurring over the base. However, their interest may go much deeper than just observing. In 1973, Investigator Raymond Fowler shocked the UFO community with one of the first credible accounts of a UFO crash other than Roswell. He was able to obtain a signed affidavit from USAF aeronautics expert, Fritz Werner (pseudonym), who claimed to have been involved in the retrieval of an actual crashed UFO outside of Kingman, Arizona. What's interesting here is that Werner told Fowler that he recognized several other officers who were also on the scene of the crashed UFO, including a highly placed official from none other than Griffis AFB in Rome, New York. If true, this would help to explain Griffis's extreme interest in pursuing any UFOs in their area.[228]

Airport Confirmed Sightings

MUFON Field investigator Jim Bouck has investigated several New York UFO cases firsthand. During his investigations, Bouck says he received calls from the staff at Albany International Airport confirming that they have had strange sightings on their radarscopes that couldn't be explained. Philip Imbrogno reports that he also received official confirmation from Air Force sources of several New York UFO encounters that had been confirmed on airport radar scopes.[229]

Talk Show Host Confirms Cover-up

Getting UFO information to the general public has proven to be problematic, as perhaps shown by the experiences of author and Long Island Cable Talk Show host Joel Martin. At one point during his career, Martin says he was offered a lucrative talk show deal with a major network. However, he was told specifically that he would have to steer away from UFOs and the paranormal. He declined the offer because he believes that the government's current position on the UFO cover-up is untenable. As he says, "It is a case of the government saying, 'We can't release information about something we already said isn't there.'"[230]

Montauk

Undoubtedly one of the strangest and most controversial stories to come out of New York is known as "the Montauk Project" named for the North American Indian Spirit guide "Manatu" — a shape-shifter and time traveler. First revealed by authors Preston Nichols and Peter Moon in their book by the same name, the Montauk Project allegedly involves a secret United States government project involving time travel.

Montauk is probably most famous for its landmark lighthouse. It is also home to a former Air Force Base, reportedly decommissioned in 1969.

The story begins in 1971, when Preston Nichols went to work for a Long Island defense contractor. As one of his own private and personal research experiments, he began working with psychics, including Duncan Cameron, to study mental telepathy. One day in 1974, Nichols noticed that every day at the same hour, the psychics were unable to transmit. He believed the problem was that a 410-420 megahertz radio frequency was jamming their brainwaves. He mounted an antenna to his car and determined that the frequency was coming from Montauk Air Force Base.

In 1984, long after the base was allegedly abandoned, Nichols explored the area and discovered various electronic equipment, which he acquired.

Around this time, Nichols says he was recognized by numerous people, such as Cameron, who told him that he had worked at the base and that the base had conducted numerous top secret experiments in everything from weather control, time travel, telepathy, and mind control using psychotronic weapons.

Before long, Nichols began having flashbacks that he had, in fact, worked at the base. According to Nichols, he was a victim of botched government brainwashing experiment. He recalled that he was actually the director of the Montauk Project and that they used powerful psychics and alien technology to travel through time. Their project used the same or similar technology that was first used during the well-known Philadelphia Experiment that involved the invisibility and teleportation of the U.S.S. Eldridge Battleship and its crew.

At some point, Nichols felt like the people in charge were abusing the technology to dangerous levels. On August 12, 1983, says Nichols, the Montauk project ripped a whole in space-time. The time had come to end the research and he took steps to sabotage the project.

The directors of Project Montauk, however, took swift and immediate action. The base was emptied and abandoned. Everyone who was associated with the project was rounded up, debriefed, and brainwashed to forget everything.

The story gets increasingly bizarre. Nichols and Moon wrote two additional books, which stretches credibility to the absolute limit; for example, including accounts of going back in time to meet Jesus. The authors admit that the books are "an exercise in consciousness" and that many people may choose to read them as science fiction.

True or not, the books contain accounts of teleportation, time travel, strange bigfoot-like beasts, and alien encounters all stemming from a secret base located at Montauk.[231]

Long Islanders Brainwashed?

Investigators have long noticed that many UFO witnesses experience memory problems in conjunction with their UFO encounters. For most people, this seems to be limited to experiencing missing time during the actual encounter. However, in some cases, these memory problems may become more pervasive.

For example, John Keel reports that he taped several interviews with Long Island UFO witnesses. However, when he returned a year or two later, the witnesses had no idea who Keel was, nor did they retain any memory of their UFO experiences. All appeared genuinely shocked when Keel told them of their UFO connections.[232]

Animal Mutilations?

According to LIUFON researcher John Ford, New York State has been the site of several animal mutilations. Ford says that he investigated a few bizarre cases from Southampton, in which pet dogs were found dead and drained of blood. There was a rash of UFO sightings in conjunction with the mutilations, which seemed to start around February 1988 and continued strong for at least a year. According to Ford, about sixty mutilations cases have turned up in areas including Manorhaven, Pachogue, Manorville, and Southampton.

In one case, a large St. Bernard dog was found on the grounds of Creedmore State Hospital. The body was found by nurse at the hospital who described it as having been turned "inside out."

Another case from Suffolk County involved a lamb that had also been turned inside out, though in this case the bones were stripped and placed in a neat pile, and the organs of the animal were placed on top of the carcass. According to Ford, during their investigation into the mutilations, they discovered that the parks were being monitored by federal authorities, including frequent over-flights by unmarked black helicopters.

Another case involved a dead heifer found in Brookhaven hamlet. Says LIUFON member Richard Stout, "All the blood had been drained from it." Later Ford and Stout returned to investigate the site and claimed that they were harassed by two low-flying unmarked black helicopters.

There have been rumors – and a few apparently confirmed cases – of human mutilations. New York UFO researcher Bill Knell tracked down one rumor to a medical examiner in Westchester County, who informed Knell that several morgues in the area and been "hit" and "fresh human cadavers" were mutilated in the same style as the well-known cattle mutilations.

In this case, the damage included the partial removal of the face and total removal of the eyes, thyroid, stomach, and genitals. Knell was informed by the unnamed medical examiner that the morgues in question quickly enacted a cover-up, and that the public was never told the truth.[233]

How Many UFOs are There?

The actual number of UFO encounters that have occurred over New York is very hard to estimate. In 1999, James Bouck Jr., then state regional director New York MUFON, and Mike Scritchfield, a UFO field investigator for the New York-based research group Skywatch, reported that their files showed a steadily increasing number of reports through time, starting with seventeen cases in the 1950s, forty-six in the 1960s, fifty-five in the 1970s, eight in the 1980s, and sixty-four in the 1990s. Of course, this doesn't even scratch the surface of the actual number of cases. Writes Phillip Imbrogno in 1989, "In the Hudson Valley area alone, there have been more than 7,000 reports of UFOs over the past seven years."

In 1993, Imbrogno wrote, "From 1982 through 1990, there were over 3,000 sightings of triangular and boomerang shaped UFOs."

In his book, *Night Siege*, he wrote, "At a conservative estimate, more than 5,000 people have seen a triangular or boomerang-shaped object as big as or bigger than a football field, usually moving very slowly or hovering just above the earth, sending down beams of light."

Imbrogno found about four hundred reports of UFOs hovering over bodies of water. In nearly every case, the reports came from artificially-constructed reservoirs and not natural lakes. Writes Imbrogno, "There were no low-altitude body of water encounters over natural lakes! This information seemed quite fascinating since there was a pattern emerging."

He reports that out of the thousands of sightings, about eight hundred were "a very close encounter."

As of October 2007, the National UFO Reporting Center has received 1,760 reports, ranking the state in fifth place, between Florida with 1,970 and Arizona with 1,630.

Combining these statistics, the number of reported encounters is approximately 4,000 to 5,000. However, because less than one percent of UFO witnesses report their encounter, it is safe to assume that the actual number of witnesses is undoubtedly much higher, at least 400,000.

New York's population currently hovers at just under twenty million. According to Gallup polls, approximately ten percent of the population report seeing a UFO. That would mean that about two million people in New York have seen UFOs, which might actually be the most accurate figure.[234]

The Crash of TWA Flight 800

On July 17, 1996, the single worst airline disaster of the year occurred. Tragically 230 people lost their lives when TWA flight 800 exploded in mid-air just off the coast of Long Island, a mere twelve minutes after take-off. There were no survivors.

This disaster would be like any other jet crash except for one fact: there is a strong and undeniable UFO connection. Evidently before, during, and after the accident there was unusual light activity witnessed by a large number of reliable witnesses. Was a UFO involved in the crash of TWA flight 800?

Here are the facts: 230 people boarded the doomed 747 that took off from JFK Airport bound for Paris, France. The take-off was normal and the jet continued its ascent. At approximately ten miles off Long Island, near East Moriches Harbor, and at an altitude of 14,000 feet, something caused the central fuel tank to explode, effectively blowing off the entire front section of the fuselage. The remaining section flew for about one minute before crashing into the Atlantic.

Instantly investigators converged on the scene, including people from the National Transportation and Safety Board (NTSB), the local police, and more than five hundred FBI agents.

The reason for such a strong FBI presence was because of heavy suspicion that terrorism was responsible for the tragedy. But why would investigators suspect terrorism? Here's where the story begins to get interesting.

Evidently, immediately preceding the explosion of Flight 800, dozens of witnesses along the nearby coast and even in other aircraft spotted a strange light in the vicinity of the doomed 747. Witnesses one by one began to tell of something that looked like a streak of light heading directly for the jumbo jet, which then exploded and fell into the sea.

At first these reports received little attention. But as the number of witnesses mounted, it became impossible to ignore. Before long, numerous witnesses appeared on T.V. relating what they saw.

Four men sitting outside on a patio each saw "a streak of light" move across the sky and apparently hit the aircraft.

Civil Engineer Michael Russo says that he saw a bright flash of light similar to a camera flash but not as intense. Says Russo, "...There was a glint, quick and sharp...wish I hadn't been here...I wish I hadn't seen it."

Another witness who saw the streak of light told news reporters, "You've got to explain that white light to know exactly — in my mind, to comfort me. That would have to be explained, what that white light was."

Then came the clincher: an actual photograph of the object. Taken at the time of the accident and in the exact area, the photograph shows a cylindrical object lit at one end, moving through the air. New York resident Linda Kabot snapped the photo from a location a few miles south of the tragic accident.

Her husband Lance was the first to notice the object in the photo, which they describe as "a long cylindrical object high in the sky. It is in a roughly horizontal position, although its left end is tilted downward. Its right end seems to be brightly lighted." Because of all the attention generated by the controversial photograph, the Kabots were forced to hire an attorney to handle the media frenzy. The FBI requested and received the photo and negative. The photo has been published in newspapers, but remains copyrighted.

The above testimonies and photograph apparently caused the FBI to suspect that a missile may have been launched at the plane. But then came the very compelling testimony of Major Fred Meyer, who was actually flying inside a National Guard helicopter in the area at the time of the accident. Says Meyer, "I saw what I've described as a light in the sky that had the characteristics and trajectory of a shooting star...the difference was, this was broad daylight and I was immediately curious because I've never seen anything like that in broad daylight."

Meyer was interviewed many times about what he saw. In another statement about his sighting, he said, "[It was] a streak of light. It was the same trajectory of a shooting star, across the sky in front of me, gently descending from a higher to lower altitude." Meyer said that it was different from a shooting star not only because it was orange-red instead of white, but because "you don't see shooting stars in broad daylight."

Meyer is also sure that what he saw was not a missile. He should know as he has had missiles actually fired at him on a number of occasions. Says the Major, "I've seen missiles fired at me, Sam 1s, Sam 2s, Sam 7s — they're 1960s Vietnam vintage missiles and is the last time anybody shot at me — and I do not attribute or ascribe to this any of the characteristics of those missiles." Meyer has repeatedly insisted that the object could not be a missile. "I've seen missiles...nothing in my experience says missiles," he says.

Further evidence against the missile theory surface when the wreckage from the plane was finally pulled from the ocean bottom and examined. The evidence showed only that the central fuel tank had exploded. There was allegedly none of the telltale marks pointing to a missile attack, which include among other things, small pitted marks imbedded in metal fragments and residue of explosive material.

So if it wasn't a missile, what was it? The idea that the plane was struck by a meteor was brought up, but this seemed too farfetched and didn't explain the observations of the witnesses. All kinds of wild theories were tossed around. Some said it was a bomb (though this was proven false in the same way that it couldn't have been a missile). Some even speculated that the airplane had hit a pocket of flammable methane gas rising from the rotting vegetation lying on the ocean floor. There were even questions raised that maybe some agency within our own government was responsible, and that 'friendly fire' was the cause of the accident.

As outrageous as this last theory sounds, it quickly gained considerable popularity. *Aviation Week and Technology*, the *New York Times*, and *Newsweek* all printed articles seriously speculating on this possibility. On "Larry King Live," while interviewing victims' family members, Larry King asked two of them what they thought of such a possibility. Neither was willing to rule it out. Finally, there's the report of retired United Airlines pilot Richard Russell of Daytona, Florida, who claims directly that "TWA Flight 800 was shot down by a U.S. Navy guided missile ship…" Russell says that he was given this information by someone who attended a "high-level briefing" in Washington following the airline disaster. Even the FBI admitted they were looking into the possibility.

As the investigation progressed, two major camps developed: those who believed the plane was brought down by a spark in the central fuel tank, and those who believed it was brought down by some outside force (i.e.: missile, bomb, unknown weapon, UFO?). The NTSB did eventually conclude that the probable cause was mechanical failure. However, the FBI announced that they were still investigating the possibility of terrorism. Nobody, it seemed, was able to account for the mysterious "streak of light."

And then came the reports of more UFOs. Incredibly they came from a very reliable source: the captain and crew of a Saudi Arabian 747 jumbo jet. It was a December evening and the jet was coming in for a landing at JFK airport, descending at an altitude of 12,000 feet. They had just reached the area where TWA Flight 800 had crashed five months earlier when they saw something very strange. The captain and crew reported seeing a "green flare-like object," which evidently hung over their plane for an undetermined period of time. The flight was diverted to land in Dulles Airport in Washington DC, where Federal officials were waiting to question the captain and crew. The press caught wind of the incident, and an airport official released a somewhat garbled statement about the incident, saying, "It might turn out to be completely nothing. I can't say there is anything to it. Obviously if someone reports something, they have to check it out. That's standard."

Despite the fact that officials remained tight-lipped about the UFO sighting, the fact that they felt it was important enough to divert the Saudi Arabian jet to Dulles Airport and question the captain crew reveals that they thought the incident was significant.

Interestingly, the day after this new UFO report surfaced in the media, CNN was told by the FBI that the report "could be explained by a meteor shower." This brief segment supposedly explaining the sighting was aired over and over again on the news.

However, what most of the news reports didn't say is that the Saudi crew not only sighted the "green flare-like object," but it actually appeared on their onboard radar. Let's see... a glowing green object that "hung over" the plane and appeared on radar; obviously, this was no meteor.

Here's where the story begins to get really strange. It turns out that the Saudi Arabian crew was not the only ones who had encountered UFOs in that area. Yet a third large jet airliner saw another UFO in the exact same spot, only one month earlier. News of the sightings was effectively suppressed until the Saudi Arabian Jumbo Jet UFO encounter was leaked to the press.

The news of the sighting was only aired briefly and many stations didn't carry it. However, in November of 1996 the captain and crew of a Pakistani jumbo jet were flying over the same spot when they saw a UFO. According to FBI investigator Bob Ropelwski, "I'm interpreting it as they saw a single beam or point of light bright enough to attract their attention."

As if three UFO sightings by three 747 jumbo jets over Moriches Harbor aren't enough, on August 9, 1997 there was a fourth incident, again involving a 747. According to an article that appeared in the *Toronto Sun*, Swissair Flight 127 was cruising over New York at 23,000 feet at 5:07 p.m. opposite JFK Airport, "near the area where TWA Flight 800 went down July 17, 1996."

The pilot was addressing the passengers on another issue when he cut his transmission short to alert the NTSB of a "near-miss by a round white object."

According to the NTSB, the following conversation occurred between Air traffic controllers in Boston and the pilot of the Swissair 747 jumbo jet. The object had just streaked past the plane when Swiss Air radioed in to Boston, Massachusetts:

> SWISSAIR: Sir, I don't know what it was, but it just flew like a couple of hundred feet above us. I don't know if it was a rocket or whatever, but incredibly fast in the opposite direction.
> CONTROLLER: In the opposite direction?
> SWISSAIR: Yes, sir. It was too fast to be an airplane.

The controller located another aircraft in the area, and asked the crew if they saw anything like a missile in the area. The response was negative. The controller then asked the Swissair pilot how close the object was to his plane.

> Swissair: It was right over us, right above, opposite direction, and I don't know, two, three, four hundred feet above... [We] saw a light object, it was white, and very fast.

The FBI's official explanation of the TWA streak of light and the Saudi Arabian and Pakistani jet UFO sightings is meteorites. They made no announcement about the Swissair sighting. However, obviously by now credulity has been stretched to the limit. Could it really be a coincidence that on four separate occasions, four crews of four different jumbo jets each encountered an unidentified flying object in the same exact location, all within the space of one year? It hardly seems possible.

UFO investigator John Romero has noticed another strange coincidence. In his article, "Just As UFOs Enter the Flight 800 Mystery, the Case is Closed!" he points out that as soon as the UFO connection became undeniable, Federal investigators immediately came up with an explanation for the cause of the crash. He writes, "The diagnosis effectively bumped the mystery of Flight 800 out of the news...but the explanation was curiously timed. It came just as reliable witnesses had reported a possible UFO connection to the explosion and crash that killed 230 passengers and crew on the Paris-bound 747. Its their one way ticket out of here, said an accident investigator. James Kallstrom, heading the FBI investigation, said he was surprised at the NTSB explanation. Funny, isn't it, how quickly an explanation surfaced the moment UFOs came into the picture. Case closed? Perhaps not?"

All three 747s that sighted the UFOs were flying at the same approximate altitude over Moriches Harbor off Long Island. Could there be something about this harbor that is attracting UFOs?

Here's where the story gets truly incredible. None of the major networks picked up on the connection, however, the truth behind what really happened to TWA Flight 800 may lie with the mysterious events that have occurred over Moriches Harbor in the recent past.

Long Island, as we have seen, is a virtual hotbed of UFO activity, and Moriches Harbor just happens to be the location where, according to LIUFON, on September 28, 1989 a UFO was allegedly shot down by none other than some agency of our own government using secret Star Wars technology.

So what are we to make of all this? The question remains, what brought down TWA Flight 800? What was the mysterious "streak of light?"

Interestingly, just over a month after the accident, yet another pilot, this time for American Airlines, was flying off the coast of Virginia when he was shocked to see what appeared to be a missile flying alongside his plane. He reported his sighting to authorities who referred him to NASA, who actually admitted that the missile was, in fact, ours. NASA spokesperson Chris Chiames confirmed the sighting and said that it was only one of a dozen experimental rockets that are fired each year from Wallops Island, which is used by NASA to conduct top secret testing with unmanned rockets. When he saw the missile, the American Airlines pilot was flying over Wallops Island, which incidentally is located about two hundred miles south of the TWA accident site.

And that's not all. A 1997 Discovery Channel special on the TWA Flight 800 disaster revealed more interesting information. Although the program mentioned the streaks of light seen by dozens of witnesses, it played down the UFO angle as much as possible. What the program did reveal was that, at the time the accident occurred, the United States Navy had a number of ships offshore of Long Island, near the area where the 747 went down, performing top secret maneuvers that reportedly included satellite reconnaissance.

Could it be that those strange "streaks of light" seen by the witnesses of the TWA crash might have an alternate explanation? Could they have seen evidence of Star Wars technology in action? Could it be a coincidence that that UFOs were shot down over the same exact area? More than one researcher doesn't think so.

Writes Elaine Douglas, "And there's that curious coincidence about Moriches Bay, which more than a few persons have pointed out. Moriches Bay is where John [Ford] said that the United States brought down an alien craft in 1989, and Moriches Bay is where TWA Flight 800 mysteriously crashed... The cause of that crash, readers are aware, has so far eluded federal investigators, and in particular investigators are unable to explain the reports of more than twenty persons who say that saw an unaccountable light streaking towards Flight 800 before it went down."

Peter Moon, co-author of *The Montauk Project*, asserts that Flight 800 was, in fact, a victim of friendly fire using Star Wars technology acquired from the ETs. Says Moon, "The rumor in my circle has it that it was the particle accelerator at Brookhaven Labs on the Montauk Point, part of the SDI [Strategic Defense Initiative] program. The plane was passing in the vicinity of a military exercise where a heat-generated target was being pursued, but something malfunctioned. The beam was accidentally fired up from the ground, hitting the deactivated missile, and activating it. The heat-seeking missile passed through the hull of the plane, destroying it, and leaving no trace of itself. The government can't investigate too deeply because it's part of the supposedly defunct Star Wars system."

While these assertions remain unproven, obviously the crash of TWA Flight 800 is unlike most other jet crashes. While the UFO literature contains numerous examples of small-planes crashing or disappearing in conjunction with UFO activity, and near-misses with UFOs and larger jets, no other jumbo jet disaster has had such a UFO connection.

A final bizarre twist to the story comes from an abduction case investigated by respected English UFO researcher Tony Dodd. According to Dodd, Stephen X., a UFO abductee from Middlesex, England, was taken onboard a UFO and, like many UFO abductees, was given prophecies of future events. In this case, however, the prophecy turned out to be nothing other than the crash of TWA Flight 800. Writes Dodd, "On one occasion he 'saw' an airliner crash. He asked the aliens if they could stop this from happening and was told 'no.' Two weeks later, TWA Flight 800 crashed into the sea off Long Island."[235]

Chapter Thirteen:

New York UFOs Today (2000-2007)

UFOs show no signs of leaving, and instead, seem to becoming increasingly brazen in their behavior. The New York record for the new millennium shows that activity continues at a steady rate across the state. Again, while the UFOs seem to be putting on displays, they continue to remain an elusive and slippery phenomenon.

Cylinder with 40 (400?) Lights

Larry Clark of New York MUFON reports that at 9 p.m. June 8, 2000 a huge cylinder with an estimated forty to four hundred lights was spotted by numerous witnesses over Staten Island. Clark reports that his friend was a firsthand witness, and said that the object was at least four times the apparent size of the full moon, cylindrical-shaped, and covered with flashing lights. It hung motionless and silent high in the sky. He turned away for a minute and when he looked back it was gone. However, according to Clark, five other witnesses reported the object, and he observed a police car cruising down Jefferson, "practically an abandoned street that the police never go down."[236]

UFO taped during Tour

On October 6, 2000 the Fox television program "Sightings" played a short segment of home video taken from a couple who were taking a helicopter tour of New York City when their helicopter was apparently buzzed by "disc-shaped" object. They were already videotaping when a disk came out from behind a building, zoomed towards the helicopter, and darted away at high speed. The entire maneuver was caught on the videotape, though the pilot doesn't appear to react. MUFON video experts viewed the footage and their preliminary assessment is that it is NOT a hoax. As of the year 2001, the footage was posted on the program's website www.sightings.com. The episode that carried the segment was #4032. The video was subsequently played on Fox News and has now been duplicated on countless Internet sites.[237]

Glowing Disk over Westbury

Says the witness, "My wife and I are educated professionals who were driving northbound on the Wantagh Parkway in Nassau County at 8:45 p.m. [October 20, 2000]. As we approached the Hempstead Turnpike, I noticed a glowing disk in the sky...The color of the light was whitish blue. I pointed it out to my wife, who also had the same reaction of awe as I did."

The object was at a low altitude and reminded the witness of the television documentary footage he had seen of alleged flying saucers. The object veered to the east, then to the north, then scooted westbound where the witnesses lost it behind some trees. Says the main witness, "Because of its appearance and movement, we knew it could not have been a plane, helicopter, or even a blimp. I assumed it would be clearly seen by thousands."[238]

Daylight Disks

Most UFO sightings occur at night, making it very difficult to identify what exactly is being seen. Of much greater evidentiary value are daylight sightings, particularly when they involve what appear to be solid, metallic objects.

A good example occurred January 20, 2001. A former pilot from Dutchess County reports that at 9:53 a.m., he saw a saucer-shaped object that glowed red on the bottom half. It was moving very quickly from the northwest to the southeast, then suddenly accelerated with such a speed that it appeared to vanish from sight. Says the witness, "I have never seen anything like this, nor have I ever seen an object just vanish from sight just as quickly as it appeared."

Another example occurred six months later on the afternoon of June 21, 2001. Yonkers artist Paul Grecco was driving along FDR Drive when he saw a "large orange disc" hovering not far above a group of buildings. Says Grecco, "I couldn't go as far to say that it was an alien craft, but it was definitely something unusual."[239]

Pilot Encounters Boomerang

One hour after a sighting in New Jersey, twenty miles away another sighting was made by the pilot and passengers of a flight bound from Teterboro Airport, New Jersey to Martha's Vineyard. It was 6:45 p.m. June 2, 2001. The plane was a private jet. Onboard were six passengers and the pilot. There was a low cloud cover. After take off, they ascended above the cloud cover and broke out into bright sunlight, flying over Long Island. Suddenly, one of the passengers shouted out an expletive, "What the *$#@ is that?"

Says the main witness, "Immediately I looked out of my window at 7 p.m. Behind us on the right side of the plane and some distance above, perhaps 1,000 to 3,000 feet, was this large, rusty red boomerang-shaped object silhouetted against the bright blue sky. We were now above the storm and had a good view. The craft had no windows or lights visible, and was about the size of a large 747 jet aircraft. It hovered in place for several seconds before we lost sight of it. My friend, who had first sighted it for a greater duration, said it looked as if it had bulbous shapes, which joined to form the boomerang or flying chevron. We both agreed, however, on the size and color of the object... The UFO resembled nothing I had ever seen. Especially the red cherry color struck us as odd."[240]

"Birds with Flashlights!"

One of the most widely observed and fully investigated sightings of 2001 occurred on the evening of July 14-15, off Staten Island, directly over the Arthur Kill Waterway. Known variously as "The Carteret Lights" and "The Arthur Kill Sightings," the large number of witnesses and the presence of a videotape of the objects caused a media sensation on both the New Jersey and New York sides of the waterway. The sighting was later investigated by members of the National Institute for Discovery Science (NIDS), and also by Dennis K. Anderson, director of the Wagner College Planetarium in Staten Island and a member of the Advisory Committee of the Intruder's Foundation.

The Arthur Kill channel is thirty to forty feet deep, and accommodates large oil tankers moving to and from nearby refineries. Also adjacent is the Fresh Kills Landfill, one of the state's (and the world's!) largest garbage dumps. Officially, the sightings began some time just before midnight, and involved witnesses in both Carteret, New Jersey and Staten Island.

Dennis Anderson's investigation uncovered a sighting that occurred earlier that day around, 2 p.m. Three witnesses were sunbathing in their backyard when they saw sixteen to twenty "diamond-shaped, bright silver objects" high in the sky, which appeared in groups of four or five, or sometimes linked up to create the impression of a much larger object. The objects moved east to west, passing in and out of the clouds, and were in view for about ten minutes.

On the Staten Island side, all the witnesses were located either along Arthur Kill Road or the West Shore Expressway, both of which parallel the channel. About nine hours after the above sighting, at 11:45 p.m., Adam O. stepped outside of a sportsman club and saw, according to Anderson, who interviewed the witnesses, "six to eight yellowish-red lights in a circular or oval pattern."

John R., a computer programmer, was driving along the West Shore Expressway at around 12:30 a.m. when he observed a large, glowing yellow triangle, about one-third the size of the full moon. It moved directly away from the witness, becoming smaller and smaller until it disappeared.

At around 12:50 a.m., Carol K. and her daughter were at the tollbooths at Goethals Bridge leaving Staten Island when they saw about twelve bright, white lights that began to pulsate, blink on and off, and sometimes dart around. All the lights appeared to be directly over the Fresh Kills landfill. After five minutes, the lights blinked off and disappeared.

Around the same time, Chris B., owner of the Waterloo Café on Arthur Kill Road, stepped outside for a breath of fresh air when he saw a group of red-orange lights in a V-formation. They appeared to be attached to a single object, about fifty feet across, that was low enough to cast a red-orange glow on the roadway below.

He called out to the people in the café, and an estimated crowd of about forty to fifty people came out and watched the lights. Among them was federal police officer, Robert M., who, according to Anderson, described the lights as "orange to gold tone, in V-configuration, approaching from the northwest."

Jeff C., the café's DJ, saw the lights and agreed with the others that they were about a half mile away, over the channel. However, Lori, A., the bartender, thought the lights might be as close as five hundred feet, and about 1,000 feet in altitude.

Security guard Bryant D. observed the lights and also thought they were much closer. He saw one light that was directly over the trees in a nearby cemetery, lighting up the area.

Meanwhile, across the channel in Carteret, New Jersey, numerous other witnesses were also observing the lights. Police and news stations received the standard flood of calls, and the next day, the story was front-page news in both Staten Island and Carteret. It turned out that somebody had also caught the objects on videotape. According to Anderson, who viewed the footage, "Sixteen to twenty lights were seen in formation. The video shows a trapezoidal grouping of lights followed by a single light bringing up the rear."

Then came the possible explanations from the media. A NASA spokesperson was given the video and several days after the event offered that it might be flares dropped from a private plane. In general, the press did not take the sightings seriously and one news reporter even joked, "Must be birds with flashlights."

Anderson takes the case seriously and says, "Something not immediately recognizable penetrated the airspace over volatile oil refining facilities and invaded one of the most heavily trafficked commercial air corridors in the world...It is now known that unknown targets without transponders, some at heights of 99,000 feet, were picked up on radar at Newark International Airport. This is less than twenty miles from Manhattan. The media, the military, and the police treated it as good summertime fun not worthy of serious consideration."[241]

Toy Model Rocket Launch Attract UFOs

UFO researchers have discovered long ago that UFOs are often seen over highly technological installations. In particular, UFOs have been seen in conjunction with numerous rocket and missile launches. In the following case, it was a toy model rocket that provoked UFOs to come and investigate.

On September 2, 2001, a Lynbrook resident and father of three kids went outside to shoot off ten model rockets with class B engines. At 5:35 p.m., he saw a few strange white objects moving around one of the rockets. At first he assumed the rocket had malfunctioned and that the wadding had come loose. However, looking through a pair of binoculars, he was shocked to see several UFOs.

Says the witness, "They were roundish with a red light, but the red light was not sharply defined. Then my sons witnessed the light change from one big light to smaller lights. There were many small UFOs and two bigger ones. They seemed to hover and then move quickly in different directions. One even went in the opposite direction without slowing down. Then after ten minutes, they started to disappear. The closest one was shiny aluminum."[242]

Blue Squares & Red Diamonds

On October 1, 2001, a woman and her two young children, ages thirteen and eleven, had a dramatic encounter while driving west on Route 20 between Pompey and Lafayette in the city of Lafayette. The witness was driving, she says, when "fifteen feet in front of us were four bright blue lights moving above us. They were in the shape of a square. I stopped my car and opened my window, and there was a very loud noise. Then all the lights turned red, and the shape changed to a diamond shape. The object moved at a rapid rate of speed, then all noise stopped. There was complete silence and then the object disappeared from view."[243]

UFO Calls Cell Phone

At 2 p.m. October 15, 2001, as reported in the *MUFON UFO Journal*, a witness from New York City observed a flying triangular-shaped object moving at very low altitude. As the witness reported, "It was a chrome-like color, as big as a one story building, maybe about 250-500 feet in the air, and it glowed reddish black, and left a whitish tail. During this event the object changed colors three or four times, from a reddish-black to a very dark red. It sounded like a whistle at first, but became silent and came on again. It was similar to Morse code. I saw a dozen lights on it that were various colors. I was talking on my cell phone at the time to my wife, telling her about this, and it was coming in kind of fuzzy. Then I heard a noise coming from my cell phone (maybe a transmission) and then it went dead a couple of seconds later. The noise I heard from the phone could have been a language, but I could not understand a word of it. After my phone went dead, the UFO left a few seconds later."[244]

New Year's Wave

On December 30, 2001 at about midnight, eight friends left a restaurant in Long Island City to look at the stars. Suddenly, what they thought were stars started to move. Says the witness, "What we were looking at started to dart and shoot all over the sky. There were so many! Some lined up in order, and then just went off in their own direction, just to zip back and forth. Others looked like they were playing a game of cat and mouse. They were darting all over the sky for the longest time."

The witnesses ran back inside the restaurant and were able to call out other people to witness the event.

A few days later, on January 1, 2002, a witness from New Hyde Park was driving home at 5 a.m. when he saw a strange ball of light climbing in the sky not far from another airplane. The object was actually brighter than the airplane. After it ascended higher than the plane, it changed from white to bright yellow. The witness estimated that it was about twenty-five miles away to the west, which would put it directly over New York City. After a few minutes, the object zigzagged and disappeared.[245]

Objects over Tonawanda

While most people who see UFOs usually observe only one or two objects, it is not uncommon to observe fleets of UFOs involving dozens of objects grouped together. A good example occurred January 16, 2002 in Tonawanda. At around midnight, the witness stepped outside to smoke a cigarette when he saw approximately twenty separate, reflective, metallic objects moving overhead towards the northeast. Says the witness, "When I first noticed them they appeared to be in a formation, but they moved around in groups of about five into different formations. They appeared to be very high and moving very quickly."

The witness reported his sighting to NUFORC. One hour later, an anonymous resident of Dorchester was outside his home at 1:34 a.m. when he observed "one large dark cylinder-shaped object heading north...flying very slow."

The object appeared to be dark-colored and had no lights on it. It blended almost perfectly into the night sky, glinting only briefly enough for the witness to conclude that it was a solid object. As he watched, the object changed direction to the west and disappeared into the distance. The witness also later reported his sighting to NUFORC.[246]

UFO Poses for Photograph

On the evenings of September 8-9, 2002, one or more UFOs were sighted by multiple witnesses across the upstate area. One of the first sightings occurred September 8 at 4 p.m. over Oneida. A witness reported he was driving along the highway in Little Falls when he noticed that the traffic started to slow down while other people pulled over and scrambled out of their cars. Looking up in the sky he was shocked to see a "yellow triangle with yellow pulsing lights." Seconds later it disappeared in a puff of smoke.

Nine hours later, at 1 a.m., a lady was looking out the window of her home in Central Square when she saw the reflection of flashing colored lights on her street. She assumed at first that it was an approaching police vehicle. Instead, however, she was shocked to see a saucer-shaped object approach from the western sky. She says, "The top was shining brightly with red, green and blue lights, and the bottom had a very bright white light."

The object proceeded to perform a variety of amazing maneuvers. It slowed down, hovered up and down, and rotated at high speed. Said the witness, "It looked like the toy top I played with as a child." After forty-five minutes, the object suddenly disappeared.

However, at 2 a.m. the witness received a call from her neighbor who lived three miles away saying that she too had just seen the same object.

The next evening they waited outside to see if the UFO would return. At 9:30 p.m., they were amazed to see the object return for a repeat performance. They called other witnesses in nearby Syracuse and Brewerton who could also see the object from their homes. They took videotapes of the UFO, which hovered in various positions for two hours, before finally departing.[247]

The October 2003 Encounters

The cat-and-mouse type of behavior of UFOs has always puzzled investigators. The following three cases took place within a space of three weeks. Each involves low-flying UFOs that exhibit this bizarre confrontational behavior.

On October 1, 2002, a gentleman and his friend were outside his home in the Emerson Hill area of Staten Island. It was 7:45 p.m. and they were watching a jet fighter perform what appeared to be routine patrols over New York City. It performed a circular pattern over the harbor, the Verrazano Bridge, and Brooklyn. On its third pass, the two gentlemen simultaneously observed a bright green light appear behind the jet fighter. Says the witness, "We both saw a bright green star following directly behind this fighter jet, only by a short distance, and to the lower left hand side of it, and every move the jet made, this thing was right there with it, flying almost effortlessly."

The bright green light tailed the jet fighter for one complete circle over New York City, then suddenly took off. There was no indication that the pilot of the jet fighter was aware of the object. The witness later reported his sighting to MUFON.

Five days later, a man and his girlfriend were "buzzed" by a UFO while four-wheeling outside Watertown. It was 7:20 p.m. October 5 when the witnesses saw a "flying rectangular shape" cruise across the sky and suddenly stop. It was covered with bright red, white, and green-blue lights. As if it suddenly noticed the witnesses, the object made a sharp 180-degree turn and headed directly towards them. Says the witness, "It flew right above us, and it started to shine its light on us. My girlfriend got really scared. She told me to go as fast as I could and drive into the garage."

As they sped away, the object turned again and began to follow. They reached their home and ran inside to get further witnesses. At that point, the object accelerated and shot across the sky, disappearing into the distance.

About two weeks later, on October 21, 2002, FOX News reported on an unusual incident over Albany International Airport. An un-named witness allegedly caught a "spear-shaped" object on videotape as it passed above the airport. At the time of the incident, a large commercial aircraft was coming in for a landing. According to FOX News, the videotape has been confiscated by the FBI who is attempting to determine if the object is a missile or something else.[248]

More Low-Flying UFOs

One of the many enigmas surrounding the UFO phenomenon is the fact that they sometimes want to be seen. Dozens of cases have already been presented that show that the UFOs have the ability to become completely invisible at any time. The many cases of low-flying UFOs over crowded roadways suggest that the UFO occupants are fully aware of the reaction they are causing and are intentionally putting on some type of performance. The months of August and September 2003 produced several cases of UFOs that appeared to be showing off.

On August 20, 2003, Bruce Cornet Ph.D. visited a friend's home in Millbrook in southeast New York. The residents had reported a lot of UFO activity in the last few weeks. Most of the sightings involved a large manta ray-shaped object. On this particular evening, they went outside with a video camera with the hopes that the UFO would show up. At 9:37 p.m. they noticed a pair of lights in the distance. As they watched, the lights flared up, and began to approach. Writes Cornet, "It gave us a classic performance that lasted for a little more than five minutes!...Its altitude could not have been much more than 500 feet as a small red light located at its nose flashed regularly and irregularly."

The object approached at about ten miles per hour to within a few hundred feet, then came to a stop and made a sharp turn, which Cornet likened to an ice skater. He also noticed that the craft's many strange lights failed to illuminate the actual fuselage, which appeared to be "stealth black." The craft was silent until it was at its closest point. Writes Cornet, "It produced a whole range of different whining sounds like a series of electrical generators powering up."

This was not Cornet's first encounter. He had earlier hooked up with Ellen Crystall and had videotaped the same type of craft taking off from various fields in Pine Bush on dozens of occasions. Writes Cornet, "Each time it did something a little different, giving us more information about this enigmatic craft. The Hudson Valley sightings continue."

A half-hour after this sighting and two hundred miles away, another low-level encounter occurred over Manlius, just east of Syracuse. The anonymous witness was driving along Broadfield Road when he observed a "white glowing round object" moving north to south at about forty miles per hour. Writes the witness, "The object was low in the western sky, flying at an altitude of 300 feet. The object had the same luminescence as a bright full moon and could still be seen as it passed behind the area trees."

On September 8, 2003 at 10:35 p.m., a large metallic-looking disk-shaped was seen cruising at a moderate speed over lower Manhattan near the Brooklyn and Williamsburg Bridges. It was orange-red and had a blinking light on one end and a rotating light on the top. For the next hour, the disk remained in view, flying back and forth, not far from JFK Airport. The witness reports that, at times, the shape of the object seemed to change. After one hour, the object departed.

A few weeks later, Ed Tou contacted MUFON and reported his sighting of a low-flying triangular-shaped craft on September 27, 2003. He was driving on the New York State Thruway at the Catskill and Coxsackie exits when he saw a craft hovering over the northbound side of the freeway. Tou and several other vehicles sped up to eighty miles per hour to get a better view of the craft, which appeared to be at an altitude of only forty feet. Says Tou, "The body of the object was gray-metallic, and I had a clear sense that this craft was otherworldly."

Three days later, on September 30, an anonymous witness called police to report his observation of a bright light flashing on and off as it hovered over an open field near the same area. When a flashlight was shined on the UFO, it appeared to follow the light, making rapid 360-degree turns. Police told the witness that they were already aware of the object and had received other calls. When the witness went to call somebody else, the object quickly darted away.[249]

A UFO with Phoenix Symbol

UFOs come in all shapes as sizes. Sometimes they have windows or port-holes, other times they appear to be smooth-skinned and featureless. On rare occasions, however, strange hieroglyphic-like symbols can be seen on their surface. One such "symbolic" UFO appeared over Bristol New York on the evening of April 30, 2004.

At 11 p.m. an anonymous witness used binoculars to observe a glowing almond-shaped object hovering over the hills near his home. Two other glowing objects appeared nearby, moving vertically and horizontally. Says the witness, "I could see almost every turn they made as they changed from almond shape to disk shaped to something that seemed perfectly round and hovered right over my house."

The two objects not only changed shape, they occasionally disappeared and reappeared in different locations. However, it was the largest central object which most impressed the witness: "There was a design on the bottom of this craft, almost like that of a phoenix or some type of geometrical design. The one that came the closest was mostly gray, but would shift into a bright blue, white, and then it would flash something red once in a while… As I watched this one come closer, I could feel a 'pull' that is hard to explain unless someone has experienced what I am talking about."

The witness reports that he watched the objects for about three hours, but admits he lost track of time. He finally became too tired and went to bed.[250]

Saucer Disappears in Flash of Light

At 8 p.m. May 23, 2004, a resident of Mohawk, New York was outside his house looking at a hawk when a UFO flew into his field of vision. The object flew in a straight line, however, says the witness, "it had no vapor trail or blinking lights like a normal plane."

The witness watched it for about one minute when "it flashed an extremely bright white light all around it, and it was gone." Shortly later he reported the sighting to NUFORC.[251]

A Flying Jellyfish Saucer

One month following the above sighting, a Richmond Hill resident was talking on the phone at 9:30 p.m. June 21, 2004 when he saw a bright red light shine through the window. Looking outside, he saw what appeared to be an extraterrestrial craft floating outside his home. Says the witness, "The object looked round like a disc, and was so bright that its light was beaming below the craft, making the object look kind of like a jellyfish, with its body hanging below it. The bright light lasted for about three seconds. About two minutes later, I saw a clearer craft. It was the same shape, and the lights were even brighter red. Both objects seemed far away, but very visible. The second craft kind of floated around wobbling like it didn't know where to go, and then it just disappeared very fast."[252]

Flying Triangle Moves at 6,000 MPH

As reported to NUFORC, an unnamed witness was on his boat in the Hudson River on the evening of July 3, 2004 when he observed a very bright light (ten times brighter than Jupiter), hovering on the northwest horizon. After remaining stationary for a couple of minutes, the object suddenly began to move. Says the witness, "It started to move toward our location at a very high rate of speed. A jet liner travels through the sky at six hundred mph. This object moved at least ten times that speed. It covered the whole visible sky, north to south in about ten seconds. As it flew over, I was looking at it with binoculars and could see the bottom that was a perfect triangle, with a dim row of lights under each edge. It was very high up. It must have been very large."[253]

Light Stalls Car

At 2 a.m. July 22, 2004, two friends were driving through the mountains in upstate New York when they decided to pull over for a break. Leaving the car headlights on, they got out to stretch their legs. Suddenly, they heard a strange humming noise. As the noise got louder, their car headlights began to dim and then went off.

The two friends became frightened and jumped back in the car. However, when they turned the ignition, the car engine wouldn't start. Says the witness, "That's when we noticed this lemon-shaped light in the sky that just sort of drifted for a minute and the strange noise stopped. And I have no idea what it was, but I'm never going upstate again!"[254]

Flying Rectangle over Queens

At 5:35 p.m. June 1, 2005, an un-named resident of Astoria reported his sighting of a large, grayish-black, rectangular-shaped object cruising slowly over Queens at an altitude of only 1,000 feet to NUFORC. The object was featureless, and appeared to be about 1,000 feet long and two hundred feet wide. When viewed from head on, it appeared to be very thin. The object performed a lazy circle-maneuver over Astoria Boulevard and the East River, turning towards Manhattan and flying southward down the west side. It was in view for about five minutes before disappearing into the distance.[255]

UFO Circles Jet Aircraft

On July 11, 2005 at 7:03 p.m., a Brooklyn resident was walking home when he saw a jet taking off from nearby JFK airport. The jet had climbed to an altitude of about 10,000 feet and was heading west. Suddenly, says the witness, "I noticed an orange/red balloon-shaped object flying east at about 5,000 feet in front of and below the jet. As the jet flew over the object, the object made a slow tight circle underneath and towards the jet, as if it were watching the jet make the turn southeast. I saw clearly this object was disc-shaped, as it waited twelve seconds and started moving smoothly straight up to 15,000 feet and out of sight. It was about 1/20 the size of the 727." The witness later reported his sighting to MUFON.[256]

A Whining UFO

On September 20, 2005 at 11:45 p.m., a resident of Brooklyn was startled to hear what sounded like a gong or churchbells ringing outside her apartment. She looked outside her 10th Street high-rise apartment building and was shocked to see an object that looked like "a cross between a small blimp and some kind of quiet helicopter." It made a strange whining sound as it moved low overhead. It was clear to the witness, however, that the object was neither. As she says, "It was flying lower than any plane, and too small to be a blimp."

As she watched, the object flew southwest over Prospect Park and Coney Island out to sea. The witness immediately called 911, but, she says, "They hung up on me." She called the FBI, and they referred her to the FAA. Unable to reach the FAA, she finally reported her sighting to Peter Davenport of NUFORC.[257]

Big Black Box Hovers over Long Island

The following case is another good example of a brazen UFO that apparently wants to be seen. At 11:13 a.m. December 13, 2005, a group of co-workers on the twenty-second floor of 1 Court Square in Long Island observed "a large, dull black object" hovering below the building tops directly above a construction site across the street. One gentleman noticed it first, and thought that perhaps it was part of a building being lifted by a construction crane. However, as it started to move, it became apparent that it was actually floating. He pointed it out to his coworkers. At the same time, they saw the construction workers themselves stop working to stare and point at the object. The object circled over 59th Street, then returned to the north side of the building. The witnesses called their co-workers who were in a nearby building in New York City. They also saw the object, which they described as "a large, black box." Witnesses later reported the sighting to NUFORC.[258]

The Poughkeepsie Triangle

Another recent sighting occurred at 8 p.m. March 8, 2006 over Poughkeepsie. An anonymous witness made the following report to NUFORC: "I saw a flying triangle with full lighting flanking on each side. One side was all red, and the other side was green. It was hovering in place for most of the time, then abruptly moved to another area in the sky for a few moments and then disappeared. The lights blinked on and off for about fifteen minutes."[259]

Another Low-Flying Object

As reported to MUFON Headquarters, on the evening of April 5, 2006 two gentlemen were driving on Brookview Road in Castleton, New York, when they noticed "an object hovering above the trees."

It was cloudy and no stars were visible. The witnesses thought the object might be a helicopter, however, as they approached they heard no sound. Soon they could see the object more clearly. Says one of the witnesses, "From what I could make out from the silhouette, the object was rectangular, with two red lights and a row of white lights, one of which was flashing. It did not have any lights on either side, which would indicate wings on a plane, and planes cannot hover. It was hovering below the clouds and above the tree line. Two or three seconds later, the object had vanished."[260]

Sphere Eludes Witnesses

There are many accounts of UFOs appearing and disappearing out of thin air. At about 9:20 p.m. May 1, 2006, a group of witnesses was driving on Route 3 through Carthage when they had the following encounter. As described to NUFORC: "In the trees to our right we saw a sphere-shaped object with red and blue flashing lights. The object appeared to be in the trees very low to the ground. We then turned the car around to go back and see what it was. It was moving away quickly, and the lights turned off. It seemed as if it was disappearing before our eyes. We kept driving back and forth trying to spot it, but there was no sight of it."[261]

UFO over La Guardia Airport

As reported to NUFORC in 2006 (exact date not given), a copilot says that after departing from La Guardia Airport and reaching a level of 30,000 feet, he noticed a "very large strobe" above and behind their plane. He asked the Captain if he could see the object, but because of his position, the object was visible only to the copilot. The object strobed brightly every seven seconds as it moved in a straight line towards the south. Says the witness, "We turned down the DUs (Data Display Units) in the aircraft to rule out any reflections from inside the cockpit. I called NY Center and asked them if they had any traffic or military traffic 20 to 30 thousand feet above and behind us, and he indicated that he had only a Falcon jet behind us going north."

The copilot reported that he could see no object, nor any position lights, just one bright strobe. He is sure it wasn't a satellite (as they don't have strobes), nor any conventional aircraft. At about 4:20, the object moved out of sight. Interestingly, however, the controller at La Guardia seemed familiar with the phenomenon. Says the un-named copilot, "The air traffic controller indicated that he was not surprised at the sighting, as he receives them from time to time."[262]

UFO on Cell Phone Camera?

Today there are many cases in which people have photographed UFOs using digital cell phone cameras. The following case is a recent and intriguing example, and was reported to MUFON by a family who prefers to remain anonymous. The main witness is the eleven-year-old daughter. On July 13, 2007, the family boarded a Delta Airlines flight from La Guardia Airport. The main witness chose a window seat. While looking out the window as the jet was in flight, the witness cried out that she saw a "thing" that was moving around the wing of the plane, moving back and forth, sometimes slow, sometimes fast, but always keeping pace with them. She recorded the object for two minutes. Says the parent of the witness, "Clearly on these videos an object can be seen moving under the wing as if it were examining or probing the primitive jet."

Nobody else onboard seemed to notice the object. However, after examining the video, the parent is convinced and writes, "I have live video proof!!! I am a believer!!!"[263]

Epilogue

Clearly, the time for debating whether or not UFOs exist is over. The evidence is overwhelming that they are here. The New York cases alone should be enough to convince even the thickest-skinned skeptic that UFOs are real. Certainly, the New York cases provide enough information to present a comprehensive picture of the UFO phenomenon in all its myriad manifestations. Many other cases could be listed, but at this point, it would only be repetitive.

Of course the Empire State has shown some unique attributes. Several New York UFO encounters have proven to be extremely influential. The New York Blackout remains the largest UFO caused power outage on record. Also, the Hudson Valley Wave remains one of only a handful of UFO "super-waves" and is largely unprecedented in terms of numbers of witnesses and intensity of activity. And of course, the Brooklyn Bridge case is also unique in UFO history.

Perhaps the most surprising information to come out of this microcosm of activity are the many cases in which people have seen UFOs and/or extraterrestrials in crowded urban locations. While these types of cases are not unique, New York City in particular seems to have produced a disproportionately large number, with UFOs whirling around the Empire State Building and hovering over the United Nations while aliens walk around inside apartment buildings, bookstores, restaurants, hotels, subways, and train stations.

The future of UFOs over New York is not hard to guess. Currently, activity remains strong and reports come into MUFON and NUFORC on a weekly basis. The UFOs are not going away. In fact, all the signs point towards the UFO activity not only continuing, but escalating. We are no longer dealing with odd objects seen at a distance in the sky. Instead, the UFOs are landing, taking people onboard, and conducting an intensive study of humanity. The exact reasons for their interest in humanity and our planet remains a matter of speculation. As we have seen, ETs appear to have various agendas ranging from genetic hybridization of their race to alerting humanity of upcoming environmental or nuclear disaster. Whatever the reason for UFO interactions with humanity, it is a very serious situation that affects millions of people.

If trends continue as they have, the time may come when UFOs will exhibit an even greater presence on Earth, and then there will no longer be any room for skepticism. Hopefully we will be ready.

APPENDIX

U.S. Air Force Project Blue Book Unidentified Cases for New York State(1947-1968)

Case #928	May 31, 1951	Niagara Falls, NY
Case #1397	July 6-12, 1952	Governors Island, NY
Case #1502	July 17, 1952	White Plains, NY
Case #1813	August 4, 1952	Mount Vernon, NY
Case #2511	March 21, 1953	Elmira, NY
Case #6446	July 25, 1959	Irondequoit, NY
Case #6663	February 27, 1960	Rome, NY
Case #7057	October 5, 1960	Mount Kisco, NY
Case #8371	Summer, 1963	Middletown, NY
Case #8739	April 11, 1964	Homer, NY
Case #8969	July 27, 1964	Norwich, NY
Case #9048	August 15, 1964	New York City, NY
Case #9806	August 19, 1965	Cherry Creek, NY
Case #10385	April 5, 1966	Lycoming, NY
Case #10917	September 1, 1966	Willsboro, NY
Case #10933	September 6, 1966	Suffolk County AFB, NY
Case #10942	September 9, 1966	Franklin Springs, NY

Endnotes

1. Clark & Coleman, 100-103
2. Trench, 76
3. Jessup, 181-186
4. Ibid, 192
5. Gormley, 1
6. Clark & Coleman, 149, 150; Flammonde, 115
7. Imbrogno & Horrigan, 185-189
8. Rife, 69
9. Blum & Blum, 60-61
10. NUFORC, (NY 4-18-33)
11. Clark, 22-23; Rife, 161
12. NUFORC, (NY 2-20-47)
13. Johnson & Thomas, 266; Kornblut, 3
14. Gribble, September 1989, 13
15. Jessup, 67
16. Dolan, 401
17. Flammonde, 272-273
18. Beckley, 1991, 96-97; UFO Photo Archives
19. Thompson, 417
20. Vallee, 1969, 202-203
21. Edwards, 1966, 56-57; Dolan, 154-155; Good, 1998, 164-165; Hynek & Vallee, 161-164; Randle, 1989, 81-85
22. Gribble, 1992, 17
23. Wilkins, 1955, 49-50
24. Post-Journal, editors, Nov 16, 2004
25. Post-Journal, editors, Feb 22, 2005; Stringfield, 1957, 50
26. Wilkins, 1955, 269; UFO Photo Archives
27. Druffel, 336-337; Fuller, 1969, 35-36
28. Vallee, 1969, 252
29. Dolan, 186-187, 409; Flammonde, 334-337; Gibbons, 144; Gribble, April 1991, 20
30. Haines, 20-21
31. Gribble, Sep 1992, 19-20

32. Vallee, 129-130
33. Michel, 241-242
34. Michel, 264-265; Vallee, 1999, 265
35. Vallee, 1965, 162-165
36. Macklin, 133-134
37. Vallee, 1966, 205-208
38. UFO Photo Archives
39. Hynek, 1977, 45-46
40. UFO Photo Archives
41. Hynek, 1972, 60-61, 265; Taylor, 7-9; Vallee, 1965, 168-170; Vallee, 1966, 42-43
42. Vallee, 1999, 301
43. Hynek, 1972, 75-76
44. Winterhalter, 2-3
45. Beckley, 1992, 23-24, 58-59; Blum, 156; Case, 10; Clark & Coleman, 228; Edwards, 1966, 259-265; Fowler, 2002, 149-150; Fuller, 1966, 203-208; Gribble, November 1990, 18-19; Huneeus, 34; Steiger, 130-132; Vallee, 1969, 320
46. Vallee, 1969, 323
47. Steiger & Whritenour, 1967, 47-48
48. Vallee, 1969, 327
49. Steiger, 1967, 49
50. Stacy & Huyghe, 104-105
51. Edwards, 1967, 78-79; Hynek, 1977, 239-244
52. Edwards, 1967, 139
53. Case, 10
54. Mastropaolo, 5-7
55. Vallee, 1969, 356-357
56. Crystall, 20
57. Keel, 74-76
58. Winterhalter, 3
59. Crystall, 19
60. Flammonde, 370
61. Flammonde, 372; Macklin, 167-168
62. Gormley, 1
63. Beckley, 1992, 15-16
64. Warren, 7-12
65. Beckley, 2002, 100-101

66. Beckley, 2005, 101
67. Bloecher, 16-17
68. Kornblut, 3
69. Hynek, Imbrogno, Pratt, 190
70. Gormley, 1
71. http://mufoncms.com (NY)
72. Crystall, 22-23
73. Ibid, 14-69
74. Hynek, Imbrogno, Pratt, 5-8
75. Ibid, 8-14
76. Ibid, 17-22
77. Ibid, 24-46
78. Ibid, 67-70
79. Hynek, Imbrogno, Pratt, 46-55; Imbrogno & Horrigan, 237-239
80. Hynek, Imbrogno, Pratt, 1-3
81. Ibid, 65-67
82. Ibid, 71-77
83. Huneeus, 36-38, 60
84. Hynek, Imbrogno, Pratt, 77-80
85. Ibid, 81-120
86. Crystall, 70-84, 176
87. Editors, UFO Magazine, Vol. 5, #3, 1990; Hynek, Imbrogno, Pratt, 143-152
88. Hynek, Imbrogno, Pratt, 153-159
89. Imbrogno & Horrigan, 114-116
90. Swartz, 49
91. Crystall, 86-92, 119; Imbrogno & Horrigan, 168, 181, 190, 216
92. Hynek, Imbrogno, Pratt, 199-200
93. Walters & Maccabee, 135
94. Arledge, 1; Hynek, Imbrogno, Pratt, 204
95. Raub, 1
96. Crystall, 94-101, 178-184
97. Imbrogno, summer 1993, 20; Imbrogno & Horrigan, 160-161
98. Lesser, 1
99. Imbrogno & Horrigan, 241-247
100. Donelan, 1; Mead, 8
101. Crystall, 184-187
102. Huneeus, 60

103. Lesser, 1; Mead, 8
104. Mead, 8
105. Gorman, 1
106. Drumm, 1; Imbrogno & Horrigan, 31-32
107. Levovitz, 8-9; Mundy, 1
108. Swingle, 8; Warren, 301
109. Novotny, July 1990, 35
110. Ware, March 1992, 14
111. Gorman, 1
112. Ware, July 1993, 20
113. Ibid
114. Ware, March 1992, 14
115. Ibid, 14-15
116. Ware, March 1992, 17-18
117. Walters & Maccabee, 118
118. Burt, 332-333; UFO Photo Archives
119. Clyne, 2
120. Imbrogno, Winter 1995, 56-57
121. Caggianelli, 1-3
122. Fisher, 10
123. Herbowy, 1
124. Reisman, 2
125. Haines, 174
126. Carr, 11-12; Polise, 12-50, www.pinebushufo.com
127. Filer, Dec 1998, 9
128. Ibid, 9-10
129. Filer, June 1999, 10
130. Filer, July 1999, 13
131. Quinn, 42-45
132. Vallee, 1969, 205
133. Ibid, 259
134. NUFORC, (NY 10-15-57)
135. Vallee, 1988, 22-23
136. Beckley, 2005, 58-49
137. Vallee, 1999, 278
138. Bowen, 163-164; Green, 38-40; Lorenzen & Lorenzen, 1976, 182-183; Steiger, 1966, 100-101; Vallee, 1999, 297
139. Bowen, 164-165; Gribble, July 1989, 20; Lorenzen & Lorenzen,

1976, 183-184; Vallee, 301

140. Connelly, 186-199; Lorenzen & Lorenzen, 1976, 330-337

141. Fuller, 32-35; Galganski, 3-12; Gribble, August 1990, 19; Hynek, 170-173; Lorenzen & Lorenzen, 1968, 106-108; Vallee, 1969, 312-313

142. Vallee, 1969, 318

143. Steiger & Whritenour, 96

144. Beckley, 2005, 17-18

145. Vallee, 1999, 336

146. Davenport, 202

147. Vallee, 1969, 348

148. Ibid, 354

149. Beckley, 1992, 51-52; Good, 1998, 153-154

150. Levovitz, 1

151. NUFORC, (NY 6-10-72)

152. Filer, May 2001, 12

153. Beckley, 2005, 99-100

154. Crystall, 40-44

155. Ibid, 68-69

156. Conroy, 17-20

157. Randazzo, 1-15

158. Baker, 11; Levovitz, 1

159. Imbrogno & Horrigan, 119-120

160. Clyne, 1; Cormia, 16-17; *Times-Herald*, July 31, 1993, 6

161. Weiner, 3

162. Talbott, 7

163. Caggianelli, 3

164. NUFORC, (NY 10-1-99)

165. Filer, Jan 2004, 15

166. Strieber, 1988, 142

167. Hopkins, Feb 1981, 4-6

168. www.pinebushufo.com

169. Fry, 11-49

170. Campagna, 10; Marrs, 353-354

171. Imbrogno & Horrigan, 210-215

172. Kent, 11-124

173. Hopkins, 2003, 33-37

174. Steiger, 1988, 132-134

175. Strieber, 1987, 252-273
176. DiPerna & Shepperd, 10
177. Ibid
178. Ibid
179. Hopkins, 1987, 123-125, 185
180. Hopkins, 1981, 116-117
181. NUFORC, (NY 6-15-65)
182. Steiger & Whritenour, 1968, 49-50
183. Imbrogno, Vol. 1, #5, 1989, 10-12, 64; Imbrogno & Horrigan, 87-99
184. Holzer, 247
185. Holzer, 213-246
186. Hopkins, 1981, 111-122
187. Strieber & Strieber, ed., 206-207
188. Kent, 42-43; Scheussler, 13-14
189. Beckley, 1992, 13
190. Strieber & Strieber, ed., 146-149
191. Bryan, 334-338
192. Grimes, 92-93
193. Falk, 3-4; Hopkins, July-August 1991, 11; Lesser, 1
194. Hopkins, IF Vol. 1, #4, 3
195. Hynek, Imbrogno, Pratt, 165-168; Imbrogno & Horrigan, September 1995, 50
196. Imbrogno, Summer 1993, 19
197. Hynek, Imbrogno, Pratt, 58-63, 163-165
198. Ibid, 161-162
199. Ibid, 162-163
200. Imbrogno, November 1988, 20-22; Imbrogno & Horrigan, 70-77
201. Imbrogno & Horrigan, 78-80
202. Conroy, 189; Strieber, 1988, 1-100, 122, 143, 213-215, 232-233; Strieber, 1995, 65, 127-128, 156, 166-167
203. Imbrogno, November 1988, 19; Imbrogno & Horrigan, 62-66
204. Imbrogno & Horrigan, 145-149
205. Imbrogno, 10-11, #7, Fall 1989; Imbrogno & Horrigan, 66-70
206. Walters & Walters, 1994, 289-290
207. Falk, 3
208. Imbrogno & Horrigan, Winter 1996, 47-48

209. Greer, 129-130; Hopkins, 1996, 1-200
210. Dennett, personal files
211. Ibid
212. Bryan, 334-338
213. Maccabee, 3-7
214. Roger, 90-93
215. Filer & Twitchell, 153-154
216. Beckley, 1992, 42
217. Beckley, 1991, 34-35; Beckley, 1992, 70-75
218. Beckley, 1992, 46-47
219. Beckley, 1992, 32-36; Warren, 210-211
220. Beckley, 1992, 25-29; Forrest, 23-24
221. Beckley, 1992, 38-40; Salkin, 69-71
222. Beckley, 1981, 92-97; Beckley, Spring 1993, 55-59
223. Fowler, 1979, 46-59; Randle, 1995, 198
224. Stringfield, 105-126
225. Douglas, November 1996, 7-9; Ford, 16-22; Hepcat, 18-19; Michaels, 3-133; Steiger & Steiger, 1994, 206-211; Wood, 211
226. Filer, August 1999, 6
227. Beckley, 2005, 147
228. Fowler, 1981, 200-203
229. Caggianelli, 1
230. Cimisi, 7
231. Guy, 65-84; Nichols & Moon, 1-150
232. Davenport, 201
233. Donelan, 1; Ecker, 7; Lesser, 1; Redfern, 196
234. Hynek, Imbrogno, Pratt, 4; Imbrogno, Fall 1989, 7; Imbrogno, Summer 1993, 20
235. Barry, 1, Dennett, Summer 1997, 30-37; Douglas, 9; Fulghum, 32; Guy, 80; Hosenball, 43; NYT, Editors, August 17, 1996 & September 9, 1996, 18; Revkin, 12; Romero, 9; Toronto Sun, Editors, March 5, 1999, A13
236. Filer, July 2000, 19
237. Filer, Nov 2000, 10; Filer, Aug 2001, 11
238. Filer, December 2001, 14
239. Filer, March 2001, 13; Reisman, 2
240. Filer, August 2001, 10
241. Anderson, 3-6, 26-27

242. Filer, Nov 2001, 14
243. Ibid, 13
244. Filer, December 2001, 15
245. Filer, February 2002, 13
246. Filer, March 2002, 17; Filer, March 2003, 13
247. Filer, November 2002, 15
248. Filer, December 2002, 13
249. Filer, October 2003, 12; Filer, November 2003, 13-14
250. Filer, June 2004, 13
251. Filer, July 2004, 15
252. Filer, August 2004, 15
253. Ibid, 14
254. Filer, September 2004, 17
255. Filer, November 2005, 17
256. Ibid
257. Filer, December 2005, 16
258. Filer, February 2006, 16
259. Filer, May 2006, 17
260. Filer, June 2006, 17
261. Filer, July 2006, 17
262. Filer, June 2006, 17
263. http://mufoncms.com (NY)

Bibliography

Books

Beckley, Timothy Green. *MJ-12 and the Riddle of Hangar 18*. New Brunswick, New Jersey: Inner Light Publications, c. 1981, 1989.

Strange Encounters. New Brunswick, New Jersey: Inner Light Publications, 1992.

Strange Saga. New Brunswick, New Jerseu: Global Communications, 2005.

UFOs Among the Stars: Close Encounters of the Famous. New Brunswick, New Jersey: Global Communications, 1992.

Blum, Ralph & Judy Blum. *Beyond Earth: Man's Contact With UFOs*. New York, New York: Bantam Books, 1974.

Bryan, C.D.B. *Close Encounters of the Fourth Kind: Alien Abduction, UFOs and the Conference at M.I.T.* New York, New York: Alfred A. Knopf, 1995.

Burt, Harold. *Flying Saucers: 101*. Los Angeles, California: UFO Magazine, 2000.

Clark, Jerome and Loren Coleman. *The Unidentified: Notes Towards Solving The UFO Mystery*. New York, New York: Warner Paperback Library, 1975.

Connelly, Dwight. *The World's Best UFO Cases*. Martinsville, Illinois: Bookseller, Inc., 2004.

Conroy, Ed. *Report on Communion*. New York, New York: Avon Books, 1989.

Crystal, Ellen. *Silent Invasion: The Shocking Discoveries of a UFO Researcher*. New York, New York: Paragon House, 1991.

Davenport, Marc. *Visitors from Time: The Secret of UFOs*. Tuscaloosa, Alabama: Greenleaf Publications, 1992.

Dolan, Richard M. *UFOs and the National Security State: Chronology of a Cover-up, 1941-1973*. Charlottesville, Virginia: Hampton Roads Publishing Co., 2002.

Druffel, Ann. *Firestorm: Dr. James E McDonald's Fight for UFO Science*. Columbus, North Carolina: Wild Flower Press, 2003.

Edwards, Frank. *Flying Saucers: Here and Now!* New York, New York: Bantam Books, 1967

Flying Saucers: Serious Business. Secaucus, New Jersey: Citadel Press, 1966.

Flammonde, Paris. *UFO Exist*. New York, New York: Ballantine Books, 1976.

Fowler, Raymond E. *UFOs: Interplanetary Visitors*. New York, New York: Bantam Books, 1979.

UFO Testament: Anatomy of an Abductee. Lincoln, Nebraska: Writer's Showcase/ iUniverse, Inc., 2002.

Fry, Dr. Daniel W. *The White Sands Incident*. Louisville, Kentucky: Best Books, 1966.

Fuller, John G. *Incident at Exeter*. New York, New York: Berkley Publishing, Inc., 1966.

Gibbons, Gavin. *The Coming of the Space Ships*. New York, New York: Citadel Press, 1958.

Good, Timothy. *Alien Base: The Evidence for the Extraterrestrial Colonization of Earth*. New York, New York: Avon Books, 1998.

Green, Gabriel & Warren Smith. *Let's Face the Facts About Flying Saucers*. New York, New York: Popular Library, 1967.

Greer MD, Steven M. *Hidden Truth – Forbidden Knowledge*. Crozet, Virginia: Crossing Point, Inc., 2006.

Guy, Timothy. *Aliens over America*. Tarzana, California: AOA Press, 2000.

Haines Ph.D., Richard F. *CE-5: Close Encounters of the Fifth Kind*. Naperville, Illinois: Sourcebooks, Inc., 1999.

Hall, Richard. *Uninvited Guests: A Documented History of UFO Sightings, Alien Encounters & Coverups*. Santa Fe, New Mexico: Aurora Press, 1988.

Holzer, Hans. *The UFOnauts: New Facts on Extraterrestrial Landings*. Greenwich, Connecticut: Fawcett Publications, 1976.

Hopkins, Budd. *Intruders: The Incredible Visitations at Copley Woods*. New York, New York: Random House, 1987.

Missing Time: A Documented Study of UFO Abductions. New York, New York: Richard Marek Publishers, 1981.

Witnessed: The True Story of the Brooklyn Bridge Abductions. New York, New York: Pocket Books, 1996.

Hopkins, Budd & Carol Rainey. *Sight Unseen: Science, UFO Invisibility and Transgenic Beings*. New York, New York: Atria Books, 2003.

Hynek, J. Allen. *The UFO Experience: A Scientific Inquiry*. New York, New York: Ballantine Books, 1974.

Hynek, J. Allen; Philip J. Imbrogno & Bob Pratt. *Night Siege: The Hudson Valley UFO Sightings*. New York, New York: Ballantine Books, 1987.

Hynek, J. Allen & Jacques Vallee. *The Edge of Reality: A Progress Report on Unidentified Flying Objects*. Chicago, Illinois: Henry Regnery Company, Inc., 1975.

Imbrogno, Philip J. & Marianne Horrigan. *Contact of the 5th Kind*. St. Paul,

Montana: Llewellyn Publications, 1997.

Jessup, Morris K. *The Case for the UFO: Unidentified Flying Objects*. New York, New York: Citadel Press, 1955.

Johnson, Dewayne B. & Kenn Thomas. *Flying Saucers over Los Angeles*. Kempton, Illinois: Adventures Unlimited Press, 1998.

Keel, John. *The Mothman Prophecies*. New York, New York: E.P Dutton & Co, Inc, 1975.

Kent, Malcolm. *The Terror Above Us*. New York, New York: Tower Books, 1967.

Lorenzen, Carol. *Flying Saucers: The Startling Evidence of the Invasion from Outer Space*. New York, New York: Signet Books, 1962.

Macklin, Milt (Editor). *The Total UFO Story*. New York, New York: Dale Books, 1979.

Marrs, Jim. *Alien Agenda: Investigating the Extraterrestrial Presence Among Us*. New York, New York: HarperCollins Publishers Inc, 1997.

Michaels, J. B. *UFO Encounters: The True Story Behind the Brookhaven & Carp Incidents*. Stamford, Connecticut: Longmeadow Press, 1995.

Michelle, Aime. *Flying Saucers and the Straight Line Mystery*. New York, New York: Criterion Books, 1958.

Nichols, Preston and Peter Moon. *The Montauk Project*. Westbury, New York: Sky Books, 1992.

Place, Marian T. *Bigfoot All over the Country*. New York, New York: Dodd, Mead & Company, 1978.

Polise, Vincent. *The Pine Bush Phenomenon*. Victoria, British Columbia, Canada: Trafford Publishing, 2005.

Randazzo, Joseph. *The Contactees Manuscript*. Studio City, Calilfornia: UFO Library Limited, 1993.

Randle, Kevin. *A History of UFO Crashes*. New York, New York: Avon Books, 1995.

Redfern, Nicholas. *The FBI Files: The FBI's UFO Top Secrets Exposed*. New York, New York: Simon & Schuster, 1998.

Rife, Philip L. *It Didn't Start With Roswell: 50 Years of Amazing UFO Crashes, Close Encounters and Coverups*. Lincoln, Nebraska: Writers Club Press, 2001.

Stacy, Dennis & Patrick Huyghe. *The Field Guide to UFOs: A Classification of Various Unidentified Aerial Phenomena Based on Eyewitness Accounts*. New York, New York: HarperCollins Publishers Inc., 2000.

Steiger, Brad and Joan Whritenhour. *New UFO Breakthrough*. New York, New York: Award Books, 1968
Flying Saucer Invasion: Target Earth. New York, New York: Award Books,

1969.

Flying Saucers Are Hostile. New York, New York: Award Books, 1967.

Steiger, Brad and Sherry Hansen Steiger. *The Rainbow Conspiracy.* New York, New York: Pinnacle Books, 1994.

Steiger, Brad. *Project Blue Book: The Top Secret UFO Findings Revealed.* New York, New York: Ballantine Books, 1976.

Strangers from the Skies. London, Great Britain: Tandem Publishing, Ltd., 1966.

The UFO Abductors. New York, New York: Berkley Books, 1988.

Strieber, Whitley. *Communion: A True Story.* New York, New York: William Morrow & Co., 1987.

Transformation: The Breakthrough. New York, New York: William Morrow & Co, 1988.

Stringfield, Leonard. *Inside Saucer Post...3-0 Blue.* Cincinnati, Ohio: Civilian Research Interplanetary Flying Objects.

UFO Crash/Retrievals: The Inner Sanctum – Status Report VI. Cincinnati, Ohio: Leonard H. Stringfield, July 1991.

Thompson, Richard L. *Alien Identities: Ancient Insights into Modern UFO Phenomena.* San Diego, California: Govardhan Hill Publishing, 1993.

Trench, Brinsley Le Poer. *The Flying Saucer Story.* New York, New York: Ace Books, 1966.

Vallee, Jacques. *Anatomy of a Phenomena – UFOs in Space: A Scientific Appraisal.* New York, New York: Ballantine Books, 1965.

Vallee, Jacques and Janine. *Challenge To Science: The UFO Enigma.* New York, New York: Ballantine Books, 1966.

Vallee, Jacques. *Dimensions: A Casebook of Alien Contact.* New York, New York: Contemporary Books, 1988.

Passport To Magonia: On UFOs, Folklore and Parallel Worlds. Chicago, Illinois: Contemporary Books, Inc., 1969, 1993.

Walters, Ed and Frances Walters. *UFO Abductions in Gulf Breeze.* New York, New York: Avon Books, 1994.

Warren, Larry & Peter Robbins. *Left at East Gate: A Firsthand Account of the Bentwaters-Woodbridge UFO Incident, Its Cover-up and Investigation.* New York, New York: Marlowe & Company, 1997.

Wilkins, Harold T. *Flying Saucers Uncensored.* New York, New York: Pyramid Books, 1955.

Magazines/Newspapers/Journals

Anderson, Dennis K. "The Arthur Kill Sightings: July 14-15, 2001." *The International UFO Reporter.* 2457 W. Peterson Ave, Chicago, Illinois: The J. Allen Hynek Center for UFO Studies. Summer 2003, Vol 28, #2.

Arledge, H. L. "South Louisiana Ranks in UFO Top Ten." *Sauce.* Gonzales, Louisiana – October 1998. (See also UFO Newsclipping Service [UFONS]. Editor/Publisher Lucius Farish. 2 Caney Valley Dr, Plumerville, AR 72127-8725. November 1998, #352, 4)

Baker, Carole. "This Week in UFO History." *Islander.* Pensacola Beach, Florida – September 27, 1995. (See also: UFO Newsclipping Service [UFONS] Editor/Publisher Lucius Farish, 2 Caney Valley Drive, Plumerville, AR 72127-8725; October 1996, #315, 11)

Barry, Dan. "Photo Taken Day of TWA Explosion Shows What Could Be a Missile." *Observer.* Charlotte, North Carolina – Aug. 26, 1996.

Beckley, Timothy Green. "Did a UFO Crash in New York's Central Park?" *UFO Universe.* Vol. 3, # 1, Spring 1993.

"Muhammad Ali's Nights of Dramatic Close Encounters." *UFO Universe.* Vol. 1, # 1, February-March 1991.

Bloecher, Ted. "Woman Drives Beneath UFO." *Skylook – The UFO Monthly.* Quincy, Illinois: Dwight Connelly, March 1976, #100.

Caggianelli, Kathryn. "Investigating Things That Go Bump in the Night." *The Record.* Troy, New York – October 13, 2006. (See also: UFONS, November 2006, #448, 3)

Campagna, Darryl. "Man Not Alone Retelling Tale of Alien Abduction." *Times Union.* Albany, New York: May 16, 1997. (See also: UFONS, October 1997, #339, 10)

Carr, Scott C. "The Rise and Fall of Pine Bush: New York Hotspot." *MUFON UFO Journal.* November 1998, No. 367.

Case, Dick. "What Twinkles in the Night Sky – Little Stars or Big UFOs?" *Herald Journal.* Syracuse, New York – August 3, 1994. (See also: UFONS, August 3, 1994)

Cimisi, Jerry. "The Long Island UFO Network." *Bridgehampton Journal.* Bridgehampton, New York – December 9, 1988. (See also: UFONS, March 1989, #236, 7)

Clark, Jerome. "Airships: Part 1." *International UFO Reporter.* January/February 1991, Volume 16.

Clyne, Mary L. S. "Mohawk Valley Journal: The Columbia Crop Formations — 'Intense Energy Beam or Vortex?'" and "A UFO Investigator Believes ET Visited Us This Summer." *Observer Dispatch.* Utica, New York – September 18, 1993. (See also: UFONS: October 1993, #291, 5)

Cormia, Jim. "New York Crop Formation Investigation." *MUFON UFO Journal*. May 1994, #313.

Dennett, Preston. "Deadly Crash of Flight 800 – Case for the UFO Connection." *Unsolved UFO Sightings*. New York, New York: GCR Publishing, Vol. 5, #2, Summer 1997.

DiPerna, Rob and Walt Shepperd. "Snatched By Aliens: Central New Yorkers Tell their Tales." *New Times*. Syracuse, New York – November 11-18, 1992.

Donelan, Jennifer. "Are Aliens Investigating Earth?" *Village Times*. New York City – March 2, 1989. (See also: UFONS, May 1989, #238, 9)

Douglas, Elaine. "The Ordeal of John Ford." *MUFON UFO Journal*. November 1996, #343.

Drumm, Russell. "Montauk UFO." *East Hampton Star*. East Hampton, New York – February 9, 1989.

Ecker, Don. "N.Y. Wave of UFOs, Mutilations." *UFO*. Los Angeles, California: California UFO. Vol. 4, #1, March-April, 1989.

Falk, William B. "That Alien Feeling." *Newsday*. New York, New York – April 12, 1993.

Filer, George. "Filer's Files: Bright Blue Square in New York" and "Sphere Reported in New York." *MUFON UFO Journal*. PO Box 369, Morrison, CO 80465: Mutual UFO Network. November 2001, #403.

"Filer's Files: Bright Cylinder Spotted in New York." *MUFON UFO Journal*. July 2000, #287.

"Filer's Files: Car Stalls in New York." *MUFON UFO Journal*. September 2004, #437.

"Filer's Files: Glowing Disk in New York." *MUFON UFO Journal*. December 2000, #392.

"Filer's Files: High-Flying Metallic Objects in New York." *MUFON UFO Journal*. March 2002, #407.

"Filer's Files: Flying Triangle in New York" and "Hovering Saucer in New York." *MUFON UFO Journal*. November 2002, #415.

"Filer's Files: Lights over Long Island, New York." *MUFON UFO Journal*. February 2002, #406.

"Filer's Files: New York." *MUFON UFO Journal*. August 1999, #376.

"Filer's Files: New York Blimp-Shaped UFO Reported." *MUFON UFO Journal*. May 2001, #397.

"Filer's Files: New York Flying Triangle." *MUFON UFO Journal*. December 2001, #404.

"Filer's Files: New York Flying Triangle." *MUFON UFO Journal*. November

2003, #427.

"Filer's Files: New York Flying Triangle." *MUFON UFO Journal*. June 2004, #434.

"Filer's Files: New York Flying Triangle" and "New York Saucer & Flash." *MUFON UFO Journal*. August 2004, #436.

"Filer's Files: New York Fox News Video" and "Second Chevron Report – This One from New York." *MUFON UFO Journal*. August 2001, #400.

"Filer's Files: NY Intruder and Light?" *MUFON UFO Journal*. January 2004, #429.

"Filer's Files: New York Large Black Object." *MUFON UFO Journal*. February 2006, #454.

"Filer's Files: New York Object." *MUFON UFO Journal*. January 2001, #393.

"Filer's Files: New York Rectangle" and "Object Follows Jet in New York." *MUFON UFO Journal*. December 2002, #416.

"Filer's Files: New York Sphere." *MUFON UFO Journal*. July 2006, #459.

"Filer's Files: New York Teardrop." *MUFON UFO Journal*. December 2005, #452

"Filer's Files: New York Triangle." *MUFON UFO Journal*. May 2006, #457.

"Filer's Files: New York White Circular Saucer." *MUFON UFO Journal*. July 2004, #435.

"Filer's Files: Rectangle With Lights In New York." *MUFON UFO Journal*. June 2006, #458.

"Filer's Files: Saucer-Shaped Object Reported in New York." *MUFON UFO Journal*. March 2001, #395.

"Filer's Files: Sightings TV Show Has Video." *MUFON UFO Journal*. November 2000, #391.

"Filer's Files: Unlighted Cylinder in New York." *MUFON UFO Journal*. March 2003, #419.

Fisher, Carol. "What About Those UFOs?" *Special-E-Fects*. Ellicottville, New York – August 19, 1994. (See also UFONS, December 1994, #305, 10)

Ford, John. "The Great UFO Crash Near Brookhaven Laboratories." *UFO Universe*. New York, New York: GCR Publishing Group, Inc. Vol. 3, #4, Winter, 1994.

Forest, Ricardo. "UFOs in Rock 'N Roll." *California UFO*. Los Angeles, California: January-February 1987.

Fulghum, David A. "The TWA Probe: Eyewitnesses Reject Missile Theory." *Aviation Week & Space Technology*. July 29, 1996, 32.

Galganski, Robert A. "Incident At Cherry Creek." *International UFO Reporter*.

Fall 1996, Vol. 21, #3.

Gorman, Raymond. "'UFOs over Long Island' Debuts in Brookhaven." *This Week*. Farmingdale, New York – April 7, 1990. (See also: UFONS, April 1990, #249, 1)

Gormley, Michael. "More Reports of UFO Sightings, More Watching Skies." *Advance*. Staten Island – November 1, 1999.

Gribble, Bob. "Looking Back: April 1956." *MUFON UFO Journal*. April 1991, #276.

Grimes, Jack. "UFO Forum: Abduction Tale." *Fate*. Lakeville, Montana: Fate Magazine, Inc., January 2005, Vol. 58, #1, Issue #657.

Gruber, Bill. "The UFO Enigma: For Some UFO Enthusiasts, Seeing is Believing." *Sunday Republican Magazine*. Waterbury, Connecticut – April 2, 1989.

Hepcat, Harry. "Long Island's Ordeal." *MUFON UFO Journal*. January 1997, #345, 18-19.

Herbowy, Alexia. "UFO Investigator Pursues Data on Recent Sightings." *Daily Sentinal*. Rome, New York – January 3, 1995. (See also: UFONS, February 1995, #307, 1)

Hopkins, Budd. "Probable Childhood Abduction." *MUFON UFO Journal*. February 1981, #156.

"Two Drawings of an 'Eye Implant' Operation." *New York IF: The Bulletin of the Intruders Foundation*. New York, New York: Intruders Foundation. Vol. 1, New York #4.

"UFO Abductions at the Event Level." *International UFO Reporter*. Chicago, Illinois: J. Allen Hynek Center for UFO Studies. July-August 1991, Vol. 16, # 4.

Hosenball, Mark. "TWA: The Anatomy of a Rumor." *Newsweek*. September 23, 1996, 43.

Huneeus, Antonio. "Flying Saucers over Manhattan." *UFO Universe*. Summer 1989, Vol. 1, #5.

Imbrogno, Philip J. and Marianne Horrigan. "The Hudson Valley UFO Mystery." *Fate*. September 1995, Vol. 48, #9, Issue 546.

Imbrogno, Phillip J. "Hudson Valley's Close Encounters of the 4th Kind." *UFO Universe*. New York, New York: Condor Books. Vol. 1, #3, November 1988.

"Mysterious Eclipses and UFO Sighting Waves." *UFO Universe*. Vol. 4, No. #4, Winter, 1995.

"Saga at Indian Point: Part Two." *UFO Universe*. March 1990, Vol. 1, # 5.

"UFO Power Stations." *Unsolved UFO Sightings*. Spring 1997, Vol. 5., #1.

"UFOs – Are They Here Draining Our Lakes and Reservoirs?" *UFO Universe*. Vol. 3, No 2, Summer 1993.

Imbrogno Philip and Marianne Horrigan. "A New Dimension in UFO Activity." *New York UFO Universe*. Winter 1996, Vol 5, #4.

Kaplan, Lisa Faye. "For UFO Trackers, the Sky is Not the Limit." *Reporter Dispatch*. White Plains, New York – July 14, 1988.

Kent, Barbara. "UFO Abduction." *Fate*. St. Paul, Montana: Llewellynn Worldwide. September 1994, Vol. 47, New York # 9, Issue 534.

Kirby, Paul. "'This Is Not Airplanes.'" *Reporter Dispatch*. White Plains, New York – February 21, 1988.

Kornblut, Anne E. "Hey, We Gotcha UFOs Right Here in the City." *Daily News*. New York, New York – July 13, 1997. (see also: UFONS, September 1997, #338, 3)

Lesser, Harriet. "UFOs Sighted Here: Close Encounters of the 5-T Kind." *South Shore Record*. Hewlett, New York – January 26, 1989. (see also: UFONS, February 1989, # 235, 1)

Levovitz, Ron. "Close Encounters of the Queens Kind." *New York Tribune*. Flushing, New York – October 26–November 1, 1989. (See also UFONS, December 1989, #245)

"Looking Back: Forty Years Ago – September 1949." *MUFON UFO Journal*. September 1989, #257.

"Looking Back: September 1957." *MUFON UFO Journal*. September 1992, #293.

"Looking Back: Twenty-Five Years Ago." *MUFON UFO Journal*. July 1989, #255.

"Looking Back: 1965." *MUFON UFO Journal*. August 1990, #268.

"Looking Back: 1965." *MUFON UFO Journal*. November 1990, #271.

Maccabee, Bruce. "Flying Peanut/Double UFO Video Seems to Be Authentic." *MUFON UFO Journal*. January 1999, #369.

Marx, R. J. "Westchester Boomerang, Years Later." *New York Record Review*. Bedford, New York – February 27, 1998. (See also: UFONS, March 1998, #344, 10)

Mastropaolo, Gerald M. "UFOs on the Hudson." *New York UFO Universe*. #7, Fall 1989.

Mead, Julia C. "Close Encounters of the Long Island Kind." *New York Suffolk Life*. Hampton, New York – April 12, 1989.

Mundy, Jean. "Unexplainable Events." *East Hampton Star*. East Hampton, New York – April 27, 1989. (See also: UFONS, May 1989, #238, 9)

Novotny, George. "Astounding Series of UFO Photos Taken by UFO Universe

Reader." *UFO Universe*. July 1990, Vol. 1, #5.

Post Journal, editors. "Information Center: In Years Past – 50 Years Ago." *Post-Journal*. Jamestown, New York – November 16, 2004. (see also: UFONS, April 2005, #429, 7)

"Information Center: In Years Past – 50 Years Ago." *Post-Journal*. Jamestown, New York – February 22, 2005. (see also: UFONS, April 2005, #429, 7)

Quinn, Ron. "My Encounter With the Little Man." *Fate*. May 2004, Vol. 1, #5, Issue #649.

Raub, Deborah Fineblum. "UFOs Seem to Bypass Rochester." *Democrat-Chronicle*. Rochester, New York – August 16, 1988.

Reisman, Phil. "For UFO Believers, Things Are Always Looking Up." *Journal News*. Yonkers, New York – April 9, 2006. (See also: UFONS, May 2006, #442, 9-10)

Revkin, Andrew. "Conspiracy Theories Abound on Cause of TWA Jet Crash." *New York Times*. New York, New York – September 17, 1996.

Roger, Pauline Darcy. "UFO Forum: Alien Meditation." *Fate*. March 2004, Vol. 57, #3, Issue #647.

Romero, John. "John As UFOs Enter the Flight 800 Mystery, the Case is Closed!" *Vortex*. Ventura, California: Mutual UFO Network, Ventura Chapter, February 1997.

Salkin, Harold. "John Lennon's Close Eerie Close Encounter." *UFO Universe*. Vol. 1, #1, July 1988.

Scheussler, John F. "Physiological Effects from Abductions." *MUFON UFO Journal*. February 1998, #358.

(Staff) *Sun*. "Pilot Saw 'Rocket' Near TWA Crash." *Sun*. Toronto, Ontario, Canada – March 5, 1999. (See also: UFONS, May 1999, #358, 7)

Swartz, Tim. "Reporting on UFOs: How the Mainstream Press Avoids UFO Stories." *Fate Magazine*. St. Paul, Montana: Fate Magazine, Inc., July 2006, Vol. 59, #7, Issue 675. 49.

Swingle, Chris. "80 Residents Called Sheriff About UFO." *Journal*. Ithaca, New York – July 18, 1989. (See also: UFONS, August 1898, #241, 8)

Talbott, Nancy. "Crop Circle Analysis Shows that Most Are Not Hoaxes." *MUFON UFO Journal*. September 1998, #365.

Taylor, Herbert S. "Satellite Objects and Cloud Cigars." *International UFO Reporter*. Chicago, Illinois: J. Allen Hynek Center for UFO Studies (CU-FOS). Spring 2004, Vol. 29, #1.

Times Herald Record, staff. "UFO, or Folks Feeling Their Oats?" *Times Herald Record*. Rochester, New York – July 31, 1993. (See also: UFONS, August

1993, #289, 6)

UFO Magazine, (Editors). "Incident at Indian Point." *UFO*. Vol. 5, #3, May-June 1990.

Valenti, Chris C. "Bigfoot Seen – and Photographed – on Long Island." *UFO Universe*. New York, New York: GCR Publishing Group, Inc., Vol. 6, #2, Summer 1996.

Ware, Donald. "Current Case Log: #910702E, #910703E, #910801E." *MUFON UFO Journal*. August 1991, #280.

"Current Case Log: #910601E, #910802E, #911101E." *MUFON UFO Journal*. March 1992, #287.

"Current Case Log: #9305053, #930506E." *MUFON UFO Journal*. July 1993, #303.

Weiner, Mark. "What Goes Around Comes Around: Second Crop Circle Appears." *Herald Journal*. Syracuse, New York – August 28, 1994. (See also: UFONS, October 1994, #303, 3)

Williams, Malcolm and Judy. "UFO Photographed over Lake Eerie." *New York UFO Universe*. Spring, 1994. Vol. 4, #1.

Winterhalter, Matthew. "The NCCC FILES – Have Unidentified Objects Visited the Cataract City?" *Niagara Gazette*. Niagara Falls, New York – September 28, 2005. (See also: UFONS, December 2005, #437, 2-3)

Websites

www.mufon.com

www.nuforc.org

www.pinebushufo.com

www.prestondennett.com

A metallic UFO, taken July 28, 1952 by August Roberts. The Empire State Building is in the background. Roberts was later questioned extensively by the FBI who expressed extreme interest in the photograph. (UFO Photo Archives)

#1 of four photographs taken May 15, 1955 by Warren Seigmond from the roof of his apartment building in New York City. Seigmond reports that the UFO appeared to glow with light, and when it hovered in place, it appeared to vibrate at high speed. (UFO Photo Archives)